Market Intelligence

Market Intelligence

Building Strategic Insight

Per V. Jenster

&

Klaus Solberg Søilen

Copenhagen Business School Press

Market Intelligence
Building Strategic Insight

© Copenhagen Business School Press, 2009
Printed in Denmark by Narayana Press, Gylling
Cover design by BUSTO | Graphic Design
1st edition 2009

ISBN 978-87-630-0202-8

Distribution:

Scandinavia
DBK, Mimersvej 4
DK-4600 Køge, Denmark
Tel +45 3269 7788
Fax +45 3269 7789

North America
International Specialized Book Services
920 NE 58th Street, Suite 300
Portland, OR 97213-3786
Tel +1 800 944 6190
Fax +1 503 280 8832
Email: orders@isbs.com

Rest of the World
Marston Book Services, P.O. Box 269
Abingdon, Oxfordshire, OX14 4YN, UK
Tel +44 (0) 1235 465500
Fax +44 (0) 1235 465655
Email Direct Customers: direct.order@marston.co.uk
Email Booksellers: trade.order@marston.co.uk

Table of Contents

In Memory of our friend and colleague David Hussey

Foreword

The aim of this book is to provide managers with a book on market intelligence and analysis which is helpful, practical, and able to provide guidance for the practical application of sound concepts in real situations. It has also been to integrate a number of loose ends in the huge flora of the intelligence-related literature.

Most managers take little interest in theories, but are concerned about what works in practice. Hence in this book, it is our hope that the reader will find each chapter conceptually sound and useful to reflect the needs of managers whilst giving proper acknowledgement to the originators of the concepts and ideas. The emphasis is on the use of the concepts and methods, rather than on the academic argument.

Business school faculty and students concerned with the application of theories will hopefully find this book to be a supplement to the more academic texts available. At the same time the book also presents much original European research, some of which has not been published to an English speaking audience before.

The aim is to give the reader clear guidance on how to make market intelligence work in his or her own situation, while at the same time ensuring that the text does not over-simplify a given topic. Of course, it is for you, the reader, to judge whether we have succeeded.

Per V. Jenster & Klaus Solberg Søilen

Preface

This book was born out of frustration that, although much has been written about competitive analysis, we could not find a practical text which covered the broad spectrum of the subject, supported by examples and case histories across different academic cultures concerned with the topic of Intelligence Analysis. There are many good books which have made a major contribution on intelligence related topics, and these have been helpful in shaping many of the concepts which this book discusses. However, the practical aspects of making use of the concepts in real situations have had less prevalent treatment. In other words, the *why* and *what* of competitive analysis has been covered, but we have found few writings on the *how* and *when* which have been practical, comprehensive, and conceptually sound. Academic communities occupied with intelligence related subjects still tend to be rather local, maybe because of the perceived sensitivity of the subject.

The book opens with an examination of the theoretical foundation for competitive and intelligence analysis. Chapter 2 examines a number of issues around competitive strategy in both attack and defence modes. We hope that this will demonstrate the need for a vigilant study of competitors.

Chapters 3 and 4 cover industry and company analysis, first from an examination of the basic principles, then with practical ways of using the concepts in business situations. Chapter 4 includes a set of tools for analyzing the information and communicating it to others which has been found particularly useful in consulting assignments.

Critical success factors are important both for self-analysis and for an examination of competitors, and the concepts are discussed in detail in Chapter 5 together with a wide presentation of other analytical tools.

Chapter 6 focuses on about how to build an effective business intelligence system. Chapter 7 emphasizes the organizational role of intelligence and Chapter 8 is discussing Business Intelligence Systems. In chapter 9 we cover the essential implications of the ethics in intelligence work. No training in intelligence analysis can be complete without it.

This is a book we have enjoyed writing, and which we hope will make a useful contribution to the understanding and application of the subject. Our acknowledgement goes to researchers and colleagues whose work we are building on, and to the students and clients who taught us through the years. We also would like to express our gratitude to Cheng Yiting for all her patience in editing and formatting the text. The book is dedicated to the memory of David Hussey, who not only contributed to much of the thought in this book, but who was also an excellent strategist and friend.

CHAPTER 1

Converging Foundations of Intelligence Analysis

A seminar on competitor analysis with a group of managers from a large multinational company reminded us of the old adage about the elephant and the six blind men. Each of the blind men tries to explain his perception of what he is encountering. One man, feeling the leg of the elephant, believes it to be the pillar of a grand building; another, touching the trunk of the elephant, thinks it is a slithering snake, and so forth.

In our discussion, a sales manager described the system for tracking different competitors' prices within a particular product line. A marketing manager talked about comparing brand positioning of different competitors. In production, attempts were made to benchmark the cost position of competing manufacturing sites, and the head of R&D was describing the technology path of various feuding organizations. A couple of corporate staff members described how the firm attempted to track competitors' acquisition paths, in order to assess the emerging build-up of market positions and competencies.

The point is that all these managers discussed some form of competitive analysis, but used the term to convey very different meanings. This lack of one common language is also reflected in the world of academic theories.

A considerable amount of research has been conducted to help managers understand competitive phenomena. The problem with most of these contributions is that they are dispersed among a large number of independent research bodies. The competitive advantage literature starts with Adam Smith[1] and follows an all but straight line to Michael

---

[1] See Smith, A. (1776/1977).

Porter and his many contemporary inspirers.[2] Matters of intelligence are today studied by a diverse research community. Contributions made to help the state on a national, regional and local level (public intelligence), the military (military intelligence), non-profit organizations (NPO intelligence) and private companies (private intelligence) are often kept separate, even though they have much in common, first of all a certain working methodology.[3]

The study of intelligence also differs much from one country to another. In the US, the study of private intelligence was separated from military intelligence in the 60's, in an attempt to discover general theories of intelligence work.[4] To this end, it first took the title, Business Intelligence,[5] followed by Corporate Intelligence[6] and then Competitive Intelligence.[7]

The term Business Intelligence has survived, but now often refers to the technology applied. In France most of this research is still studied under Geopolitique or as Intelligence Economique. In Germany, it is studied as Wirschaftsspionage or hardly at all,[8] and in Sweden as Omvärldsanalys, loosely translated to "surrounding world analysis". There is a need to bring all this research together and to develop a general methodology for studies of intelligence. In this book, we have chosen to call it Intelligence Analysis.

We want to provide the reader with an overview of the most important tools and concepts relevant to intelligence analysis for strategic decision making. Our focus will not only be competitors, but also customers, suppliers, and a range of other influencers. Even though this book focuses on private enterprises, it will be apparent to the reader that the same analytical framework may be used to understand the intelligence process in public organizations or the nation state. We will start this chapter with some thoughts on important dimensions to consider before engaging in any competitive analysis. We will discuss a

---

[2] Porter, M.E. (1990).

[3] For an in-depth explanation as to how these forms of intelligence differ and coincide, see Solberg Søilen, K. (2005).

[4] See Knorr, K. (1964).

[5] See Greene, jr., Richard M. (ed) (1966).

[6] See Eells, R., Nehemkis, P.(1984).

[7] The term was established with the appearance of the journal The Competitive Intelligence Review. The journal, which was edited by SCIP and published by Wiley, came out between 1995 and 2001. It has been replaced by The Journal of Competitive Intelligence and Management (JCIM), edited by Craig S. Fleisher and John E. Prescott.

[8] Solberg Søilen, K. (2004).

number of factors which may aid the analyst in delineating the problem and clarifying the boundaries of her work.

We shall also attempt to explore the various theoretical schools of thought in academia which have contributed to a greater understanding of the whole intelligence field. Additionally, we will provide some of the analytical tools used to analyse both micro and macro factors in the organization's environment to better predict future outcomes in decision making.

In an effort to alleviate confusion, let us highlight some of the differences among organizational intelligence functions. Economic Intelligence is defined as the intersection between state intelligence and private intelligence. All other forms of intelligence are illustrated in Figure 1.1. The model makes no distinction between national and international intelligence functions. This is primarily a distinction for state intelligence services, and less so for private intelligence.

The intersections between the different forms of intelligence are in part based on the theoretical development of the field, and partly on common practice. Competitor intelligence is primarily, but not only, an academic interest within the fields of marketing and strategic management. It also concerns a growing interest for public intelligence, as regions are becoming more aware of their competitive situation vis-à-vis other regions, both nationally and internationally.

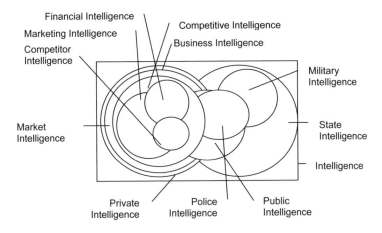

Figure 1.1 Intelligence Studies

13

The Venn diagram shows the relation between different intelligence studies. It basically shows that there are two major areas of intelligence studies: private and state. Within state intelligence studies, public intelligence is the major domain. Market Intelligence (dotted line) is mostly about business activities, but also public organizations participate in these markets. Within private or market intelligence, it is business and competitive intelligence which are the major areas of study. There are also smaller fields of intelligence study, which cannot fit into the model without making it too detailed; such an example is Exhibit and Trade Show Intelligence.

It is important for analysts, especially those in larger companies, to get an overview of all of the organization's intelligence activities, understand the boundaries, to coordinate efforts and achieve economics of scale and scope in generation, interpretation, dissemination, systems and incorporation into decision making.

It Depends how you Look at It

An organization does not obtain any long term competitive advantage just by focusing on its products and internal processes alone. Instead, it must try to understand the broader environment in which it is conducting its business. This permits a perspective on matters of competitive advantage and intelligence which is more complex than the static phenomenon often described in neo-classical economics, in which a given number of firms compete under similar assumptions, with similar products or closely related substitutes, and where perfect knowledge of market conditions exists among customers and firms.

The literature and evolving management practice reveals that analysis of customers, complementors and competitors takes on varying forms, and it thus becomes critical to develop an appropriate context and a broader perspective by building on multiple streams of research.

The necessity of delineating the scope is not only felt by academics. In working with senior managers, strategic planners and marketing executives, we often observe their frustration over the quality of competitor analysis conducted within their organizations. These frustrations in management teams seem to centre around issues, such as:

1. How do we define and identify current and potential competitors and what criteria should be used to define the competitive landscape to be investigated?
2. What allows us to understand emerging customer needs or the technologies which can be used to serve these?

3. How do we overcome the limitations of traditional listings of strengths and weaknesses, which mostly reflect historical, gut-feel snapshots, rather than a dynamic future-oriented picture?
4. Inability to cope with the vast amount of data from different information sources, which needs to be integrated into the analytical process.
5. The conflict which arises from the paradox that most analyses are general in nature, whereas the decisions to be made are specific and situation dependent.
6. The sheer magnitude of the analysis, which is often presented in large volumes of reports which nobody reads, and thus results in no action.
7. The analysis is only available to a few insiders in the analysis unit, rather than a broad base of line managers responsible for decision making.

The academic intelligence and competitive advantage community feels it has achieved great advancements when it comes to putting concepts and tools intended for competitor analysis into the hands of practicing managers. This is particularly true when one considers questions of competitive behaviour, both at the firm level, as well as from institutional perspectives. At the same time, the academic literature mirrors the confusion experienced by practising managers, in framing the scope of the problems to be examined in the intelligence analysis.

We will therefore start by discussing the point of departure of any intelligence analysis, of competitive behaviour, namely, the definition of "the focus of the analysis".

Focus of the Analysis

One of the first impressions one gets when discussing competitive intelligence analysis with practicing managers is their general confusion with what is meant by the term. For example, in discussions with sales managers, competitor intelligence analysis will centre on comparisons of price points and features, sales force coverage, seniority, professionalism, terms and conditions, service, and quality. Marketing managers will often be concerned about issues such as market share, brand positioning, advertising expenditure, distribution coverage, and product breadth and depth. In the research and development function, the competitive questions may be examined based on critical technologies among competing companies, patents, innovation performance, and so forth. In manufacturing, concerns such as competing companies‘

manufacturing base, economies of scale, supply chain performance, etc. are considered the most important. At the chief executive level, competing companies may be benchmarked on levels of operating returns and leverage, partnering relationships, etc. At the corporate level of large international organizations, competitive intelligence analyses may include such comparisons as technological platforms, degree of vertical integration, geographical coverage and locations of operating entities, and synergies between divisions.

The point is that the questions you would like to have defined and clarified depend on your point of departure. Accordingly, one uses different theoretical concepts and frameworks employed to study the phenomenon in question, explain competitor behaviour, predict future competitor activities and assess profitability of markets.

We find it useful to distinguish between a number of related dimensions which should be considered before engaging in any competitive intelligence analysis activity. The list should not be seen as exclusive, but rather as a proven group of variables which tend to influence the academic concepts and frameworks used for the inquiry, the nature of the information search, as well as impacting the shape of the conclusions to be reached from the exercise.

Decisional "Altitude"

The first dimension to observe in conducting any competitive intelligence analysis relates to the relevant organizational level of departure for the types of decisions demanding an inquiry, sometimes referred to as the unit of analysis. As already alluded to in our examples, we need to understand if the intelligence analysis in question relates to:

- a sales representative who is attempting to assess a relevant bidding situation,
- a sales manager assessing the outcome of a new pricing strategy,
- a manager of a division or strategic business unit attempting to position his or her unit in the marketplace,
- a CEO attempting to develop an acquisition plan, or
- a governmental office wanting to assess antitrust matters, evaluating the impact of state subsidies or the future of foreign direct investment flows to different countries or regions of the world.

Behind a desire to define the relevant unit of analysis lies an important recognition: Ultimately, it is not organizations that compete, but the coordinated market performance of different activities embedded in hierarchical structures and the associated networks with other organizations. This recognition becomes particularly important when performing an intelligence analysis for the purpose of developing a platform for business strategies.

In this book, we will also examine how competitive analysis can be performed at the level of a country, in relation to other countries, in competing to attract foreign direct investments, or as suggested in Michael Porter's seminal book on the competitive advantage of nations, with the analysis of the underlying reasons why certain industries tend to congregate in specific countries.[9]

In examining the different types of competitor analysis performed at various organizational levels, the literature has often attempted to distinguish between operational, tactical and strategic analysis of the competitive environment.[10]

Decisional Scope

The reference to operational, tactical and strategic analysis becomes a second dimension to consider, and centres around the immediacy of the issues, the functional base of concepts and information sources, and thus makes an implicit reference to the hierarchical nature of the decision-making unit. This can be illustrated in Figure 1.2. This view suggests that immediate competitive issues are not strategic, but operational in nature, a view not shared by most practicing managers.

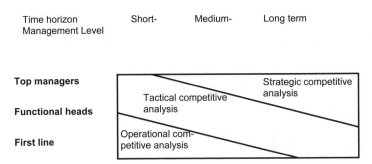

Figure 1.2 Management Levels and Scope of Analysis. Modified version by Jenster[11]

---

[9] See Porter, M. (1990).
[10] See e.g. King, W.R. & Cleland, D.I. (1979).
[11] See Jenster, P.V. (1992).

Rather, our definition of "strategic issue" emphasizes the impact on the value of the firm. To us, a strategic issue is one where the outcome or resolution has a significant impact on the value of the firm. Defining what is meant by "strategic issues" is important because this distinguishes "nice-to-know" as opposed to "need-to-know" information.

A tactical issue does not in itself have such a substantial impact on the firm, but may, in conjunction with other challenges, lead to the situations which may place the organization in a strategic quandary.

Following this line of thinking, an operational issue identified in an intelligence analysis is usually related to a specific customer or regional area and does not have a significant impact on the firm's value. In planning terms, tactical planning will typically have a horizon of 1 to 3 years, although this time span should not be taken too literally, as it is dependent on the contextual setting of the planning effort. This does not mean, however, that competitive analysis at the operational level is unimportant and should not be pursued. Lack of attention to operational competitive discrepancies can quickly accumulate and become of vital importance. For example, we came across a situation with a Dutch food manufacturer who had had problems in shipments to a large retailer. The third time a shipment arrived late, the food manufacturer was de-listed from the shelves of this retailer for a six-month period. The retailer happened to buy 20% of the firm's production volume. In turn, this created the opportunity for a much smaller competitor to enter this market and ultimately establish itself as the "category captain" by this retailer, thus managing the category assortment for the retailer. The result over eighteen months was a devastating slide in market share for the organization. What would have been considered merely an operational problem by many, escalated to a tactical issue, and then became a strategic problem.

Customer/Market Scope

The third dimension of crucial importance in competitive analysis is the delineation of a precise customer/market definition. The definition of scope of any analysis is vital as it provides the boundaries within which the inquiry takes place. An analysis of competition in men's shoe retailing in Denmark would be distinctly different from a study of the men's shoe market in Europe, which again would differ from a discussion of the global shoe industry. This illustration also highlights the different shades of grey in the distinction between market and industry analysis which has often created confusion in the literature.[12]

Another example illustrates how a company made an effort to understand the competitive situation in the Scandinavian Electrical Installation Material Industry (EIM). The investigation started with a delineation of the dimensions relevant to a definition of the sector to be studied in order to provide a picture of the competitive dynamics in the years to come.

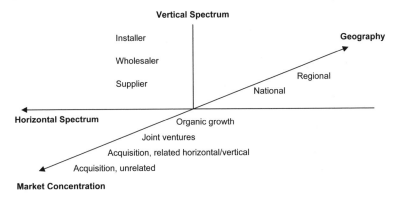

Source: Thesis by C. Schmidt under the supervision of Professor P. Jenster, CBS

Figure 1.3 Model for the Electrical Installation Materials Industry

In Figure 1.3, we show a model where the vertical spectrum defines the various critical dimensions relevant to the business; that is (installers), Wholesalers, and Component Suppliers. The horizontal spectrum includes Lighting, Cables, Hardware Accessories and Plumbing Suppliers, as well as those related to the Telecommunications, EDP, TV and other electronic companies, which need to be investigated in order to understand the EIM situation. In addition, both the geographical dimension and the market strategies pursued by various organizations were clarified. This framework led to an interesting, but also challenging effort to understand the development of a number of different, but related industries, as depicted in Figure 1.4.

---

[12] See Hayes, M.H., Jenster, P.V. & Aaby, N.E. (1996).

In a very similar way, it was necessary to understand the different client groupings among the customers to whom the industry was providing its services. In Figure 1.5, we have illustrated how the mapping of competitor formation among Electrical Installers was defined by the various companies active in related and overlapping activities, which in one way or another are competing or have the potential of competing.

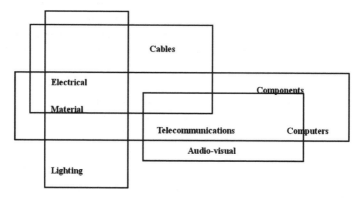

Source: Thesis by C. Schmidt under the supervision of Professor P. Jenster, CBS

Figure 1.4 Illustration of the Overlapping Industries Impacting the Scandinavian Electrical Installation Materials Industry

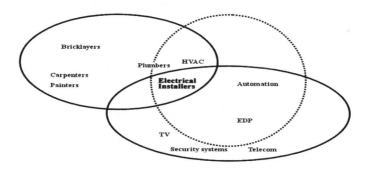

Source: Thesis by C. Schmidt under the supervision of Professor P. Jenster, CBS

Figure 1.5 Defining the Customer Scope for Electrical Installers' Materials Wholesaling

20

Product and Technological Scope

A fourth dimension to consider before starting a competitive analysis is the definition of the product and technology boundaries framing the inquiry to be conducted. Here, a relevant aspect of "product and technological scope" is the degree of integration to consider in the analysis of competitive behaviour. That is, relatively early, we must come to an agreement as to which of the critical activities involved in bringing products and services to the customers need to be considered in the discussion. This definition is particularly challenging in certain industrial settings where the technological base, and particularly the related emerging technologies, can be very difficult to assess in the context of current and future competitors.

The following example illustrates how a high-level group within Hewlett-Packard, called the Metaframe Group, approached the problems of finding an appropriate way of examining different competitive scenarios and communicating its findings to senior management. The firm was facing a dramatically changing marketplace and the team was appointed to "get its hands around the company's future". The task included establishing the criteria for selecting joint venture partners out among its competitors.

The task force began by searching the academic community, including that of IMD and Harvard, to find useful tools which could help them in the analysis. One such useful tool to define the competitive space was identified in B. Compaine's 1985 book entitled Understanding New Media. The team adapted this framework and used the graph and a colour overlay from this book to visually map out what set of competencies would be needed for the office of the future.

The Metaframe Group then developed the idea of colour-coding the competencies of different competitors or possible joint venture partners to map where various companies were positioned vis-à-vis "the office of the future". By using colour overlays, they were able to capture information about several companies at the same time. This also enabled the team to simulate different competitive scenarios (for example, "What if DEC makes a joint venture with ATT or buys Apple?"[13]). Although this analysis of the competitive space and the various competitors was most useful in that the two dimensions (product/service dimension and degree of content versus conduit character-

---

[13] DEC was acquired by Compaq in June 1998, which subsequently merged with Hewlett-Packard in May 2002. Hewlett-Packard started a long awaited joint venture to supply Apple iPods with HP devices in 2004.

istics) helped to "flush out" possible new competitors, the team felt that more in-depth analysis was needed.

In particular, the Metaframe Group wanted to do a more detailed analysis to capture competitive information along a number of dimensions. It was, nevertheless, felt that the colouring scheme was a unique and useful way of producing comparative data on competitors as well as possible partners. This led the DEC team to develop a unique mapping process for competitive data which was awarded US Patent 4,936,778. Each category was further divided into subcategories, where data, such as market share, technological sophistication, skills or competency, could be shown for different competitors. This method gave the team the ability to capture massive amounts of information for analysis and, subsequently, to present it to senior management.

The above example illustrates how competitive analysis must concern itself with the definition of the competitive space, the structuring of massive amounts of information for analysis, as well as the effective communication of the analysis in a way which can be readily understood by busy executives.

Network Definition

As suggested in the illustration of the Scandinavian Electrical Installers Material Wholesalers, it is essential but often difficult to define the relevant degree of horizontal and vertical integration appropriate to consider in the analysis. This decision will be impacted by some of the previous considerations in the definition phase, as well as the nature of the transactional relationships binding the relevant activities in the value-creation chain. For example, can the textile cleaning industry be looked at as a part of, or separated into, garments, floor mats, general or more specific laundry services to hotels, hospitals, restaurants, etc.? From one perspective, a number of the issues are similar across segments; from others, they are very different.

Temporal Dimension

The temporal dimension of how far back in the history and how far into the future the analysis should extend, that is, the time span to be covered in the competitor assessment. For example, are we to assess the evolution of European competition within electrical utilities from the start of this century? The question may rather be one of price dynamics of sales of Christmas trees in Stockholm during the month of December.

Competitive Battlefield

In recent years, the task of competitive analysis has been impacted by three major trends which have dramatically changed how practising managers are addressing the topic. These major trends are (a) the fusion of industries, (b) the globalization of trade and (c) the improvements in information and communication technologies. Needless to say, other trends influence the field of competitive analysis, but we feel that these three have had the greatest impact.

The first trend which seems to have changed the way in which firms pursue competitive analysis is the introduction of new configurations of business models. Most recent is the emergence of e-commerce sites, which are so different from traditional purchasing channels that one must decide if it is relevant to assess competitive players in the traditional sectors without including online alternatives. For example, 2CheckOut.com, a banking service which only exists on the internet, is taking small and midsize business customers away from major banks all over the world. Its services are often quicker and less expensive than those of its competitors. 2CO does not have the large infrastructure and headquarters to worry about, it does not have a tradition of high transactions fees, and it does not have to pay for extra office space. As long as the company continues to be good at detecting internet fraud and securing against it, there are, as of now, few limits to how far it, and other similar businesses, can grow in the banking industry.

Globalization, the disappearance of trade and regulatory barriers and geographical distances as constraining factors for commerce, have created competitive challenges in many markets. The opening of borders has accelerated the flow of goods and funds. For example, the strategic planners of the Danish mortgage banking firms are well advised to consider the challenges that the European Monetary Union presents, when commercial developers and international firms often prefer to avoid the currency risks of mortgaging in Danish Kroner (as Denmark has chosen to remain outside the EMU), and prefer an international lender. Similarly, globalization has made it more difficult to retain price differentiation in different countries. A buyer from a large retailer recently told us that as soon as his department observed price differences in Europe of more than 3-4% on fast-moving consumer goods, he would look into so-called "grey market transfers" of products. This means buying original products such as Nescafe in one country and transferring them to another, to take advantage of differences in the manufacturer's list prices.

A final development is changing the way we view competitive behaviour and conduct analyses. This is the rapid development of information and communication technologies which, through speed and volume, can provide buyers, sellers, and competitors access to information which was previously unimaginable. The last decade's proliferation of Internet usage has radically altered our view of competition. This development is likely to continue, and our ability to use this technology will be a deciding factor in the survival of any business in the future.

Academic Perspectives

The academic literature has concerned itself actively with competitive analysis for more than half a century. It is striking that the theoretical foundation and underlying assumptions vary significantly across the academic disciplines. There are, of course, several reasons why the various academic disciplines have started from different viewpoints, related to their underlying paradigmatic vantage points and the different purposes of discourses.

Most students of classical and neo-classical economic theory have often found themselves with few normative tools and little guidance when faced with these problems.

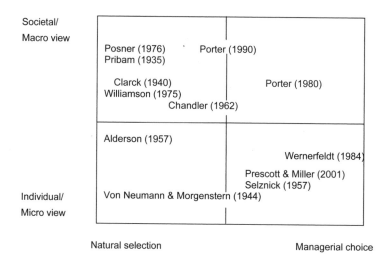

Figure 1.6 Illustrative Map of the Theoretical Orientation of Various Authors on Competitive Analysis

24

On the other hand, the marketing and strategic management literature has been more concerned with frameworks that are not only descriptive, but which also explore normative and decision-making heuristics. In Figure 1.5 we have attempted to provide the reader with one framework to understand the various streams of literature on competitive analysis and their placement in a framework mapping the various schools of thought.

Figure 1.6 places several of the more important authors, who represent specific streams of literature about competitive analysis, along two dimensions. The vertical dimension shows the scope of the perspective taken by the authors, ranging from a macro perception of societal implications to a micro level related to individual business actions. The horizontal dimension is on a spectrum from authors who assume a deterministic view (where markets are governed by a natural selection, predetermined by laws of economics), to assumptions of managerial choice (where rationality is at best limited, and influenced by both psychological and sociological phenomenon).

The underlying thrust of this illustrative map of the literature on intelligence analysis is to point out varying perspectives and thus potentially differing outcomes in analysis and description of competitive situations, and the potential normative implications of such analysis. Thus, it is useful to reflect on one's choice of analytical toolbox. and the opportunity for selecting both complementary perspectives to underscore a certain problem set and even opposing perspectives in an effort to test the treatment and robustness of a certain analytical exercise.

It should be mentioned, however, that the framework introduced in Figure 1.6 represents only one viewpoint of how the literature on competitive analysis can be mapped. Other examinations of the literature, such as that of Day and Reibstein[14] or recently by Knip, Dishman and Fleisher (2003), have looked at a number of different perspectives to Intelligence analysis, encompassing broad areas such as management, marketing, policy, and strategy. A preliminary list of the major academic approaches to these issues would be:

1. A resource-based point of view, popularized by Prahalad and Hamel, focusing on the firm's resources or assets and capabilities, and how these may provide advantages for rivals.[15]

---

[14] See Day, G.S. & Reibstein, D.J. (eds) (1997).
[15] See Prahalad, C.K. & Hamel, G. (1990).

2. The positional view, most closely associated with the work of industrial economics, also sometimes referred to as the "Structure-Conduct-Performance" school of competitor analysis, which examines different competitors' relative positions in the industry and the forces which allow firms to sustain strategic positions.[16] In their discussion, Day and Reibstein emphasize that the resource-based approach is concerned with what advantages are needed and the positional view is concerned with how to create advantages.[17]

3. Game theory, from its early development in ancient Chinese writings to an academic discipline, examines moves and countermoves of competitors. Whereas this school of thought is based firmly on rational behaviour, the next stream of literature reminds us that competitors' movements may be far from rational.[18]

4. Behavioural theory examines the cognitive and behavioural properties of decision making in competitive environments, including psychological biases and motivational forces.[19]

5. Public policy has, particularly in a US context, been concerned with the antitrust implications of competitive behaviour in an effort to shield the public from undesired effects of firm strategies: In many ways, the body of literature stands in contrast to the underlying motives of most of the strategic management literature which aims at equipping managers with knowledge which can help create market imperfections.[20]

6. The Competitive Intelligence literature in the US as it developed around the Society of Competitive Intelligence Professionals (SCIP) and the journal Competitive Intelligence Review (CIR); now the Journal of Competitive Intelligence and Management (JCIM), has taken a practical intelligence perspective on the topic of competitive advantage, with parallels to military intelligence practice and research.[21]

7. The French Intelligence Economique and Geopolitique literature and tradition tends to take a macro perspective on these issues.[22]

8. The German tradition treats competitive intelligence under

---

[16] See Porter, M.E. (1985).

[17] See See Day, G.S. & Reibstein, D.J. (eds) (1997).

[18] See e.g. Teck, H.H. & Weigelt, K. (1997).

[19] See Meyer, R. & Banks, D. (1997).

[20] See e.g. Areda, P. (1986).

[21] See e.g. Fleisher, C. S., Bensoussan, B. (2002), and Prescott, J. E. (1993).

[22] See e.g. Delbecque, E. (2006) and Chauprade, A. (2003).

Konkurrentz-Analyse, Beobachtung and Wettbewerbsforschung.[23] Or as Wirstchaftsspionage when there is an unethical, or illegal component or otherwise as a part of subjects like marketing or strategy.[24]

9. The Swedish tradition of "omvärdsanalys" tends to treat the topic from a broader, interdisciplinary perspective with emphasis on the intelligence methodology.[25]

Among academics, we use a saying that "there is nothing more practical than a good theory". What the above listing of various theoretical directions should point to is that the problem to be analysed may benefit from one or more theoretical perspectives, and that one cannot necessarily be said to hold a patent on the truth in the area of competitive analysis. What is needed, on the other hand, is a cross reading by these academic communities, not only between research communities, but also across cultures. To present this perspective is one of the aims of this book.

Conclusion

It would be appropriate to start a book on assessment of competitors by remembering that competitive analysis uses a broad set of analytical tools which are used to describe market phenomena and produce decision-relevant information for managers at different levels in organizations. This requires managers and other leaders to think about competitive analysis from a context-specific viewpoint and not as a generally applicable methodology.

It is important to remember that the area of competitor analysis is evolving as a result of developments in globalization of trade and commerce, restructuring of industries, and the evolution of information and communication technologies. These developments are forcing managers to go beyond the traditional definition of their businesses in terms of what they produce and market, to look at new and different configurations of how products and services are transformed in the long journey to reach the end customer.

---

[23] For a summary see e.g. Michaeli, R. (2004).
[24] See e.g. Ulfkotte, U. (1999), or Solberg Søilen, K. (2004).
[25] See Solberg Søilen, K. (2005), or Hedin, H. (2004).

We conclude that the academic world has been concerned with competitive analyses for many years, but that there is a call for a more integrated view to build an analytical platform from which competitive behaviour can be better described and predicted. Contributions by Ganesh, Miree and Prescott (2003) to take the competitive intelligence research agenda from one that is consulting-based, to one based on double-blinded peer reviews, is also a welcome step in the right direction. Together, these perspectives and initiatives may lead to a healthy convergence in Intelligence Studies.

REFERENCES
Alderson, W. (1957). *Marketing Behavior and Executive Action*, Homewood, IL: Irwin.

Areda, P. (1986). *Antitrust Law: An Analysis of Antitrust Principles and Their Application*, Boston, MA: Little, Brown.

Chandler, A.D. Jr. (1962). *Strategy and Structure*, MIT Press, Cambridge, MA. Clark, J.M. (1940). Toward a concept of workable competition. *American Economic Review*, 30, June, 242-56.

Chauprade, A. (2003). *Géopolitique*. Paris: Ellipses.

Day, G.S. & Reibstein, D.J. (eds) (1997) *Wharton on Dynamic Competitive Strategy*, New York, NY: Wiley.

Delbecque, E. (2006). *L'Intelligence économique: une nouvelle culture pour in nouveau monde*, Paris: PUF.

Eells, R., Nehemkis, P. (1984). *Corporate Intelligence and Espionage*, New York, NY: MacMillian Publishers Company.

Fleisher, C.S., Knip, V., and Dishman, P. (2003). Chronological and Categorized Bibliography of Key Competitive Intelligence Scholarships. Part 2 (1990-1996). *Journal of Competitive Intelligence and Management*, Vol. 1, Nr. 2, pp. 11-86.

Fleisher, C.S., Bensoussan, B. (2002). *Strategic and Competitive Analysis: Methods and Techniques for Analyzing Business Competition*, Upper Saddle River, NJ: Prentice Hall.

Ganesh, U., Miree, C.E., Prescott, J. (2003). Competitive Field Research: Moving the field forward by setting a Research Agenda. *Journal of Competitive Intelligence and Management*, Vol. 1, Nr. 1, pp. 1-12.

Greene, jr., R.M. (ed.) (1966). *Business intelligence and espionage*, Homewood: Dow Jones-Irwin.

Hayes, M.H., Jenster, P.V. & Aaby, N.E. (1996). *Business Marketing: A Global Perspective*, Irwin, Chicago, IL.

Hedin, H. (2004). Evolution of Competitive Intelligence in Sweden. *Journal of Competitive Intelligence and Management*, Vol. 2, Nr. 3, pp. 56-75.

Jenster, P.V. (1991). DEC-ITT case. *Planning Review*, September/October, 20.

Jenster, P.V. (1992). Competitive analysis: understanding the nature of the beast. *Journal of Strategic Change*, 1, 28.1-4.

King, W.R. & Cleland, D.I. (1979). *Strategic Planning and Policy*, New York, NY: Van Nostrand Reinhold.

Knip, V., Dishman, P., and Fleisher, C.S. (2003). Chronological and Categorized Bibliography of Key Competitive Intelligence Scholarships. Part 3 (the earliest writings – 1989). *Journal of Competitive Intelligence and Management*, Vol. 1, Nr. 3, pp. 10-79.

Knorr, K. (1964). Foreign intelligence and the social sciences. *Research paper, Nr. 17*, Center of International Studies, Princeton University.

Meyer, R. & Banks, D. (1997). Behavioral theory and naive strategic reasoning. In Day G.S. & Reibstein, D.J. (eds) (1997), *Wharton on Dynamic Competitive Strategy*, New York, NY: Wiley.

Michaeli, R. (2004). Competitive Intelligence in Germany. *Journal of Competitive Intelligence and Management*, Vol. 2, Nr. 4, pp. 1-6.

Porter, M.E. (1980). *Competitive Strategy: Techniques for Analyzing Industries and Competitors*, New York, NY: The Free Press.

Porter, M.E. (1985). *Competitive Advantage*, New York, NY: The Free Press.

Porter, M.E. (1990). *The Competitive Advantage of Nations*, New York, NY: The Free Press.

Posner, R.A. (1976). *Antitrust Law: An Economic Perspective*, University of Chicago: University of Chicago Press.

Prahalad, C.K. & Hamel, G. (1990). The core competence of the corporation. *Harvard Business Review*, May/June, 79-91.

Prescott, J. E. Miller, S. H. (eds) (2001). *Proven strategies in competitive intelligence : lessons from the trenches*, New York, NY: Wiley.

Prescott, J. E (1993). *Global Perspectives on Competitive Intelligence*, Alexandria, Va.: Society of Competitive Intelligence Professionals.

Pribam, K. (1935). Controlled competition and the organization of American industry. *Quarterly Journal of Economics*, 49, May, 371-93.

Selznick, P. (1957). *Leadership in Administration*, New York, NY: Harper & Row.

Smith, A. (1776/1977). *The wealth of nations*, Harmondsworth: England. Penguine books.

Solberg Søilen, K. (2005). *Introduction to private and public intelligence*, Lund: Studentlitteratur.

Solberg Søilen, K. (2004). Wirtschaftsspionage in Verhandlungen aus Informationsökonomischer und Wirtschaftsethischer Perspektive - Eine

REFERENCES

Interdisziplinäre Analyse. *Dissertation*. Wirtschaftswissenschaflichen Fakultät der Universität Leipzig, Deutschland.

Teck, H.H. & Weigelt, K. (1997). Game theory and competitive strategy. In Day,G.S. & Reibstein, D. (eds) (1997), *Wharton on Competitive Strategy*, New York, NY: Wiley.

Ulfkotte, U. (1999). Marktplatz der Diebe, *Wie die Wirschaftsspionage deutsche Unternehmen ausplündert und ruiniert*, München: Bertelsmann.

Von Neuman, J. & Morgenstern, O. (1944). *The Theory of Games and Economic Behavior*, New York, NY: Wiley.

Wemerfelt, B. (1984). A resource-based view of the firm. *Strategic Management Journal*, 5, 171-80.

Williamson, O.E. (1975). *Markets and Hierarchies: Analysis and Antitrust Implications*, New York, NY: The Free Press.

CHAPTER 2

Strategies for a Competitive Advantage

Seeking a Competitive Advantage

Development, maintenance and execution of a robust organizational strategy lies at the heart of all intelligence activities; the ultimate purpose being to ensure superior performance through sustainable competitive advantage.[26] This cannot be done in isolation from the market and the rest of the industry, because being better than a competitor will not guarantee success, if what is offered gives little value to the customer. Any conclusions that might be drawn from competitive analysis must be considered in conjunction with these other factors.

So far, the most prevailing competitive models have tended to focus on two groups, customers and competitors. In a cooperative world, other factors such as supportive business organizations (collaborators or organizations with related technologies) government institutions, financial actors, universities (research) and cooperative institutions (industry organizations, chamber of commerce, institutes for keeping and improving quality, standardization, and supportive cluster organizations) play a major role. These are often excluded from the competitive perspective, especially in macroeconomic studies.[27] Michael Porter defines national prosperity, not as the sum of the means a state can undertake to increase its wealth though its own direct activities, but as a function of the competitive advantage of its companies.

The competitive advantage literature is of concern to intelligence analysts, because it sets out the roadmap of the modern organization, especially the Multi-National Enterprise (MNE). Moreover, competi-

---

[26] For recent research on competitive advantage theory, see e.g. Nilsson, F., Rapp, B. (2005).
[27] On clusters, see Porter, M. (1990).

tive advantage constitutes the overall framework of our free market economy.

In the early part of the 20th century, Austrian philosopher Ludwig Wittgenstein introduced what was later called the Linguistic Turn, the idea that language itself constructs reality. At the turn of the 21st century, economists understand that information is changing the way we obtain economic growth. We could call this the Information Turn, or what is sometimes referred to as the Information Revolution.

"Every business consists of two elements; the physical and the virtual...the information revolution provides organizations with an unparalleled opportunity to move elements of their business from the physical domain to the virtual".[28] Even though this realization is not new to theorists and academics, our organizations have not yet adapted themselves to this new reality; our management methods are still firmly rooted in the physical. We continue to manage people rather than intellectual capital.[29]

We also continue to work independently, instead of working according to the model of "work-learn-share".[30] Our organizations need to "capitalize on the information they own about their customers, suppliers and partners. To take an example, research at Federal Express suggests that when customers assess perceived service value, the information about the package is as important as the package itself. This insight has impact the service configuration, and has become a part of the value proposition for sustainable long-term growth.[31]

The quest for global dominance within any given market has never been more outspoken among business leaders of MNEs.[32] Competitive or Business Intelligence is considered to be of vital importance to these companies, as they can only prosper through a close connection with each other and an active and direct involvement in political institutions.[33] "With every passing day, it is becoming more obvious that managers must view every industry as a global industry and every business as a knowledge business."[34] Managing knowledge, which may be defined as "the collection and processing of disparate knowl-

---

[28] See Czerniawska, F., Potter, G. (1998), Preface. p. viii.
[29] Idem p. 134.
[30] Idem p. 197.
[31] Hurd, M., Nyberg, L. (2004), p. 2.
[32] Title of a book by Govindarajan, V., Gupta, A.K. (2001).
[33] See e.g. Sölvell, Ö. (2004).
[34] Govindarajan, V., Gupta, A.K. (2001), preface, p. Xvii.

edge in order to affect mutual performance",[35] is the art of managing the invisible – the heart (emotional commitment) and the head (the intellect) – of people around the world".[36]

At the same time, as pointed out by Rothberg and Erickson, knowledge management is not enough. "Knowledge has value, but intelligence has power".[37] "Possessing knowledge is important, but to be truly useful, knowledge must be used, [and] knowledge must become intelligence".[38]

Knowledge Management and Intelligence are therefore highly interrelated areas of research. We may say that while Competitive intelligence is highly operational, Knowledge Management is strategic. Knowledge Management practices are about capturing the intellectual capital of the firm, and the goal of Knowledge Management can be expressed as collecting knowledge that is tacit and making it explicit.[39]

From an academic perspective, we may treat every business discipline related to the Information Turn under one established term, namely Information Economics, where each area of study must define itself in relation to the others. For example, Customer Relation Management (CRM) and Data Mining (DM[40]) are closely related areas. The boundaries between these fields of study are changing with new technology and customer demands. For example, the Swedish Software company Brimstone Intelligence discovered that it had moved from being predominantly a Business Intelligence firm to a CRM company.

Data Mining is the process of automating information discovery.[41] DM automates the process of discovering useful trends and patterns[42] through the construction and use of models. For the DM models to be of use, the data has to be "cleaned", meaning it must be consistent. It must also be updated and complete. When this is achieved, data can be merged.

Central to data mining is the process of model building. It is often used in connection with direct marketing, trend analysis, and forecasting,

[35] See Montano, B. (ed) (2005), p. 1.
[36] See foreword by Prahalad, C.K. in Govindarajan, V., Gupta, A.K. (2001), p. xv.
[37] Rothberg, H.N. , Erickson, G.S. (2005), p. 3.
[38] Idem.
[39] Idem, p. 33.
[40] Not to be confused with Direct Marketing.
[41] See Groth, R. (1998), p. 1.
[42] Idem, p. 2.

and often sold with consultative services.[43] CRM is the use of these abilities to recreate the old 1-to-1 marketing relationship. As anyone who has used Amazon.com understands, we can now profile customers as never before, adding new products and services. Most companies have not even started this value-added adventure.

At the same time, many companies are now seeking to gain a competitive advantage through their investment in information technology.[44] Data mining is already used heavily in banking and finance, in retail and consumer marketing, telecommunications and the healthcare industry. Behind these developments lie significant advances in computational power and the application of new algorithms.[45] Data mining and competitive and business intelligence thus go hand in hand, as does Database Administration (DBA), Marketing Analysis, and Business Marketing Intelligence. As the marketing function remains the single most important application for this new area, we shall use an entire chapter to present this field.[46]

The Organization's Strategic Options

We shall continue by exploring the different strategic positioning options available to firms. Figure 2.1 gives one view of the strategic moves that are available to any competitor. For the purposes of this diagram, industry should be interpreted as including suppliers, competitors and buyers, and therefore the requirements of the market. Chapters 3 and 4 will look in much more detail at industry and company analysis, including the "Five Forces Analysis" approach of Porter (1980).

Every company has strategic options, although this does not mean that all options are sensible for every company. The matrix in Figure 2.1 looks at the things a company might do to build a competitive advantage.

The firm may choose to operate within the "rules of the industry, without major change to what it offers. This is the top left-hand cell of the matrix. The options here include a stronger focus on a niche strategy, seeking to identify and exploit segments where its products would have an advantage, or what might be termed improvement strategies. Those shown on the matrix are seeking ways of giving added value to customers, or becoming more efficient through attention to costs. Under

---

[43] See Groth, R. (1998).

[44] Kalling, T. (2000).

[45] On neural networks, see Hopfield J.J. (1988).

[46] See chapter 7, Marketing Intelligence.

all these strategies, most of the changes the company would make would be internal, examining its processes and making only incremental adjustments to what is basically the same family of products. These options do not preclude the launch of new products, but would be of a similar nature to the current offering.

ACTIVITY

		Same	Novel
INDUSTRY STRUCTURE	**Same**	Niches/segmentation Improved value for customers (quality, service, price, cycle time) Cost reduction	New products New niches/ Segmentation
	Change	Acquire competitors Strategic alliances	Change the nature of the industry Change how the industry operates

Figure 2.1 Strategic Options (Developed from a diagram in Hussey, 1994)[47]

The top right-hand cell suggests a more fundamental change to some of the things the organization does, without any significant attempt to alter how the industry operates, or the balance of power between the industry firms and other actors such as buyers and suppliers. Strategies might include paying attention to niches and segments in a more innovative way than the first cell implies, with a willingness to add new lines. Or the company could pursue an aggressive policy of new product launches. An example might be an automotive manufacturer which adds a new type of sports car to its list, when previously it had offered only staid family cars.

At the bottom left-hand corner there is a group of strategic options which are designed to change how the industry is structured but without any fundamental change to what the organization does. This might in-

---

[47] See Hussey, D.E. (1994).

clude actions to reduce the number of competitors through acquisition, subject of course to national monopolies legislation. Rationalization of an industry has been a traditional strategy followed by competitors anxious to improve their market position. Strategic alliances may be used for a similar reason, although, as will be seen below, there may be better reasons for making alliances. A third group of strategies is to attempt to change the channels the industry has traditionally used. Here we find companies like Avon Cosmetics which do not follow the typical wholesaler/retailer route to the customers, and sell direct instead. Not on the chart but in the same category might be an attempt to work much more closely with a supplier, in a way that makes it difficult for competitors to use that supplier in the future.

The bottom right-hand cell reflects a reinvention of the company and of the industry. It is this type of activity which Hamel and Prahalad argue should lie at the heart of competitive strategy: "...the goal is to fundamentally reinvent existing competitive space (First Direct's Telephone Banking Service in the United Kingdom) or invent entirely new competitive space (Netscape's web browsers) in ways that amaze customers and dismay competitors. Sustainable profitable growth is not the product of a deal, it's the product of foresight. In turn foresight is not the product of perspicuity, but of unconventional out of the box thinking".[48] Hamel and Prahalad argue that in order to be able to reinvent the industry, the organization must identify its core competencies, and concentrate on building the competency it will need to make the necessary leaps to a different future. This notion was further developed in W. Chan Kim and Renêe Mauborgne's work on Blue Ocean Strategy.[49]

It is not all about Aggression

It is noteworthy to observe that in many industries not all the competitors are in contention with each other. This does not mean that they may not become rivals at some time in the future, which may be a good reason for studying them, but it also provides an opportunity to gain a competitive advantage through collaboration. Let us hasten to add that we are not advocating illegal actions, such as price fixing, and, as is the case throughout the book, our stance is that businesses practices' should be both legal and ethical.

There are three obvious examples of non-competing "competitors":

---

[48] See Hamel, G. & Prahalad, C.K. (1994/1996), p. xi.
[49] See Chan Kin, W., Mauborgne, R. (2004).

- The segmented market, where competitors at different ends of the spectrum offer products which are not really substitutes for each other, and have few (if any) customers in common. An extreme example can be found in the car industry with Rolls-Royce and the old Reliant Robin.[50] Both companies make cars, but have little in common besides this, not even the number of wheels on the car. It is not readily apparent what either of these companies could gain from collaboration. If we had said Rolls-Royce and Morgan, both expensive cars but not competing for the same customers, it might be possible to see areas where there could be benefit from collaboration, such as benchmarking each other's processes, exchange of technological information, or sharing dealer networks overseas.

- The second type of non-competing competitor is the company which makes similar products to yours, but for various reasons does not offer them in the countries in which you trade. Possibly neither organization has the resources to move quickly to become global. Here a strategic alliance might be beneficial to both. This might be achieved by sharing technology, distribution facilities, or plants so that both can gain the benefits of being global, without all the costs that would otherwise be involved. Much more might be gained by both organizations, than if they began to move piecemeal into each other's markets, and began to become competitors in earnest. All the commonsense rules of creating a successful alliance apply, not least being the need to understand each other's objectives for seeking an alliance, and a shared vision of what the alliance should achieve.

- A third type of competitor may be one that is in contention with you now, but perhaps to a limited extent, and which can be removed or neutralized by collaboration. Here, we are thinking particularly about the peripheral activities of someone whose original reason for establishing the competing activity was to provide services to its own organization. Activities such as corporate training colleges, training, physical distribution, and various other services have often been set up to serve the organization and also offer their services in the market as a whole. Where there are competitors of this type, it may be possible to collaborate with the parent organization and effectively take over the competitor by persuading its owners to enter into an outsourcing deal.

---

[50] The production of Reliant Robin stopped in October 2002.

When the Harbridge Consulting Group (HCG) wanted to offer a Europe-wide management training service to multinational companies it could have followed a risky and expensive program of setting up an office in every country. This could have taken a long time, but the opportunity existed immediately: to be able to offer a common, highly tailored training program, which could be delivered in a variety of European languages. The alternative chosen was to create a capability through cooperation. Selecting alliance partners from competitors in each country meant that there were mutual benefits. Although some of the revenue went to the alliance partners, it created assignments and revenue for HCG that would otherwise not have been obtained. In Germany office facilities were set up within the premises of a non-competing consultancy. Although there was much more to the pan-European strategy than this, collaboration was a far more attractive method of achieving a Europe-wide presence than any of the other options.

Such methods are not open to every industry, or every organization, but they act as a counterbalance to the attack and defence strategies which may be another outcome of competitive strategy. The aim of competitive strategy is not primarily to "kill" the competition, but to build a position of sustainable competitive advantage. Indeed it is possible to argue that every organization needs competitors, as without them there is less incentive for creative thinking, and a tendency for the organization to become complacent and less effective.

Deterrence

> *The concept of deterrence is as old as military conflict. Deterrence is a strategy to prevent conflict, by persuading a rational competitor that you are willing and able to punish non-compliance with your clearly expressed and understood wishes. Deterrence is a strategy for an acceptable peace rather than a war, and is a battle won in the mind of the competitor through psychological pressure rather than by physical combat.*
>
> *James, B. (1985)*[51]

In business terms deterrence is a strategy to:

---

[51] See James, B. (1985), p. 27.

1. Persuade new entrants that the market is not worth entering, because of the way you will react, or
2. Try to stop encroachments into a segment of the market which is important to you, or
3. Attempt to keep a competitor from increasing its market share.

An example is provided by the insurance brokerage industry in the UK, which for decades held off the threat that the insurance companies whose products they sold would compete with them by selling directly to the market. The threat was that all brokers would cease to recommend any company that took this action, and the insurance companies held off because the speed at which they feared they would lose revenue was greater than the speed at which direct sales were likely to take off. It is only in the past decade that this threat has been eliminated, and this was mainly because a new entrant to the market, Direct Line, set up to offer a direct general insurance service over the telephone, took a large market share because it was able to offer lower prices, and in many cases offer better customer service.

The best deterrence is a strong position, which makes it difficult for an attacker to gain a foothold without investing a lot of capital. This is not achieved merely by having the largest market share. Indeed sheer size and past success often breeds complacency, despite the achievements of the past. It is notable that neither Xerox nor IBM, both of which can be said to have re-created their industries, was as invulnerable as they believed. IBM did not take action early enough to erect a strong position in the personal computer market, and Xerox put too much reliance on its network of patents. In both these cases, the judgments appeared to be from the inside looking out, rather than undertaking an examination of what an attacker might see as vulnerability.

A strong position has market share as a component, and this may be most important when the learning curve effect means that high volumes give lower costs, which in turn allow prices to be set which other competitors find difficult to meet. But it is also about technological foresight, adequate levels of research and development, and giving customers value in all respects, so that they have little incentive to change.

Michael Porter terms the tactics by which one competitor communicates with another as "market signals", and points out that they can be bluff or real.[52] Bluffs are intended to mislead competitors into either

---

[52] See Porter, M.E. (1980).

doing or not doing something. In one study we made of the UK detergents industry, we found that one competitor had sales that were considerably higher than its capacity. Investigation showed that it had announced the installation of additional capacity, but had given the impression that it was to replace old plant. In fact it was incremental, but the confusion enabled it to implement its strategy to increase market share without attracting defensive actions from competitors. Sun Tzu wrote in his treatise on the art of war some 2400 years ago: "All warfare is based on deception". He argued that deception can have its place in the competitive battle. However, there is at least one added element in business battles, which is that while you may want to deceive the competitor, you rarely want to confuse the customer.

Michael Porter gives examples of market signals, including: early announcements of new product launches, intended to persuade buyers to defer a purchase decision of a competitor's new product until both were available; announcement of capacity expansion, which is large enough for all unfulfilled marketing requirements, to deter others from planning more capacity; and speeches which try to get competitors to hold the line on prices, by giving forecasts of raw material cost increases, and expressing fears that profits are now inadequate to support the research and development needed by the industry.

When Shell Chemicals published their analytical technique, the Directional Policy Matrix, which provided an objective way of looking at prospects for different streams of products, they may well have done so for altruistic motives. Perhaps even more likely was an attempt to persuade the industry to look at data objectively, so that the then-prevailing pattern in the industry of capacity expansion based upon "gut instinct" was changed to a more predictable decision process. A second signal might well have been to tell competitors that they should not think on a single-country basis, as the industry had become truly global.

James suggests that a deterrence strategy must have four elements:[53]

- It must be credible, for if the competitor does not believe it, it will have no effect.
- The company applying a deterrence strategy must have the resources to carry it through, as well as the willingness to do so. If your competitor knows you can afford a price war for much longer than it can, a price war may well be avoided.

---

[53] See James, B. (1985).

- By one means or another actions and counteractions must be communicated between the competitors, without infringing any competition laws.
- The actions should try to persuade competitors to behave in a rational manner, so that disruptive actions which are damaging to all are avoided.

Deterrence strategies do not always work, and are unlikely to be effective against a competitor who is changing the rules of the game. We once saw a pamphlet issued by a manufacturer of radio valves (and it would be no surprise today if many readers have no idea what these are) arguing that the newly invented transistors had only limited use, and that radio valves were the long-term future of the industry. Firms who may have been leaders in duplicating machines and the older-style photocopiers could not hope to defeat the advances of the far superior Xerox machines, when these came on to the market in the 1960s. Electromechanical telephone exchanges had to give way to electronics in the 1970s. The gramophone record had almost disappeared by the end of the 1980s, in the face of competition from the CD, as the CD is threatened by a combination of internet + iPod today. In the 1990s, the shape of the information industry had been changed by developments in telecommunications and computers. At the start of the 21st century, record stores are closing down everywhere as users download their music onto their PCs via the internet, whether legally or by means of piracy. This last form of activity is leading to a steady and dramatic loss in record companies' earnings. A new generation is growing up which has never used a fax machine, who will smile at the sight of a fax number on a business card. Lines drawn in the sand are not credible when a competitor faces such fundamental changes.

Attack Strategies

We have chosen to deal with attack strategies next, because it is logical to consider how competitive attacks may be made, before looking at defence. Sun Tzu, whose ancient writings on strategy are said to have influenced many modern Japanese companies, argued that the most important thing is to attack an enemy's strategy. Disrupting his alliances is the next best thing; next best is to attack his armies; but the worst option is to attack his cities. For competitive strategy we need to think in somewhat less murderous terms, but the underlying principle of minimum force/resources to achieve maximum advantage is good advice.

- *Attacking the strategy of a competitor.* This can pull the rug out from under the competitor's feet, and leave him in a weaker position. The most effective way has already been mentioned; strategy of applying creative, entrepreneurial thinking to a base of sound knowledge and analysis, thus changing the competitive arena. Another example might be to pre-empt a competitor by getting to the market first with a new product, in an area which is known to be of strategic importance.

- *Attacking the competitor's alliances.* An example of this was the acquisition of Rover by BMW. There were undoubtedly many reasons for this acquisition, but one effect was to cause Honda to withdraw from the alliance it had operated for many years with Rover, and its predecessor British Leyland.[54] Similar patterns of alliances changing allegiance have been observed in the airline industry.

- *Attacking the competitor's armies.* This is akin to choosing segments or geographical areas to attack, where the competitor may be weakest, or least able to mount a defence. Sometimes it may be the first step in a longer-term plan of attack, and may not be seen as a major threat in the first instance. When Japanese motorcycle companies entered the European market they started with the low-priced segments, but also began to expand those segments by appealing to different groups of people. This was the spearhead for a long-term attack on the market, which eventually meant that they achieved dominance in all segments. Ryan air is doing the same in the airlines industry.

- *Attacking the competitor's cities.* This is akin to a frontal attack where a competitor is strongest. Risks are higher, and the action ensures that the competitor so attacked will respond.

The first rule of any attack strategy is to know the industry, the market, and the competitors being attacked. If the weak points of the competitors are known, and their likely reactions predicted, the attacker is more likely to arrive at a successful strategy. It is this rational analysis which enables a decision to be made about whether the rewards of success outweigh the costs, and whether the chances of success are

---

[54] In February 1999, after years of heavy losses, BMW's board fired its company chairman Bernd Pischetsrieder, the man behind the Rover acquisition. Rover was sold to Ford but the production of Rover cars has seized. Ford keeps the brand much to protect the Land Rover brand.

high enough to justify the move. The structure of the industry is, in essence, the terrain upon which the battles will be fought, and will affect both what is possible and how obvious any full-scale attack might seem. In a highly fragmented market, such as management consulting, where there are no dominant leaders and a long tail of small organizations, it is possible that any attempt by any individual small competitor to seize market share will pass largely unnoticed. This is because a quadrupling of sales of a company with, say, a 0.25% market share means that the impact on any one of the several hundred competitors is likely to be negligible, and even if the impact is seen, the reasons for it may not be obvious. In an industry with four or five competitors of roughly equal share, every player will be watching the others very carefully, and is more likely to notice the effect of any attack and who is doing it. Where there is a dominant player at, say, 60% market share, a follower with 25%, and three other companies sharing the rest of the market, the position may be less straightforward. It may be easier for a small company to move against the others than for either of the top two to try to improve their positions. This is because a large increase in sales of a company with a small market share may have little impact on the big company. The other companies may restrain themselves from responding aggressively, because to do so would be construed as an attack on the dominant company and invite a response.

Some modern military principles can be used to guide strategy in a business situation. A comparison of the US Army field manual and principles defined by a writer on business strategy appears in Caplan.[55] They are:

- The objective: every action must be directed to the achievement of a clearly defined and attainable objective.
- Mass: adequate resources must be concentrated at the right time and place to achieve the objective.
- Economy of force: to use only the amount of effort that the situation requires.
- Manoeuvre: leave room for flexibility.
- Unity of command: ensure that all action is coordinated to achieve the objective.
- Security: take actions to avoid being surprised by the actions of competitors.

---

[55] See Caplan, R.H. (1965).

- Surprise: attack the enemy when, where and how the attack is not expected.
- Simplicity: the simple plan is usually the best.

Business is not warfare, and the objective of most competitive attacks is to secure an advantage in profit through growth, market share, or longer-term positioning, rarely the annihilation of a competitor, and in any case in many countries there are laws designed to prevent many of the actions that might achieve this.

The classification of attack strategies follows the thinking of Kotler[56] and James,[57] although there are differences between these two authorities.

1. The frontal attack. This is the commercial equivalent of Sun Tzu's worst case: the attack on the enemy's cities. It implies a head-on confrontation where the defence is at its strongest. Some such attacks mirror the defendant's marketing strategy, and hope to achieve results through sheer perseverance. Others have only one point of difference: price. By cutting price for what is otherwise a matched offering, the attacker hopes to be able to persuade customers to switch. Only in markets where there are many niches is it possible to use the full frontal attack selectively. It clearly does not hurt Rolls-Royce car sales if the cheapest Fiat is discounted, because the products are not comparable. In markets where the products are more similar to each other, an attack on one competitor is really an attack on all of them. In full frontal attacks, the victory usually goes to the strongest. However, a dominant competitor is less likely to make a full frontal attack on a competitor, unless it is a niche operator where the effects of the warfare can be isolated. The reason is that someone with, for example, a 70% market share who has to cut prices across the board to attack a smaller competitor may find that the negative impact on profits is greater than the amount of extra market share that may be gained. Frontal attacks were best in industries where very large cost reductions can be gained from increases in volume; and where price reductions may stimulate growth in the market as well as stealing share from competitors. This is a feature of markets such as pocket calculators, and

---

[56] See Kotler, P. (1994).
[57] See James, B. (1985).

various consumer electronic products, where gains in volume can bring considerable competitive benefit.

2. The flanking attack. Instead of attacking where a competitor is strongest, the flanking attack goes for areas of weakness. This may be to find geographical areas where the competitor is not performing as well as elsewhere, or to identify segments of the market which have either not been spotted by the competitor, or are not catered for as well as they might be. In both of these situations the attack may be partly concealed, because if that portion has not been served well, attention to it may expand the market as well as taking sales away from the competitor. If the product has been specifically designed for the segment, it may be some time before the defender can respond. One example of the flanking attack is provided by Simon Aerials in the USA. This was a company that made truck-mounted aerial platforms, of the type that would hoist a worker to the top of a tree or building, and provide a secure platform from which tasks could be undertaken. These heavy vehicles were also used on construction sites, but were not ideal for all jobs because of their size and weight. The company designed a vehicle specifically for the construction industry. It was a fraction of the size and height of the trucks, but would give the same weight, with greater capability to reach awkward places because of the way the lift mechanism worked. Its smaller size meant that it could work inside a building, and had greater manoeuvrability and flexibility. It could also be manufactured at a much lower cost, and could be offered at a cheaper price than the less suitable vehicles traditionally used on construction sites. Because the vehicles were smaller, a greater volume could be made in the existing plant, thus capacity was increased without major investment. This flanking attack was successful, as there was little that the competitors could do in the short term, since cutting prices to meet the new machine would have been uneconomical, and would have resulted in unwanted losses in the other markets in which the machines were sold. In any case, the new machine was still better for the construction industry. A comparable product could not be offered until it had been developed by existing players, much later.

One example of geographical flanking attacks is the supermarket which erects its new store in an area where its rivals are weakest. Another is First Direct which established a telephone retail banking operation, which not only eliminated the need for branch offices but also enabled the company to accept only the business it wanted, thus cherry-picking the more profitable segments. EasyJet, a small company, established a cut-price service from the UK to various destinations on the continent of Europe, taking from British Airways both low-margin holiday traffic and some of its premium business travel. Flanking attacks have also been carried out successfully on companies that supply products like tires and batteries to an original equipment manufacturer. Traditionally Original Equipment Manufacturer (OEM) sales have been made at low margins, in order to gain the more lucrative after-market for replacements. The flanking attack applied here, is where competitors enter the replacement market, by possibly offering a price advantage, thus picking off a slice of the more profitable business, and leaving the OEM business untouched.

3. Encirclement. Under an encirclement strategy the attack is made on several fronts at once. Successful encirclement strategies usually attempt to identify and exploit new niches, and to beat the offer made to the customer by competitors. The attempt by US retailer Sears Roebuck to change the financial services industry in the USA was an encirclement attack on competitors from several different industries at the same time. The in-store credit card was converted to Discovery, a full credit card. A chain of real estate agents was acquired, as was a major securities organization. Allstate Insurance had been part of the Sears Roebuck group for many years. The new niche the company hoped to conquer was the private consumer who wanted one-stop shopping: to buy a house, furnish it, obtain all necessary loan facilities, and insure everything in any Sears store. The strategy failed, because the niche was not large enough. The acquisitions therefore did not disrupt the competitive situation in their industries, and the Discovery credit card became a frontal attack on existing credit card competitors. At one time Sears was reported to have secured the record for signing up the largest number of defaulting clients in the shortest time!

4. Unconventional or guerrilla warfare. This is a continuous series of attacks on the competitor's weak areas, particularly where it is possible to avoid a crushing response. The aim is to build market share and thereby gain a stronger overall position. In marketing terms, it may mean attacking in countries or regions which may not be of large importance to the competitor, or following a policy of selective price discounting. Guerrilla actions may also include deliberate attempts to entice executives away from a competitor, a frequent occurrence in the financial services industry, or exploiting any op-

portunities in the legal process (for example, anti-monopolies legislation, and planning applications) to increase the competitor's
costs, or frustrate its intentions.

The military analogies are useful, but they show how actions might be
applied, rather than what actions to take. The list below owes much to
Kotler,[58] but extends the list of headings that he suggested.

- Price discounting. The aim is to offer a comparable product at a
  lower price. However, the buyer has to be convinced that it is a
  comparable product, and will take other factors into account, such
  as after-sales service. The strategy will bring more economies to
  the challenger if it is linked to actions to reduce the overall costs of
  the challenger, through actions such as business process
  re-engineering or the experience-curve effect.
- Lower price, lower quality. In essence, this strategy tries to appeal
  to that segment of the market which believes that the current offerings are over specified. The Ratner jewelry chain in the UK expanded the retail jewelry market, and achieved large growth between 1984 and 1991,[59] by virtually creating a new segment of the
  market for very cheap jewelry. This brought the resources which
  enabled the group to buy chains that operated in the higher–
  price/quality segment. This was the same strategy once used by
  Amstrad. This British company obtained considerable success in
  the PC market by producing a low-priced product which exploited
  obsolete technology. Because of the rapid changes in technology,
  component suppliers had large stocks of 8-bit computer components, which ran on the CP/M operating system, instead of the
  modern DOS. There were also stocks of obsolete 3-inch drives and
  disks. Amstrad designed a computer around the old technology,
  taking advantage of the very low costs of these components. It had
  the user in mind, and drives, computer, monitor and printer were
  easily connected, and were plugged into the mains by one ready-fit
  plug. It was promoted as a word processor that would do other
  things, and was the first serious computer to penetrate the home
  market in volume, as well as appealing to small businesses and

---

[58] See Kotler, P. (1994).
[59] In 1993 the company changed its name to *Signet Group plc* after the owner, Ge-
rald Ratner, had made a statement saying that their own products were "total crap".
The incident is remembered as one of the biggest gaffes in business history.

schools. Here was a low-price product which could match the specifications of the DOS machines, but which nevertheless gave its users the quality and reliability which they found acceptable. The same phenomenon and commercial logic is not all that different in the PC market of today.

- Same price, higher quality. The offering of a better product at the same price as that of the competitor. How many times do you see "new and improved" on a product label as you walk around a supermarket, and how many times do you believe it? Success depends upon that the customer acknowledging the quality is higher.

- Higher quality/higher price. Kotler terms this a prestige goods strategy. Essentially it is an attempt to serve a niche which the competitor has neglected.

- Product proliferation. Under this strategy the product category is expanded by the launch of additional variations of the product, giving more choice to the buyer. So instead of a copy of the competitor's product, several varieties are offered.

- Product innovation. An innovative version of an old product, or in some cases a new way of packaging it, may be the main feature of an attack. Miller increased its US market share to second place by the introduction of a light beer, in an innovative package. Such a strategy, if successful, usually works by satisfying a niche that had previously been overlooked. In the UK, the introduction by Mars of an ice cream bar version of the chocolate-covered Mars bar not only gave them a good position in the ice cream market but also changed the market, as competitors strove to launch products to compete with it.

- The innovative product to bypass the competitors. The hardest strategy to devise, and the hardest for competitors to react to, is one that we have mentioned earlier. It is the innovative attempt to change the industry so that new norms are established and the existing competitors are all left isolated, with obsolete products based on old technology. The fax, for example, drove out the telex because it was simpler to operate and the machines had steadily come down in price over time. Its introduction dramatically expanded the market for the transmission of hard copy over the telephone system. Today the fax is being substituted by email, PDF documents, different e-commerce solutions and a system of IP verifications over the Internet.

- Innovation of distribution. New ways may be used to get the product to the ultimate buyer, either through the creation of new channels or the modification of old ones. The example of First Direct has already been mentioned.

- Advertising and promotion. A significant increase in advertising and promotion may be used. However, it should be remembered that a brand share may have been built up over many years of promotion matched by the performance of the product, and merely outspending the competitor for a short period is unlikely to be effective unless there are weaknesses in its position.

A few of these strategies are mutually exclusive, but most can be used in combination with other actions. So it is a question of choosing the most appropriate mix to achieve the objective which lies behind the attack.

Defensive Strategies

Competitive positions are being attacked all of the time. Strategies of deterrence may not hold off the enemy for ever, and in any case are not available to every competitor. Smaller competitors in a market where there is a dominant leader may be able to offer few credible deterrents.

The first issue is to know when there is an attack. Sun Tzu stressed the importance of information. In all markets there is competitive activity, but this does not always imply a serious threat and may be countered by what might be termed the normal actions of marketing. The danger signs are:

- New entrants to the market
- Existing competitors who are trying to move into different segments
- Attempts to change how the market works, which may be through technological change, alterations in the channels of distribution, or changes in relationships with buyers and suppliers
- Abnormal marketing activity, that is outside the expected pattern, such as the enlargement of the sales force, price cutting, expansion of capacity beyond that justified by current market shares, large increases in advertising, or increases in R&D capability.

When a market position is under obvious and serious attack, the first decision is whether it should be defended at all. This decision should take into account the fit of the activity with the strategic vision of the company and an assessment of the resources needed to mount a successful defense. There is a caveat, in that retreat from one segment can strengthen the attacker, and put it in a good position to attack the next segment. It may not be long before the core of the business is vulnerable. The companies in the British motorcycle industry followed a path of segmental retreat in the face of competition from Honda, and eventually surrendered the whole market. The belief that Honda and other Japanese companies would stop at the bottom rung of the ladder because they did not have the engineering skills to make quality medium-sized and large motorcycles was a total misreading of the competitive situation.

However, there are times when it is better to give up than to fight for something which is not seen as important for corporate success. Retreat may be a question of letting the market decide, and taking no particular actions to counteract the actions of the attacker. It may be a question of selling the activity, probably to a competitor which may even be the aggressor, thus recovering capital. Alliance may also be a way of reducing the level of commitment needed to resist a determined attack, in that a joint venture between two competitors may mean that a position can be defended at a shared cost. However, if the motivation of one of the parties is to reduce commitment to the market, this may well be a recipe for failure.

- Position defense. In military terms, this is the defense of a previously prepared strong position, the "cities" of Sun Tzu, or the French Maginot Line of the Second World War. The aim is to build an impregnable position, through product differentiation: achieved through image, levels of service, design, quality, reliability, and every other possible way, and by being a low-cost producer. This all-round bastion is better as a deterrent than as a defensive strategy, since a protracted siege may be costly to the attacker: however, if it starts it may also be costly to the defender. Kotler[60] argues that position defense is often a form of marketing myopia, and it is all too easy for a strong position to turn out to be something the attacker can get around. Position defense implies matching what the attacker does, which leaves the initiative with the aggressor. Sun Tzu advises against a protracted war, as it leaves even the winner in a weak state and vulnerable to further attacks from elsewhere.
- Counterattack. The counterattack is an attempt to ward off the intrusions of the attacker. The most effective counterattacks are those

---

[60] See Kotler, P. (1994).

which identify an area of weakness in the attacker, and result in carefully chosen, cost-effective responses. It is sensible to examine the competitor as a whole, and not just the brand or product, as it may be better to attack something important to the competitor than to mount an expensive defense of the product being attacked. This may be a product or a geographical counterattack.

For example, if you and your competitor both make canned cat and dog food, and one of your product lines is attacked on price, it would be worth considering whether to defend this product or to choose the product that contributes the most to the competitor's profits, and make a massive attack on this instead. Or if the competitor is attacking your organization in a country where its present market position is weak, consider attacking it in one of the countries which is more important to its profit and loss account. In this sort of game, there are advantages to the competitor which not only operates in many countries but also has a global approach to marketing, because this gives it the information and the capability to switch the attack to a different country. Companies which operate as a series of local businesses, with local managing directors held responsible for their own profitability, find it much harder to respond in this way, and are easier to attack because of this.

The strategic options available for a counterattack are largely those listed under the attack strategy. The difference is that they are the tools of response rather than aggression, and should be chosen in relation to the attacker's strategy. Would the best counterattack to a massive advertising campaign by a competitor be to respond in kind, to bring forward the launch of a new and improved product, an innovative packaging change, or a money-off promotion? The right answer, and this is not a full list of options, depends on the nature of the attack, and the weaknesses identified in the competitor.

In the Simon Aerials example mentioned earlier, there was little short-term action the competitors could take. The product's price differential was too great to allow for an effective reduction of prices, and it was much more suited to the purpose for which it was aimed than the competitor's products. The medium-term response was to accelerate development of competitive products. As contractors would not all replace their old equipment at once, this meant that competitive products launched within a reasonable time would have a chance of capturing sales. So the main defensive strategy they might have used would be to persuade previously loyal customers that a

51

better version of the product was on its way, and that they should delay any decision to change.

- Pre-emptive strike. Anticipating a competitor's moves and frustrating them by attacking first carries the advantage of surprise. In Chapter 8 we give the example of an advertisement which gave information about the recruitment of a large number of additional sales posts as part of an expansion plan in a particular market segment. A pre-emptive strike might do much to reduce the impact of these moves. There is an old story, probably apocryphal, that when Heinz first suspected that Campbell might be planning to enter the UK market with a range of condensed soups, they frustrated the move for many years by launching a range of condensed soup which was clearly inferior to the traditional canned soups. This established that canned soups were an inferior product to the real thing. The story may well be untrue, but it helps to illustrate the ingenuity which may be used in formulating a preemptive strike.
- Flanking defense. The flanking defense is an attempt to create positions peripheral to the core of the business, which may either make it more difficult for a competitor to attack or may serve as a basis for counterattack. In this example, we have had to disguise the product and the industry, but the actions are substantially correct. The global market leader in the manufacture of a particular type of plant had suffered a series of attacks in Europe from a much smaller competitor which, for the sake of this example, we will say was based in Holland. This was a country that the multinational had avoided because of the extremely strong position of the competitor, and a belief that it would be impossible to make profits there. In turn this meant that the competitor had an extremely profitable home market, which enabled it to fund its gradual erosion of the larger organization's global market share.

  The flanking strategy was to establish an operation in the competitor's home base, accepting that it would make losses for a long period. This would also provide a base to counterattack the competitor where it might hurt most, should this become necessary in the future.

Both attacking and defensive strategies are most effective when based on a sound knowledge of the competitive arena, and of the key actors in your industry. This is the journey we begin in the next chapter as we go from strategy to actual Intelligence Analysis.

REFERENCES

Caplan, R.H. (1965). Relationships between principles of military strategy and principles of business planning. Appendix B of Anthony, R.N. (ed), *Planning and Control Systems: A Framework for Analysis*, Boston, MA: Harvard University Press.

Chan Kin, W., Mauborgne, R. (2004). Blue Ocean Strategy, *Harvard Business Review*, October.

Czerniawska, F., Potter, G. (1998). *Business in a virtual world*, London: Macmillan Press Ltd.

Govindarajan, V., Gupta, A.K. (2001). *The quest for global dominance – transforming global presence into global competitive advantage*, San Francisco, CA: Jossey-bass.

Groth, R. (1998). *Data Mining*, Upper saddle river, NJ: Prentice hall.

Hamel, G. & Prahalad, C.K. (1994). *Competing for the Future*, Boston, MA: Harvard Business School Press.

Hopfield J.J. (1988). Artificial neural networks. *IEEE Circuits and Devices Magazine*, Volym 4 Nr. 5, pp. 3-10.

Hurd, M., Nyberg, L. (2004). *The value factor*, Princeton, NJ: Bloomberg press.

Hussey, D.E. (1994). *Strategy Management: Theory and Practice*, Oxford: Pergamon.

James, B. (1985). *Business Wargames*, London: Penguin (first published by Abacus, 1985).

Kalling, T. (2000). *Gaining competitive advantage through the investment in Information technology*, Dissertation, Lund University Press.

Kotler, P. (1994). *Marketing Management: Analysis, Planning, Implementation and Control, 8th edition*, Englewood Cliffs, NJ: Prentice Hall.

Montano, B. (ed) (2005). *Innovation of knowledge management*, Hershey, PA: Irm press.

Nilsson, F., Rapp, B. (2005). *Understanding competitive advantage*, Berlin: Springer.

Porter, M.E. (1990). *The competitive advantage of nations*, London: Macmillan.

Porter, M.E. (1980). *Competitive Strategy*, New York: The Free Press.

Rothberg, H.N., Erickson, G.S. (2005). *From knowledge to intelligence. Burlington*, MA: Elsvier.

Sun Tzu (c 400 BC). *The Art of War*, The translation used: 1993, Wordsworth Editions, Ware, Herts: translation by Yuan Shibing.

Sölvell, Ö. (2004). *Kluster och den nya näringspolitiken*, Östersund: Institutet för Tillväxtpolitiske Studier.

CHAPTER 3

Industry Analysis:
Key to Understanding the
Competitive Situation

The Importance of Industry Analysis

At the core of our framework for performing the competitive analysis is a fundamental understanding of the industry in which a firm is engaged. In chapter 3, we present our approach to Industry Analysis, before proceeding with an in-depth understanding of the firm's own situation and capabilities, discussed in chapter 4, entitled the Company Analysis.

Chapter 3 actually presents two layers of reality, one called the market environment, which represents the organization's "direct environment", and the Macro Environment, which will be shared with many adjacent organizations. Together these layers form the subject for our Industry Analysis.

Businesses do not operate in a vacuum. In order to understand the likely behaviour of a competitor, we first need to understand the context in which organizations operate. One element of this is the external business environment in a given country in which the industry operates. The second element, dealt with in this and the next chapter, is the balance of forces which determine competitor behaviour within an industry. This is not just about the relative size of competitors, but goes backwards to the relative influence of suppliers in the industry and forwards to that of the buyers.

An understanding of the principles is important because it helps us to interpret what a competitor is most likely to do in any particular situation. This is never a certainty, but even when a competitor behaves in a way that we did not expect, knowledge of the principles helps us to understand the most likely results of their behaviour. By using industry analysis in a dynamic way, it is possible to identify what actions might be taken to change the balance of power, and to identify which actors across the whole spectrum could take this action.

Industry analysis is an essential first stage in competitive analysis, and one which, if done well, helps us to ask the right questions and to make better use of the information we collect on individual competitors. It helps to bring a measure of order to the data we have about the industry, and about the individual competitors within it.

The Concepts of Industry Analysis

The credit for much of the thinking on industry analysis goes to the industrial economists, and much to Michael Porter, who assimilated and further developed much of the thinking from industrial economics about the influences of profitability of an organization in a competitive situation (see Porter, 1975, 1980), described by his well-known Five Forces model:

- Rivalry among competitors in the industry
- Bargaining power of buyers
- Bargaining power of suppliers
- The relative attraction of substitutes
- Entry/exit barriers.

Within each of the categories are factors which affect the balance of power between each competitor and its rivals, and between competitors within the industry. Later we will discuss these factors. One main value of the Porter concept is that it broadened thinking, both relating to the number of forces that should be considered and the factors within each. Traditionally some thought has always been given to competitors and to customers, but Porter demonstrated that this was inadequate to fully understand the industry.

Figure 3.1 builds on the Five Forces. It owes much to Porter's work, but makes two different points of emphasis, and adds another important force which is not seen in the Porter model. The Figure makes it clear that substitutes are really two different forces: between suppliers and the industry, and between the industry and its buyers. Entry and exit barriers have been separated, because they are totally different forces, which work in different ways. The new force is influencers: critical organizations or people, positioned between the industry and the buyer, which determine a key aspect of the buying decision. Influencers can be an individual or an organization. The most commonly seen forms are mass media, interest and lobby groups. It may also be an individual, like a doctor. Take a situation where a child is ill. A doctor determines what drug is necessary and writes a prescription: the doctor does not buy the drug, but without the prescription the chemist cannot dispense it. The parent collects the prescription from the chemist. In some countries he or she does not "buy" it, as it may be paid for by a national health service: in others cash may change hands, or there may be a minimum prescription charge which has no relation to the price of the drug. If we wanted to study the ethical pharmaceuticals industry, we need to take the doctor into consideration, for if he or she does not prescribe our product the chemist will not stock it. But in this industry, there may also be a national health service, which in one sense is the ultimate buyer, but not the user, of the product, and may influence the market by urging doctors to prescribe a generic version of our product, because it is cheaper. The complexities in this brief and incomplete example take us beyond the scope of Figure 3.1, and are something we will return to later. For the time being, the Figure describes all the relevant factors which will affect the profitability and competitive strength of any firm in the industry. Real-life situations will bring us more issues to consider, but will not change the underlying principles.

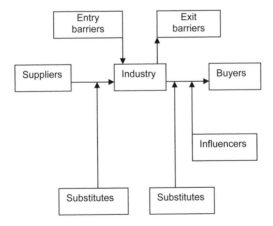

Figure 3.1 Components of Industry Analysis

Factors which Influence the Competitive Position

In a real situation, only some of the many various influencing factors will affect a particular competitor in the industry, and they are not necessarily the same factors for every competitor. It is how the individual organization manages its situation to achieve the most favourable balance of factors across all the forces that is the ultimate determinant.

In discussing the factors, and to avoid repetition, we have given a list of factors which covers both the buyer and supplier components of the model. Of course, some mental manipulation is necessary, for whereas the industry is in the position of a supplier to its buyers, it is a buyer to its suppliers. Thus, whatever strengthens the buyer's power, weakens the supplier: but when we are the buyer, it strengthens us in relation to our suppliers. The opposite applies to the factors which weaken a buyer's power.

When undertaking industry analysis it is important to remember that the profitability of the whole chain in the industry may not necessarily be driven by the competitors in the industry. For instance, in the personal computer industry, much of the power has shifted from the PC manufacturers in the favour of software suppliers, i.e. Microsoft, as well as chip-makers, i.e. Intel.

The structure of industries changes, so it is important not to rely on static analysis. A dynamic view is imperative. Failure to understand the changes that are taking place can give rise to serious strategic errors, as, for example, when Xerox failed to see the threat posed to it when Canon entered the market, and when IBM underestimated the changes that the personal computer would bring. Or when the convergence of technologies suddenly create new competitors, as is happening today when Apple is bringing the iPod, the PC and the Phone together in one unit. At the announcement of the iPhone in January 2007, Motorola, Nokia and Sony-Ericsson stock fell immediately. The future value of their stocks will depend on their ongoing reactions to this new technology.

When looking at the factors which should be considered when analysing an industry, it is important to take a balanced view. A negative impact of one factor may be cancelled out by a positive impact elsewhere. But to understand the factors, we do need to look at them separately. They will be considered in relation to the headings of Figure 3.1.

Competitors in the Industry

1. Number of firms and relative market shares. A fragmented industry where no one firm has a significant market share tends to be more

fiercely competitive than one which is a clear market leader who is in a dominant position. The lack of a clear market leader may be explained by the fact that the industry is emerging and is in a condition of considerable turbulence and uncertainty, or it may be seen in more mature industry where there are low entry barriers and few advantages to size. The ferocity of competition is also affected by the degree of "protection" given by locality. There may be thousands of hairdressers in a country, but because they serve a relatively local market, the strength of competition is related to the size of the local market in relation to the number of firms in that market. In this situation, market share may be less important than whether or not there is enough demand to allow profitable trading for all the competitors.

When a market has a dominant leader, whose market share is considerably higher than any of its competitors, competition may be less violent. As long as those firms holding the smaller shares do not threaten the leader, behaviour in the industry can be summed up with the word "gentlemanly". This was the position in the computer industry until the advent of the personal computer, as when IBM was the dominant player for years.

2. Growth rates in the industry. Competitive behaviour tends to be less aggressive when growth rates are maintained, because each firm can achieve its growth objectives without having to steal or take market share from others. This may not hold true for an industry at the early phase of the product life cycle, when existing competitors are striving to attain a sustainable position and high growth is attracting new entrants. What is often a trigger to more aggressive competitor behaviour is a change in growth rates. Competitors in all industries tend to take actions to maintain volumes in times of recession and may break the behaviour pattern of the past. When an industry matures and growth slows, there is often a period of intense competition as some players are shaken out of the industry. This means that an industry, whose growth rate has plunged from 10% to 1%, is likely to be more competitive than one whose growth rate has been 1% over a long period.

3. Nature of the product. A perishable product, which may be a physical product, which cannot be stored for any length of time, or a service such as a seat on an airplane or the time of a management consultant tends to be more susceptible to random moves by competitors as they strive to avoid loss. This may be offset to some degree by the success the competitor has in obtaining prices that are high

enough to cover part of the loss. Management consultancies and solicitors may be able to sustain a certain amount of downtime without slashing prices: a low-margin product, such as fresh fruit, may leave the competitors few options other than to cut prices to try to dispose of surplus stocks.

4. Degree of differentiation. The closer a product is to a commodity, the more intense the competition in the industry will be. Where product differentiation is high, and there is less of a substitute effect between the products of the various competitors, the tendency is for some protection to be obtained against the actions of competitors. Protecting against forms and degrees of different actions should be a key element of the organization's strategy.

5. General level of profits in the industry. A very profitable industry often tends to be somewhat complacent. If all competitors are profitable there is no incentive to rock the boat by aggressive actions. A decline in profitability, like a fall in growth rates, may trigger decreasing tolerance by competitors.

6. Level of fixed costs. In industries where the investment is large and highly specialized, and fixed costs are relatively high in proportion to total costs, competitors tend to "hang on", selling at less than full costs, especially when the market slumps or there is overcapacity for some other reason. Shipping, oil refinery, and petrochemicals are examples of such industries, where competitive behaviour has led to continued trading at low profits or losses over a long period of time, because the alternative is plant closure at a time when assets cannot be realized.

7. Economies of scale/experience curve. In some industries, there are clear advantages to being big, as the experience curve effect means that increases in volume bring predictable decreases in costs. When demand is elastic, such as with consumer electronic products, a lower-cost producer can expand the market, and each increase of market share fuels further decreases in cost, making it much harder for competitors to stay in the market. While these conditions are maintained, competitive rivalry will tend to be fierce.

8. New owner or new leadership. Another factor that may increase or decrease the fierceness of competition is a change either of ownership of a competitor, or of its chief executive. Often an industry will settle down to an established pattern of competitive behaviour, where certain unwritten rules become established, and each member of the industry recognizes certain "no-go" areas. For instance, in an established industry, no one competitor ever practices aggressive

price cutting, or launching products that will intentionally damage part of a competitor's business. Then, a competitor is acquired by a newcomer to the industry, and the new owner either does not know the unwritten rules, or has no interest in maintaining them. The same effect can occur when a new chief executive or senior marketing executive is brought in from another industry.

In competitor analysis, any change of this type is a danger signal. Although an increase in aggressiveness is not inevitable, it is good to be on guard for such a possibility. It is also worth challenging the assumptions under which the company's managers act.

Buyers (the converse of these factors apply to suppliers)

1. Dependencies. If one party is highly dependent on the other, its power decreases. The industry firm that depends on one buyer for most of its profits may find that it has to dance to the buyer's tune. Similarly, the sole supplier of a critical component may be able to determine its own price levels. The ratio of industry firms to buying firms is an important indicator of whether the balance of power lies with the industry or with the buyer. The position is complicated by switching costs. If a buyer can only change a supplier at some expense, which may be additional capital and revenue costs, or lost profits because of production shutdowns while the switch is being made, the firm's power will increase. This was once the position with computers: if you started with Windows, expansion and upgrading tended also to be Windows although it is not the same with personal computers; where it costs little to switch (unless to and from Apple; recently, Linux software is also starting to pose a threat to Microsoft's Windows software). Looking at ways to increase switching costs for buyers is one strategy that can be applied to help an industry firm retain the initiative, or to neutralize an advantage a buyer has over you.

2. Relative size. If the industry includes firms that are considerably larger than their customers, sheer weight of resources may put them in a dominant position. The converse may apply when the buying organizations are the largest. This is not a universal rule as other factors may outweigh it. For example, access to the UK grocery markets is largely controlled by a few supermarket chains, who not only control most of the sales volume going to consumers but also have arrangements with contract packers to make own-label products for them. These can be adjusted in volume, space, and shelf space if branded manufacturers do not toe the line. In this way, they

may determine the profitability of manufacturers, although these may be part of giant global corporations.

3. Profitability of the buying industry. The industry firms are likely to be in a healthier position when they are selling to a profitable industry. When buyers are unprofitable, or have low profits, there is likely to be strong pressure on the industry to reduce prices, or at best to hold them stable. Resistance against price increases, and an increased tendency to change suppliers, may be greater when the buyer faces an elastic demand curve and cannot pass on price increases. The modern tendency is for buyers and suppliers to try to work together so that both are profitable, but this does not apply in all situations.

4. Experience of buyers. Although experienced buyers may instigate actions to work more closely with the industry, they are also more likely to be aware of all the competitors, the levels of quality and the prices at which they are available, and to have coordinated their needs across the whole organization in order to ensure one standard price is paid to their suppliers. Less experienced buyers, or buyers in an emerging industry, may not be in such a strong position, either because of lack of information or because the requirements are changing so fast that there is no time to understand the suppliers.

5. Threat of integration. The possibility of integration forwards by an industry into its buyer's business or backwards by the buyer to the industry may be a considerable source of power. Whichever party can exercise an implied threat gains a potential advantage over the other. The threat has to be credible. It may, for example, be entirely possible that a giant multinational oil company could decide to move into the management training business, or at a minimum take in-house the training services it was buying: it is not credible that the modest-sized consultancy it was using to provide its training could offer a credible threat to challenge the oil industry. Siemens has been offering in-house university education since the late 90s, and frequently appears at educational trade shows all over the world; not so much to buy as to be seen and market themselves as an employer. The company also performs its own management research. For management education, its programs have become real alternatives to other university programs, taking away a considerable part of traditional universities' customer base. Even though the company does not compete directly with universities today for non-employee customers, nothing says that it cannot do so in the future. Another German Multinational, Volkswagen, was among the first organiza-

tions to get the new CEL accreditation given by EFMD for Distance Learning Education. In fact, among the seven organizations accredited so far, two are private MNEs, the other being L'Oreal in Paris.[61] Multinationals may indeed constitute a threat to universities in the future, especially in sectors and disciplines where there are profits to be made. Most top ranked universities today are already private institutions.

Entry Barriers

One way to think about entry barriers is to compare them to a boundary fence built around an orchard. If the fruit trees were diseased, and the fruit sparse and of poor quality, the weakest of fences would be enough to deter thieves. A good-quality orchard might find that a security fence was essential; and that even with this, some determined predators could find ways of breaking into the orchard. If the fruit had unique properties, perhaps the apples were from the original stock from the Garden of Eden, security alarms and guards might be necessary to try to keep thieves out. In other words, entry barriers which might deter a new entrant from going into a poor industry may be inadequate to keep out someone from attacking an industry with strong growth and profit prospects. So any discussion about entry barriers should be interpreted according to the specific situation.

New entrants to a market should be of considerable concern in any competitive analysis, as they are difficult to predict. There are four types of possible new entrants:

- Organizations that are in the industry already but in a different part of the world. The forces of globalization have led to an explosion in cross-border movement of companies and products, and the process has not ended.
- Organizations that are in closely related businesses.
- New businesses set up by individuals who have been employed in other firms in the industry and therefore already know the business. This is very prevalent in service businesses where entry barriers are low, but is not restricted to this, as well-connected individuals are often able to obtain financial backing which enables them to overcome many of the barriers.

---

[61] See http://www.efmd.org (2007-06-26).

- Rank outsiders, about whom little may be known. Given the movement by Sears Roebuck into financial services in the 1980s (although they had owned an insurance company for many years before this), it was not surprising to see Marks & Spencer add banking services to their activities in the UK, and it was not totally unpredictable that major supermarkets would follow suit. However, who would have expected Virgin, with (at that time) its interests in the music industry and retailing, to go into the travel and tourism business (airline, balloon flights, limousine hire), finance and banking (credit cards, home loans, insurance), and the health and medical industry (health clubs, stem cells)?

A determined entrant may try to avoid many of the barriers by alliance with, or acquisition of, one of the existing players. When such moves occur, it becomes even more important to assess the strategic reasons behind them. A change of ownership may not necessarily imply more than that, but when an organization in a related business, or the same business in another country, makes such a move there may be much greater reason for concern. For example, when Otis Elevators bought into lift companies in central and Eastern Europe it would have been a mistake for any competitors in those countries to assume that this would not affect the local competitive scene.

It is in the interests of competitors in an industry to raise entry barriers when this is possible (and legal). Not surprisingly, this is an action that can be seen in practice. The attempts by the British security services industry to obtain legal regulation of their industry have less to do with its declared intention of working for the common good than to stem the flow of new security firms, which any individual can easily establish. Although some of the high-tech parts of the industry have higher barriers, the guard and patrol business has become a commodity because of the volume of competition.

What then creates or increases the entry barriers?

- A high level of differentiation will raise entry barriers, since any newcomer will have to make a significant marketing investment to gain any significant market share.
- Patents may prevent others from competing because the technology is not open to them, but this can also create an unfounded complacency. Xerox ignored the threat from Canon until it was too late, because in order to enter the market, Canon had to develop products that did not infringe Xerox's 600-plus patents. Had the

copier industry not had high growth and profitability characteristics, it is unlikely that Canon would have expended the enormous effort to do this.

- The cost structure of the firms in the industry. If a critical element in profitability is determined by economies of scale or the experience curve, it follows that any newcomer will have to make a large investment in capacity, and may face losses and considerable risks when trying to build up to the volume needed. However, it must be remembered that many such products are no longer made on the basis of a factory in every country, and the barrier may be non-existent for a company that is not in your market but which can ship products in from operations in other countries.

- In addition to patents, there may be other factors which make it difficult for others to gain a foothold in a particular market. These may be government restrictions: for example, a new airline can only operate if it has landing slots, and as there are a finite number of these it is rare for there to be spare slots available. Long-term contracts with buyers can make it harder for others to break in. The modern tendency to have "preferred suppliers" makes it harder for another to gain a foothold. Control of distribution outlets may also create barriers, but this should not be overestimated. When Honda attacked the British motorcycle industry, there were no dealers available to distribute their products, so they set about creating new dealers by persuading bicycle retailers to convert, a task made easier because the first Honda motorcycles were not much bigger than a bicycle.

Exit Barriers

Exit barriers work in quite a different way. They imprison an organization so that it cannot escape from the industry without loss, and will therefore continue to operate as long as there is cash to support it. The oil-refining industry in Europe continued to add capacity after the OPEC oil crisis of the early 1970s; despite the fact that demand for petrol fell dramatically throughout the decade. No companies were willing to abandon partly built refineries. The industry continued to have severe overcapacity through the 1980s, with the consequent effects on competitor behaviour, until BP led a move to close down some of its refineries. Highly specialized assets may be impossible to sell when there are conditions of overcapacity, and the inability to take the capital loss (and sometimes the obligation to clean up an abandoned site) means that it is extremely difficulty to exit. The stronger these exit barriers are, the more likely it is that there will be periods of extremely competitive aggression whenever trading conditions are bad, and firms are willing to lower prices below full costs in order to retain some contribution margin.

Substitutes

For reasons described earlier, substitutes appear in two positions on Figure 3.1. However, the effect they have on the competitive arena is similar, and if we describe the impact on the industry firm/buyer relationship there should be no difficulty in reinterpreting this for the supplier/industry firm relationship. It would be possible to argue that there should be no separate consideration of substitutes, because if they exist they should be brought into the industry definition. Most people would agree that it would be pointless for a company that made canned dog food to insist that dried dog food was a substitute and not really part of the overall pet food market. The glass bottle industry would be foolish not to consider the manufacturers of PEP bottles and drink cartons as competitors. Similarly we can see without difficulty that a company which made steel cans would be very short-sighted if it excluded aluminium cans from its definition of the industry. In such examples it makes much more sense to treat the substitutes as part of the industry, and the firms in it as competitors. As we will see in the next chapter, there is room to examine various segments when analysing competitors.

When a more general view of substitutes is taken, the position is somewhat different. Although both are forms of transport, a bicycle is hardly a substitute for a plane ticket. Yet even here things change, and fast trains through the Channel Tunnel are certainly in direct competition with flights to some destinations. Often the impact of a broad substitute is on the market: a government may tax and regulate private cars so that buses and trains are used instead. This may affect the demand for cars, but it is not really realistic to consider a local bus company as a competitor to Ford or BMW.

When a substitute offers a real or likely threat to the current industry products, it should be studied in the same way as the industry. When it does not, it may be a relevant factor to consider when looking at the future of the market, but it is only a matter for industry and competitor analysis if the buyer is able to use it as a threat to gain advantage over the seller. The availability of real substitutes strengthens the position of the buyer.

Influencers

The difficulty with influencers is that they are not always obvious, but this does not make them any less important. What is important in any study of an industry is to assess whether influencers play a role in the buying decision process, and to set strategies to either influence the influencers or to reduce or eliminate their role. Governmental institutions are very significant influencers; for example, the Chinese government has played a significant role in the development of the Chinese Semiconductor Industry, by providing cheap loans, infrastructure, land etc. to local industry participants in ways which go beyond rational economic thinking. Other influencers can be organizations, such as Green Peace. A complete analysis requires obtaining good information about the influencers, their agenda or businesses which influence the industry, in order to use that information to formulate a plan of action.

The Industry and the Macro or External Business Environment

Figure 3.2 adds a further step in the analysis of an industry. This figure depicts the elements in the macro environment which affect the demand for the product and the businesses of the "actors" on the competitive stage.

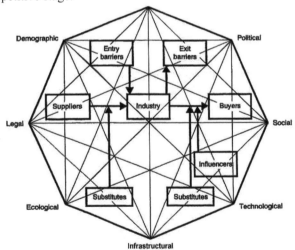

Figure 3.2 The Industry and the Macro Environment

The figure is intended to mirror the reality that every industry operates within a macro environment and that that environment is continually

67

changing. So our industry analysis diagram is set within a diagram of its external world.

The outer octagon offers some broad headings that might be used as a check list to aid thinking about what is going on in this outside world. They are, of course, very broad headings, and there are many subheadings which should be considered under each. For example, under the economic heading there are factors like the level of unemployment, inflation, growth or decline of GDP, and foreign exchange rates.

The faint lines which connect every point to every other are intended to imply that everything has a potential influence on everything else. Thus changes in economic circumstances may trigger different social trends and opinions, which may in turn cause political pressure to be brought to bear upon the factors, and eventually political changes may result in changes in legislation (See Hussey, 1998).

It is tempting to argue that macro factors affect everyone in the industry in the same way and that they are important for looking at market trends but can be ignored in competitive analysis. This would be a naive conclusion. First, the products of every firm in the industry are rarely identical, nor are they all manufactured in the same country. So changes in economic factors, such as inflation, will not hit every competitor in exactly the same way, because labour costs increases are not identical in all countries, and a different mix of components and raw materials may mean that increases in these costs are not evenly spread, even when the competitors manufacture in the same country.

The different segments where competitors have their strengths may not all be equally vulnerable to, for example, changes in unemployment levels. In fact, in some markets, if a premium segment of the market becomes smaller, it is possible that a low-priced segment may grow in size. A competitor in the higher-priced segment may be tempted to move into another segment in order to offset a decline in sales.

If we consider changes in the business environment in relation to the industry, we transfer industry and competitor analysis from merely examining the past to dynamically accessing what may be different in the future. Further ways of ensuring a dynamic view will be discussed in the next chapter.

The Life Cycle and the Industry

Figure 3.3 draws attention to another factor which affects behaviour across the whole industry. This is the position in the general life cycle of an industry. Before discussing this Figure, we should stress that it is a generalization, and what actually happens in any one industry will depend on all the factors previously discussed. If the entry barriers are high, some of the issues suggested, for example in the emerging industry, may not happen as the diagram suggests. A lot also depends on how long a phase of the industry life cycle lasts, and how dramatic the change from one phase to another is. In the modern world, many industries may move rapidly from one phase to another, and sometimes be overtaken by the merging of industries, or come under the onslaught of new technology. The figure should be used as a very approximate guide to some of the things that might be expected, rather than as a firm predictor of what will happen.

The emerging industry, particularly if the technology is new, is characterized by uncertainty, typically going through an initial period of negative cash flow, as capital requirements chase the expansion of demand, and as markets are developed. If growth is high, newcomers may enter the industry. The learning curve effect may be very noticeable in certain types of industries, such as manufactured products where demand is elastic, and the pioneers try to build volume fast in order to gain the cost advantages of high cumulative volume.

We have not illustrated what may be a fairly consistent period of growth as the industry takes off, although this growth would be experienced differently for each competitor in an industry. We join the life cycle again at a point where the industry is moving towards maturity. Growth rates are slowing dramatically, and competition might be expected to become fiercer as each competitor strives to maintain its historic pattern of growth. This may cause a fall in profits, and lead to a shake-out in the industry, depending on the number of competitors, and their relative market shares. In some situations, profits may be maintained by emphasis on costs, or attempts to extend the life cycle through product enhancements and add-ons. In many industries, the slowing growth of the industry may bring an opportunity to generate cash, as there is no longer a need to expand capacity. However, this depends on the lead time of investments. It was noticeable that the European oil refinery industry continued to expand capacity for several years after the OPEC oil crisis of the 1970s.

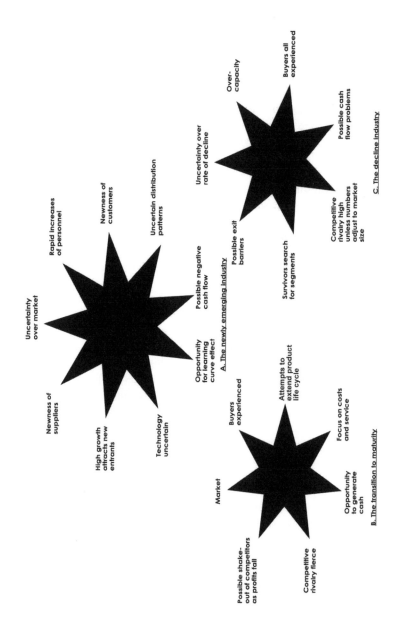

Figure 3.3 The Effect of the Product Life Cycle on Industries

Although demand slumped and continued to decline over several years as buyers were motivated to save energy, much of the new capacity was already partly built, and the oil companies felt they had no option but to complete its construction. It was not until the 1980s that the industry began to close capacity.

We have skipped the period of maturity, which can, for the reasons given earlier, be a time when the industry's cash inflow still exceeds its outflow. Such a period may last for many years: an example is the to-bacco industry: yesterday in the US and in Europe; today in developing countries where smoking has not yet declined.

Our final illustration is the industry which is in decline. Once again uncertainty is the order of the day. There may be a frantic scramble to find new segments. Unless there is a shake-out, it may be a period of low profit or even losses. Competitors are especially vulnerable to recession. In the rare situations where the shake-out leaves only one or two players, with the obvious reduction of rivalry, it may be possible to do very well in a declining industry, but this is the exception.

What is the "Industry"?
So far we have left open the critical issue of determining the parameters of the industry we are studying. When we discussed substitutes we suggested that real substitutes might be considered within our industry definition, effectively taking more of a market view of the industry than the more traditional technology view. The definition of the industry should be related to markets, but not too narrowly. In other words, it would be a mistake to analyse only the product/segment of an industry that we had chosen to operate in, and to ignore other product/segments which form part of the overall market. For example, if we only manufacture wheat beer, it would be very silly to analyse only the wheat beer market. This would deprive us of a full understanding of the whole industry, and would stop us examining competitors who did not currently make our product, but could easily do so if they wished.

Almost every marketing manager likes to be able to claim brand leadership, and this is nearly always possible if the segments are narrowed down far enough. However important this narrowing may be for marketing claims, it would be disastrous for industry analysis. We have several times had experience with organizations which once provided particular types of plant and machinery to the world but which have not kept their technology up to date, and have ended up losing markets in the developed world, and supplying only the less sophisticated markets of the Third World. However, as these markets either move to world standards for the industry, or disappear, it follows that analysing only the low-technology end of the industry can deliver misleading information.

There is another important aspect to consider. This is the geographical area under investigation. We may operate only in one country, and at this time this is our only important market. But can we sensibly think of our industry only in parochial terms? Instead of thinking, for example, of just the French industry, should we not extend our thinking to the European Union? Is there any reason why this restriction is appropriate? Shouldn't we be thinking globally?

Clearly in this case we should want to look at the French industry in detail. If we have a number of competitors which are multinational companies, we cannot begin to understand them unless, as a minimum, we extend our analysis of the competitors to their total operation, and if the market is truly global we may be forced to paint our picture of the industry on a wider canvas.

Our experience has been that often too narrow a view is taken, with the company limiting its focus to the things it does itself. Thus we have found a machine tool manufacturer who believed that it needed to consider only the British industry, because it was restricted by a technology agreement from offering its main product in other countries: yet all its competitors in its narrow product segment were from Japan or Germany. There was the fast-moving grocery products company that undertook a European analysis (restricted to the countries in which it operated). One major multi-national competitor operated in only one or two of the countries in Europe, and the conclusion was that it could almost be ignored, as its interest in the product category was so small, and appeared to be more a matter of historical activities rather than a deliberate strategy. When this competitor was considered as a total business, it was found that the company was making massive investments in this industry, acquiring marketing and manufacturing businesses in a number of countries around the world, and building up strong R&D capability in North America and elsewhere. It simply had not got round to extending the global strategy across Europe, but it was clearly wrong to assume that it had no real interest in this product area.

The guidance that can be given is to think very carefully about what is an appropriate scope for the industry. There are still some industries where a country analysis is completely adequate. There are many others where the old definitions are suspect, and there is a need to extend the thinking. By all means begin by looking at a particular country, but always be willing to extend the analysis as it progresses, and deliberately seek out any indications that this should be done. The worst assumption to make is that the industry is limited to your own current area of activity.

Industry Analysis in Practice

There is always a difference between understanding a concept and actually applying it in a real situation, and there are at least three questions that the analyst has to answer before beginning. What information do we need to undertake industry analysis? What do we have at present? How should we use that information? In considering the last point, it is worth also thinking about how the information will be communicated to others once it has been analysed.

Industries vary in the amount of good statistical data that is available, and organizations vary in the attention they have paid to collecting relevant information. As a generalization it is true to say that consumer products companies tend to have much more information about markets, channels, consumers and competitors than do industrial products companies. Professional services organizations tend to have much less hard information about their industries than even industrial products organizations. Lack of information at the start of the analysis does not mean that nothing can be achieved, but it does make it harder to get started.

The analyst's first step is to assemble the hard data that is available, and to tap into managers to obtain the "soft" data that they all possess. The term "analyst" is used here not as a job title but simply the person doing the analysis, who may be the managing director, a staff specialist or a manager in any position or at any level.

One of the things that in most organizations will become obvious the minute anyone takes the first serious step to perform the industry analysis is that the headings in the Porter Five Forces model, and even in the expanded version we have used, are often too broad. There is often a need to categorize buyers, and also to think of whether they sit at the end of the chain or are part of the channel which enables the products to reach the final consumer. Two examples will help to clarify this.

A company like Heinz will make its sales to retailers such as the supermarket chains. It may also sell to wholesalers, to cash-and-carry warehouses, and to specialist retailers who may vary with the product (chemists may be important for selling baby food but not for baked beans). All these buyers sell the products to consumers, and Heinz will be as interested in the end users as it is in its buyers. The consumers are indirect buyers but behave very differently from the trade customers. However, they do not all have the same requirements, and need to be thought of in terms of market segments, because the Heinz competitive position may vary between segments, either from choice or because of competitive rivalry. And different types of trade buyers exercise different levels of influence over Heinz, and Heinz again may have greater strengths in some channels than in others. Just as we think we have got all this figured out, we suddenly remember that Heinz products may also be sold to the catering industry, which has a different pattern of buyers and ultimate consumers. So we have to think this through too. This would then bring us to a point where we need to define the industry further. In a broad sense we can say that Heinz is in the food industry, but it is unlikely that the competitors for soups, baked beans and baby foods are the same for each classification. So although we might come to the same conclusion about the relative power of Heinz and Tesco we would probably want to make a different analysis for each of the products, as the competitors and consumers are different.

Now let us take a company which makes batteries for vehicles such as forklift trucks. There are two markets here, the original equipment manufacturers (OEMs) market for inclusion in their products and the replacement market. It is unlikely that all competitors will serve both. OEMs almost certainly will buy directly from the battery companies. Replacement sales will be made to wholesalers, service centres, OEMs, and sometimes directly to those organizations which operate large fleets of forklift trucks. So again we have a far more complex situation to analyse and consider.

The supply side of our analysis may be equally complicated. It may not make sense to throw all suppliers into one box. Every organization uses office stationery, yet the power that any one of the stationery suppliers has over their customers is almost non-existent. But what about the suppliers of chips for computers, you may ask, where there may be only a few suppliers for the whole world? Clearly we need to separate the suppliers into categories, and not waste time on detailed examination of the unimportant. But our suppliers may not be at the start of the chain, and we may need to look behind them in some cases to look at their suppliers.

There is something else we have to decide before we can really get started, and this is how much of the chain from the first raw material to the ultimate consumer we need to consider in our analysis. Take the travel agency business as an example. This divides into two businesses. One is a leisure business offering services, mainly package holidays, to the individual. The other activity is business travel, dealing with the requirements of companies for the travel arrangements of their staff. Here, package holidays are only sold to individuals in the client businesses. Business travel bookings made have to match the needs of the customer. This is straightforward so far. But, when we look at the suppliers for these two services we have to stretch the definition a little further, as they do not always follow the same separation. The leisure side deals with package holiday companies as well as with individual rail, air, ship, ferry, coach, car hire, and hotel bookings, and insurance. The package holiday companies also deal with these other suppliers, and often to a greater extent than do any of the firms of travel agents.

The situation is made more complex by the fact that some package holiday firms own travel agents, airlines and hotels. Some airlines own hotels and travel agents, although this tendency is less visible now than it was twenty years ago. Airlines are major buyers of equipment and services, the most obvious of which are the aircraft. But sometimes they lease these planes, even from competitors.

If we were leisure travel agents we would want to make a study of the package holiday companies, because some of them are also competitors in our business, and because they are our major suppliers. We might want to understand the airline industry, but we certainly would not want to consider their suppliers, such as the airframe and aircraft engine companies. However, if we were an airline, we should certainly be considering these suppliers in depth, as well as looking at both the package holiday and travel agent industries, right to the ultimate user of our services (we would also want to review charter and scheduled airline competitors, and add the airfreight business to what we had to study). Of course, today the whole leisure booking business is about to disappear as private individuals tend to book more and more often by themselves online, using services like Seat24.

The point is that although we could argue that all the suppliers and the travel agents are part of the travel industry, we would choose a different arena to perform our analysis depending on where we sat in that industry. A decision has to be made of what makes sense, and what will give useful results.

Making Sense of a Mass of Information

These brief examples have begun to show the complexity of the analysis, and we have already seen that we need to answer a number of questions, which requires the manipulation of a great deal of information. One method which was developed by Hussey is to chart the industry, creating a block diagram to represent the various groups of "actors" we want to consider, so that we have a visual picture of the industry. Key information is then recorded on this diagram in note form so that interpretation becomes easier, and communication with others is facilitated. The implications of the analysis are recorded on a separate sheet, and, of course, extra information may be added either on this sheet or in an appendix.

This approach has been used in a variety of consulting assignments, and the normal presentation has been to use A3 paper, and to bind the sheets so that the chart and the implications are on facing pages. Sometimes one such pair of pages is adequate, but more likely an organization will have several pairs to cover different products and/or geographical areas. The advantage is that complex situations can be expressed in very few pages. Typically, the analysis would be supplemented by one-page charts of key competitors, and possibly key buyers and suppliers. These contribute to the understanding of the situation, and have another use which we will come to later, for using industry analysis in a dynamic way.

The examples given here are compressed to fit the book, and the data recorded has been simplified for the same reason. Colours can be used in a real situation, and this can expand the information that can be displayed, as it reduces the amount of explanation. For example, the normal path of distribution for the industry might be shown through black lines connecting the boxes that represent the groups of actors, while your company's path might be shown in a colour. This immediately shows the difference without the need for long explanations. The percentage of product that goes through each channel may be indicated by numbers written on the lines: But we are getting a little ahead of ourselves, and need to give some examples of how to undertake this type of analysis.

The Outline Diagrams

The first step is to prepare a block diagram for the industry as you have defined it for the analysis. The starting point may be what your company does, but it would be a mistake not to check this against the broader canvas of the rest of the industry. First, we are interested in identifying all the means by which the product reaches the customer, not just the method your organization has chosen. Thus our example in Figure 3.4 is a toiletry, such as a hair care product, which most competitors do not supply direct to the consumer. To ignore this would mean that we omitted organizations such as Avon. Second, we need to ensure that the chart is not just restricted to the product activity in which we ourselves are engaged. Not all toiletries manufacturers are in the own-label business, and many companies make this their only business. To ignore this would mean we do not fully understand the dynamics of the industry.

The outline block diagrams can usually be drawn based upon discussions with managers inside the organization, supplemented by market research reports. However, our experience is that managers sometimes ignore those aspects of the industry in which they do not participate. So instead, great care should be exercised when they are the primary source of information, and a lot of prompting may be needed to ensure that every aspect is captured.

Figure 3.4 gives a reasonable initial picture of the way the industry works, and might be the result of the first round of thinking. The three key groupings of suppliers represent raw materials, packaging, etc., and there may, of course, be more than three, in which case we add more boxes. Competitors are divided into the two parts of the industry, both of which use similar raw materials, although if we wanted to include advertising services this would not be of interest to contract packers. The branded products reach the industry through wholesalers, retailers, and the hairdressers and beauty salons. Contract packers deal only through retailers.

When we move into the checking phase, other things become apparent. First, we have forgotten hotels and airlines, both of which may be customers of the branded and contract packing parts of the industry.

Second, we need to separate the different types of retailer: the supermarkets have a stronger influence on the profitability of the industry than drugstores, chains such as the British company Woolworth's, and department stores. Similarly, we should at least consider whether we should separate the different types of wholesaler. Third, we need to give thought to the consumers, and perhaps look at them in segments.

Next, we need to consider substitutes, make sure that we have not neglected to think about any influencers, and add a space to note information about entry and exit barriers. By now the sheet is getting cramped, so this could appear on the facing page. There is considerable variation in outline charts for different industries, but the principles for constructing them are the same. Further examples can be found in Hussey (1998).

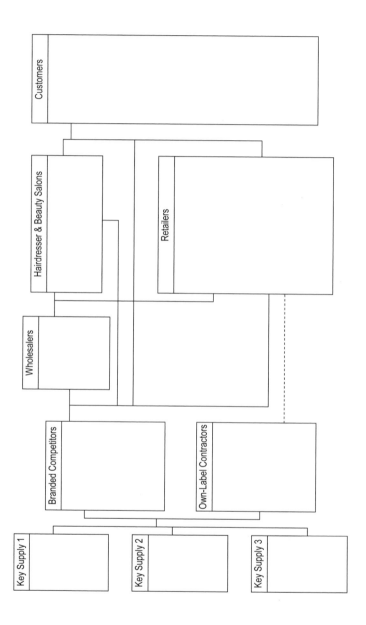

Figure 3.4 Outline Chart for a Toiletry Product Such as Hair Care

Mapping Strategic Groups

It will have become apparent by now that what has been suggested so far is only part of the competitive analysis, and that the analysis of the industry requires much detailed knowledge about all of its actors. The nature of this knowledge and how to obtain it will be the subject of subsequent chapters. However, even applying what we have looked at so far, we see that understanding may be improved if we can cluster competitors into groups that have similar strategic characteristics. This may be essential in an industry where there are hundreds of competitors and it is impractical to study every one of them in detail. It may be desirable when the numbers are manageable, but it is helpful to get a fix on who is competing and where. Porter (1980) developed the idea of "strategic groups", which could be mapped on a diagram to show the variations in competitive activity. One advantage with this is that it may reveal who the real competitors are and those which are in the same industry but are not a real threat.

Porter suggested a matrix with specialization (narrow to full line) on one axis and vertical integration (high to assembler) on the other. However, this is illustrative, and what he advocates is a matrix which shows the way in which the firms are similar to other firms in the competitive strategy they are following. In another industry, the two sides of the matrix might be "quality brand image" and "mix of channels." The groups are illustrated by circles which diagrammatically represent the collective market share of the firms in the group, and the names of the firms are written in each circle. Figure 3.5 provides an example, using two strategic parameters for the business travel industry. The circles' sizes in this example should not be taken as accurate representations of market share.

The purpose of the exercise is to help explain differences in profitability of the various competitors, identify barriers to mobility between the strategic groups, provide a basis for charting movements of competitors, to analyse trends and assess likely reactions. Although the technique is helpful, its value depends on the ability of the analyst to determine the most appropriate parameters for the matrix. Selecting two from the many options is not always an easy task, and the wrong choice will result in an inadequate assessment.

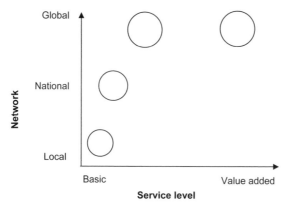

Position the business travel agents you know on this diagram.

Figure 3.5 Strategic Groups: Business Travel Agents

It follows that the only sensible route to the choice of parameters would be to begin with a larger matrix which listed all the main competitors (and some representative competitors from the lesser ones) on one axis and all the key strategic variables on the other. By marking which of the parameters is used by each competitor, it may be possible to arrive at the sort of two-dimensional map suggested by Porter.

Although it does not appear in much of the literature on industry and competitive analysis, there is some value in considering the approach suggested by Abell (1980).

He suggests a three-dimensional matrix to examine the three strategic variables which are: a). customer functions, b). customer groups, and c). alternative technologies. He suggests variations in what is examined under each heading, based on the circumstances of the industry. Customer groups may, for example, be standard business definition such as airline, banks, hospitals, etc., or they may be something about the buying requirement (as in our business travel example, where global customers want an organization that can offer a global service, something not needed by a local customer). Customer functions are how the customer is satisfied by the product. If we use the business travel example again, we can see that some customers want, and are offered, the basic requirement of travel arrangements. Additional functions, which are not offered by all suppliers, might include reducing or monitoring travel costs and other consultancy services. In another industry, the functions would be different.

Alternative technology is best illustrated through another industry: elevators. The main technologies are related to the electric lift, and most modern lifts include a fair quota of electronics. One alternative technology is the hydraulic lift, which has a particular advantage for low-rise buildings where overall roof height is limited for environmental reasons (the electric lift requires a building on the roof to house the lift machinery: the hydraulic lift has its driving force housed in a pit at the bottom of the lift shaft). A third technology is the stair lift, designed for infirm people, where the lift seat moves on rails at one side of the stairs. This is not the end of the story, but is enough for our example. There are competitors which are limited to only one of the technologies, while others could cover all three.

For illustration purposes, Figure 3.6 develops the lift example, to show the application of Abell's concept. The three-dimensional diagram could be seen as being made of a series of bricks, every competitor choosing the bricks it will use to build its own strategy: Do not take the analogy too literally, as you have to imagine that some bricks may defy gravity and be held in mid-air!

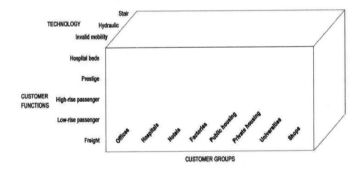

Figure 3.6 Abell's Approach to Business Definition: Elevator Industry

There is no reason why a three-dimensional approach cannot be used in strategic group mapping, although it may be easier to indicate the third dimension through colour or shading than to try to draw three dimensions on a flat piece of paper, like here. One good option is to map the strategic groups against a number of different strategic parameters, so that each delivers some insight and helps to assess whether there is likely to be migration of the firms in each group to a different position on the chart.

Taking a Dynamic View

Although we have hinted at change, much of the description so far has been about taking a snapshot of the current position. Yet we can all see how many industries have changed not just in their structure but also in the relative power of industry firms, suppliers and buyers. In Chapter 2 we discussed the idea of deliberately setting out to change an industry. If this is something which we consider ourselves, then we must accept that the other actors in our drama might have similar thoughts.

One method we have found to be useful for a more dynamic industry analysis is to chart the industry in the way described in this chapter and to complete the mapping of the strategic groups. Ideally we should have collected enough information to gain an understanding of each competitor. This is something we will explore in more detail in subsequent chapters. The best analysis will include collecting detailed information about key customers and suppliers. Our industry analysis so far helps us to see how the industry works, but as we move into a more dynamic analysis, we need to understand the motivation and capabilities of the rest of the industry, as change may be initiated at any point in the chain from raw materials through to the final consumer.

The next stage is to try to think of all the ways in which either the structure of the industry might change or the balance of power might shift from one part of the chart to another. This requires us to incorporate our insights from trends in the macro environment. The structure of an industry may undergo change because of the availability of a different technology, either affecting the product itself or how it reaches the customer. For example, automatic teller machines, now a well-established part of the retail banking system, were one of the technological advances that made it possible for the UK bank First Direct to launch an effective telephone banking service, thus changing the competitive structure of its industry.

The next step in the analysis is to examine the list of what could happen, to see which of the "forces" (suppliers, competitors, buyers, influencers, and new entrants) might initiate such a change. We can then be more specific, and examine which particular organizations shown on our industry chart could initiate such a change with success.

From this reflection it is possible to develop some scenarios of the industry's evolution and to consider our own strategy in relation to this. We may want to be the organization that causes the change, or we might want to take pre-emptive action to make it more difficult for such a change to be initiated by others. What should not be forgotten is that the structures of industries do change, and very few are static.

Dynamic industry analysis can help to prevent a competitive position from eroding because someone else has rewritten the rules of the industry.

In the next chapter we will explore the industry analysis' opposite, the company analysis, the "inside view" so to speak. Only in combination do they give us an idea of our overall competitive position.

REFERENCES

Abell, D.F. (1980). *Defining the Business: The Starting Point of Strategic Planning*, Prentice Hall, Englewood Cliffs, NJ.

Hussey, D.E. (1998). *Strategic Management: Theory and Implementation*, 4th edition, Butterworth-Heinemann, Oxford.

Porter, M.E. (1980). *Competitive Strategy*, The Free Press, New York.

Porter, M.E. (1975). *Note on the structural analysis of industries*, Harvard Business School, Cambridge, MA (a teaching note in the case study collection).

Porter, M.E. (1980). *Competitive Strategy*, The Free Press, New York.

CHAPTER 4

Company Analysis: Assessing Competitive Fitness

Introduction

The Industry Analysis (IA) presented in the previous chapter should tell us about the overall attractiveness of the industry subject to our analysis. It should also give us an understanding of the structural conditions for competition and the forces of change impacting the industry. Finally, we would expect the analysis to provide us with a picture of the possible generic strategies available for competitors and which ones are likely to yield the best result. The subject of this Chapter, Company Analysis (CA), should tell us how the organization under study is performing in its market within a given industry. We would also expect the CA to help us understand the specific constellation of products-market efforts which has yielded the results of the firm. Finally, we would expect the CA to provide us with a picture of the competencies which provides the firm with a competitive advantage and the sustainability of the advantage. Thus, the identification of competitive advantage of any organization is highly dependent on the two sets of analyses IA and CA. Regretfully, many executives do not conduct a proper review of the two, and thus fail to understand the true nature of the firm's competencies and the sustainability of its competitive advantage.

The Company Analysis

The company analysis may contain a number of distinct, functional themes, such as objectives, mission statement, value statement, a list of products and services, financial data, details about ownership, an event calendar (future events), a list of major deals (past events) and competitors. All this should give us a clear idea of what shape the company is in. Thus, it is no coincidence that KPMG defines the company analysis as a "fitness check-up", the allegory to the status of one's own body and condition.

Only upon having completed a thorough industry and company analysis can we define an efficient strategy. Once the overall strategy of the company is defined, it is of course open to change. This is due to the evolutionary nature of business life. A company and industry analysis is only good for as long as its major parameters have not changed significantly. Further, the more competition we find in any industry, the more often we would have to undertake new competitive analyses. It is therefore right to see the strategic process as an ongoing activity. Instead of purchasing expensive one-time plans the company should invest in its intelligence capability, its information gathering and analytical processes. Only such a system will guarantee the company's long-term competitive advantage.

Many companies engage in many disperse analyses of economic performance without performing an analytical integration to provide a holistic picture of the firm's situation, competitive position, its distinctive competencies and sources of competitive advantage. Ideally it should be possible to start with the industry analysis and contrast it with the company analysis as a foundation for the firm's business plan.[62]

Mid-size and larger companies may want to differentiate between their overall strategy and their tactical strategies. This is done for practical purposes; when the company analysis becomes too comprehensive, there is a need to break down the plan in order to explain to lower management what they should focus on.

The banking industry is an example of a profession which has a long history of searching for and collecting essential economic data from their client businesses. After all, it is in bankers' interest to find Key Success Factors (KSFs) when they loan money or make direct investments in companies.

We mentioned earlier that a number of different internal reports are used to make the company analysis. An illustration of the most common of these internal analyses is given in Table 4.1.

All of these internal plans may convey information essential to the company analysis. Efficiencies are not only to be discovered by study-

---

[62] Most start-up companies today will typically start by performing a business plan, consisting of a marketing ("Are you sure customers want your product?") and a financial part ("How are you going to finance the venture?"). There are good and easy-to-use pieces of software for this purpose, such as Palo Alto Software's BusinessPlan Pro.

ing financial figures and the making of better marketing and production plans. In fact, many companies are spending too much on housing or are not using their office space efficiently. If they own the offices themselves, maybe some can be rented out. If they rent facilities, maybe they can renegotiate a better contract after the lease runs out.

Plans and Strategies	Efficiency Parameter	Responsible department
Financial	Capital, People, etc.	Accounting/Finance
The Marketing Plan	Sales, Market Share, etc	Marketing and sale
Production plans	Production, Service level, Quality	Production
HRM strategies	Staff turnover, salary level	HRM
IT Plans	Infrastructure, security, uptime	IT
Facilities contracts	Office Space, off balance sheet risks	Legal
Research & Development	Technology, projects, timeliness,	R&D
Acquisitions	Capital, strategic fit	Business Development

Table 4.1 Company Analysis

The Swedish telecommunications company, Ericsson, had to cut staff due to dropping sales. From the beginning of 2001 to 2005 worldwide staff was practically cut in half, from 107.000 to about 50.000. The good financial result in 2006 was much due to this staff efficiency, not to better sales. Investors do not always ask why a company is performing better. It is often assumed it is because of higher sales. In some cases it is only cutting "dead weight", in which case it will not lead to long term improvements of the company's competitive advantage.[63]

Many foreign industrial analysts were amazed at the speed of this transformation in Ericsson; they wondered how it could be possible. It was possible to lay off so many employees due to close relations with unions, and by the company's willingness to share great amounts of information in advance. That is, Ericsson reasoned with the unions instead of forcing them.

This is a decades-old Swedish tradition, which began in the 1920's when Sweden had more strikes than any other country in Europe. In a few years, thanks to the relationship developed between the head of the unions and the head of the employers' federations, Sweden has had the lowest number of strikes in Europe. British, French and German companies have often much higher costs related to staff reductions. Such cultural differences are important pieces of intelligence for company analysts.

---

[63] Ericsson B shares fell by almost 50% in 2007.

Company analyses can be done in-house or outsourced, bought by external information and intelligence providers. Conducting a company analysis can be very resource-intensive exercise, especially if your company does not have the sufficient know-how. Even if you are capable of doing it yourself, outsourcing your company analysis may still be less expensive.

There are some other solutions. If you are doing a company analysis of your own company, it can be useful to get help with the structuring of the work from an outside consultant. He or she will then take the role of a facilitator. If you do bring in a consultant here is some advice:

1. The consultant will not be an expert on your company. Do not evaluate him or her accordingly.
2. Let the consultant start by showing you a methodology or some working practices, a good methodology is essential to save time and avoid unnecessary errors.
3. Be clear about what type of analyses are needed and which ones are superfluous; consultants are able to stay with you as long as your check book will allow.
4. Let the consultant help you to relate the individual analytical results to benchmarks
5. Set up a process by which the results of the company analysis are integrated into decision making; only then will the firm yield results from the work. Much good intelligence work fails to reach the relevant decision makers because it is not communicated well enough.

There are many outside providers of information and intelligence in the market, and this is hardly the place to suggest any one company or attempt to present them all, but some examples may still be useful. FactSet, with HQ out of Norwalk, Connecticut, started in 1978. They provide global financial and economic information. Their company analysis product "Company Explorer" is primarily targeted towards investors in publicly owned companies, and their focus is on share prices. Hoover's, "a company, industry, and market intelligence company," based in Austin, Texas, also provides benchmarking service with other companies. Another company, Lexis-Nexis, is an information provider which offers searchable archive content from newspapers, magazines, legal documents and other printed sources.

More important than who should perform the company analysis is how it should be performed. This we will discuss next.

How to Perform a Company Analysis

Some experts seem to suggest that there is only one way to conduct a company analysis. Others suggest that that there are a number of equally good methods. We subscribe to a contingency view which argues that the choice of methodology depends on the firm's situation.

To get started, we will look at a concrete example, Lexis-Nexis' suggested ten steps for conducting a company analysis: [64]

1. Determine a research goal
2. Find the company address, phone number and ticker symbol (if available) in a directory
3. Describe the company's primary business, products, and services.
4. Identify the company's industrial classification code
5. Review the company's financial statements (if available), conduct a ratio analysis, examine stock performance
6. Identify current news like dividend announcements, product news, and strategic announcements
7. Organize the information into a descriptive narrative of the current situation
8. Highlight variations, trends and relationships
9. Compare to industry or aggregate information
10. Synthesize information relative to the research goal

The first point here states the limits and the scope to the investigation. Point 2 simply states the company's contact information. At Point 3 we recognize the approach by Peter Drucker. Drucker starts at the product level, with an analysis of revenues, market share and profit contributions.[65] The industrial classification code is more of help later, when performing the Industry Analysis, and for choosing companies for benchmarking. At Point 5 it is suggested we do a financial analysis based on key ratios. Point 6 takes a larger perspective inside of the organization, looking for what is new. In intelligence analysis, it would be something like an early warning analysis, only internally. In Point 7 all the info is organized into narrative descriptions of the situation. We draw conclusions based on what stands out, such as clear patterns, or trends and relationships. In Point 9, all this is compared to the industry.

---

[64] See
http://support.lexis-nexis.com/academic/Record.asp?ARTICLEID=Academic_company_tensteps (2007-02-25).
[65] See Drucker, P. (1964).

Finally, in the last point there is a check to see whether we did what we said we would do.

The suggested process then is both a company and an industry analysis in one. Others would choose to keep these two forms of analyses separated. If we develop each analysis by itself and in full, it will often be easier to do comparisons and updates later on. This in turn will give us a clearer view as to our actual competitive advantage and position.

What kind of specific analyses are then used in the company analysis?

Many companies choose to start with some sort of SWOT analysis; defining Strengths, Weaknesses, Opportunities and Threats to the organization (see e.g. Short, 1996). His analysis also includes a short financial summary and a short competitive comparison table.

Another preferred way of starting is to define Key Success Factors (KFS), which then later can be compared with KFSs in other companies and with the industry in general, given that we chooses similar variables. Before proceeding, pause and notice for a moment what a SWOT is from an analytical perspective. It is the good old "pro and con" placed in two dimensions, the present and the future:

Effects	Today	Future
Positive	Strengths	Opportunities
Negative	Weaknesses	Threats

Table 4.2 The SWOT

It is important not to think about an analysis as a black box or standard product. It is only a standard product to the point that you need it for comparison with other companies.

To show that it is not a black box but can be altered according to needs we shall look at a number of ways in which it is possible to combine a SWOT with other kinds of analyses. Let's start with a problem. Many analysts are concerned that they are failing to see reality as it is or from their competitors' perspective. They are afraid that they are becoming too subjective, too focused on their own company, not seeing the forest for all the trees. Said differently, we often become blind to a situation when we know it too well. This is the flip side to being an insider.

One way to solve this problem is to perform a Devil's Advocate Analysis. This can be done in a number of ways, by everything from hiring external help to having an employee "play" or think like he works for a competitor or another company during meetings. Further-more, notice how a Devil's Advocate is just one of the analyses which can be combined with the SWOT.

Effects	Today	Future
Positive	Strengths from our perspective	Opportunities from our perspective
	Strengths from their perspective	Opportunities from their perspective
Negative	Weaknesses from our perspective	Threats from our perspective
	Weaknesses from their perspective	Threats from their perspective

Table 4.3 An Extended SWOT (+ Devil's Advocate)

Notice how we are breaking with the rules of standard analysis. We are in fact developing, constructing new forms of analysis depending on the problem at hand. This is the true sign of a good analyst; he does not only know the different analyses available, but more importantly he knows the language of analysis.

Another way of starting a company analysis is by the use of Porter's Value Chain Model approach.[66] In this approach, costs and value drivers are identified for each value activity, where the idea is to arrive at a suggestion which will maximize value creation while minimizing costs. A more complete list of different analyses and their use is given in Solberg Søilen (2005). The book also discusses the nature of analysis.

Whatever method we choose, the goal of the analysis is the definition of the company strategy, either operational or tactical. According to earlier contributions by Porter, we know that the company has three generic strategies to choose from. [67]

Competency/ Market Scope	Uniqueness	Low Cost
Narrow	Segmentation Strategy	
Broad	Differentiation Strategy	Cost Leadership

Table 4.4 Porter's Generic Strategies

If you operate in a narrow market you choose a segmented strategy no matter whether or not you have a unique product or cost advantage. If you are in a broad market you choose to differentiate if you have a

---

[66] See Porter, M. (1985).
[67] See Porter, M. (1980).

unique product, or you chose to focus on cost if you have a cost advantage.

Choosing an analysis is a question of where the analysis should be performed, and it is a question of what degree of quantitative techniques may be applied. As a general rule in economics we prefer quantitative methods if applicable, as the handling of numbers will tell us more than the handling of concepts. But we do not want to force the use of quantitative methods where there is no basis for such, or where numbers would not make enough sense. For instance, when testing a new product we may want to get out as much information from the customer by leading a longer discussion with him or her to discover everything about associations and feelings, and not simply whether the product was good or bad on a Likert scale from 1-7.

Where ratios give results that make sense, as in the finance department, they will continue to be used. In the same way, cost analyses are best used where cost plays the biggest role, i.e. in production. Notice also that we do not only suggest one analysis for each function. There should be a possibility for what is called redundancy in method. That is, we study the same facts or data using different and multiple analyses. The great advantage with this method is that we can see if we get the same or different results. If our results are too different, then we may evaluate whether or not to do yet another analyses, or to redo the ones we have already done to search for errors. A summary of some common methods of analyses is given in the table below.

Type of analysis/ Company Function	Qualitative	Qualitative/ Quantitative	Quantitative
Marketing	Focus groups Trend Analysis SWOT Rational Choice Theory KSF Deep interviews	Questionnaires Benchmarking	Forecasting Game theoretical approaches
Finance	SWOT Rational Choice Theory	Questionnaires Benchmarking	Ratio analysis Cost analysis
Production	SWOT KSF	Questionnaires Benchmarking	Cost analysis

Table 4.5 Choosing an Analysis

Why Perform the Company Analysis[68]

There are a number of reasons for conducting a company analysis. It may be that we are preparing a Strategic Plan, that we need to do a Review of our Strategic Situation, that we are planning a Merger or an Acquisition, a Divestment, or that we want to do an Analysis of Synergies.

Preparing a Strategic Plan

All companies should be concerned about strategy. The difference lies in the amount and the quality of work put into the process. Small companies often do not even bother to write their plans down. They have few employees and the roadmap to success is something which is often just known to those who run the company, something they think about the whole time, but which is never put down on paper. Other small companies often have a written business plan, and may or may not update what it says about strategy in this document.

It is first when we enter the mid-size and large companies that strategy becomes a real concern in practice. For most of these companies, and often for each department or product level, there is an annual update of strategy. The understanding and the enthusiasm put into this exercise varies greatly. Some see the necessity in rethinking where the department is going, while others see it as something which has to be done but which bears little consequence on their everyday work.

There is a contradiction in strategy work. In many companies, even in larger ones, the strategy document does not change very much from year to year. Instead it is mostly a copy of last year's. It is often performed by a person who has too many other things to do. Besides, it is done in December, the end of the financial year, and everybody seems to be asking for reports at the same time.

Unfortunately, as it does not lead to any immediate returns, the strategy Plan does not seem all that important. Instead of allocating more resources to conduct the plan, we find ourselves trying to defend a number of assumptions: next year will probably not be that much different from this year, there will be no major shift in technology or any new competitors or competitive situations we do not know about. There will be no disasters; our clients will continue to ask for the same products; and our suppliers will provide the same services they are de-

---

[68] See Jenster, P., Hussey, D. (2001), pp. 11-19.

livering today. Everything will be more or less the same, at least for next year, or so we think.

At the same time, we know that the business world is at a state of continuous change and that these changes are becoming more numerous as the competitive climate intensifies. Competition is getting ever fiercer and new technology is changing consumers' preferences. There exists in other words a fallacy whereby many leaders seem to think that change is something that happens to others. It does not, and companies are taken by surprise every day. So there is every reason to take the strategic plan seriously.

The company analysis prepares you for the Strategic Plan. The more resources and qualified work is put into this process, the smaller the chance of being taken by surprise. In addition, each new strategic plan demands a fresh pair of eyes, a critical mind, by someone who is qualified to ask tough questions.

To know were we are going, we need to know where we are. That is what the company analysis tells us. When compared to the industry analysis – which tells us where all the other actors in our industry are positioned– we can conclude what our competitive position is. This will also tell us what we need to do to become more competitive. Many books and consultants will try to present both the company and the industry analysis in one and the same document. The result is often that we take lightly on one or the other part, e.g. we do a very good company analysis, but when it comes to the outside world we fail to give it our full attention.

It may be that we are not used to performing these kinds of analyses. It may be that we are more insecure about what goes on in the industry, outside of the company. From a purely psychological perspective, it is often good to keep the company and the industry analysis as two different documents. We can then compare them, saying "well, this one explains where we are", and "… this is where all the others are." This division into two separate documents can also make comparisons much easier, and it can facilitate fruitful conversations about where we should be, and what we need to do to get there.

This is all done to make, correct or adjust the Strategic Plan. The Plan should tell us where to go and how to get there, and nothing more. If it tries to say too much, chances are we will miss out on what is really important. So it is better to stick to the core questions, the *where* and the *how*.

Review of the Strategic Situation

There are many good reasons to perform a review of the strategic situation. It may be that a new manager is assigned to a department, or that an existing manager takes on new assignments. These are situations when the Strategic Plan is open for a new, extraordinary, revision, not due to its quality or because it is simply time, but to organizational circumstances. The new manager likes to start by making sure that he or she understands where we are going and to what degree he or she agrees with these directions.

It may be that the new situation calls for external assistance, especially if the company or the department is performing badly and existing resources are not sufficiently qualified. In this case the predecessors' SWOT is not likely to do the trick. After all, if the previous management knew which variables to include and how to deal with them, there would most likely not be a problem. Instead the new manager will be looking for those variables which the previous management failed to recognize, and therefore could not include in their analysis. This, more than anything else, calls for a complete revision of the company's or department's actual standing.

Mergers and Acquisitions (M&As)

M&As are alternative ways for a company to achieve rapid growth. However, growth does not necessarily mean better net results. The problem is very much as follows: one and one does not always make two. It does if you are counting money, inventory and production hours in a table. But it does not if you are counting employees, their knowledge, and willingness to work, not even when you count customers.

In many cases, new groups of employees from the merged company perform less efficiently because they do not get along, and it may be that our customers preferred to buy from us because we were small and local. In the words of Cartwright and Cooper (1994) the psychological contract is often broken, becomes unclear or has to be re-established or negotiated. The larger the cultural differences in M&As the greater the possibility for malfunctions. Transnational merger and acquisitions are particularly demanding. The DaimlerChrysler merger has never really worked, largely due to cultural reasons. The company was struggling to become a unified global organization, and the merger is now an openly declared failure.

Firstbrook (2007) defines four key drivers for a cross-border M&A to work. These are:

1. Develop a clear and compelling strategy
2. Do your homework
3. Value your new people
4. Carry out your executions early

We should first know and articulate what purpose and direction we want from the merger or acquisition. This could be the result of a thorough Industry Analysis. Then we need to do an analysis of the targeted company. It is paramount that this analysis is not just another Due Diligence. Take it from one of the authors with a background in a large Auditing Firm: Auditors are trained to analyse accounting figures, not to assess the value and potential of employees and customers' preferences. "Cultural Due Diligences" are better left to experts. This seems like common sense, but judging by statistics on all the failed mergers and acquisitions, there is still a lot of work to do in this area. Research by the Northeast Human Resources Association (NEHRA) suggests that up to 65% of failed mergers and acquisitions are due to 'people issues'. Of approximately 14,000 corporate acquisitions in the US in 2003, savants estimate that 60-80% were failures. In the same year, 1180 US-listed companies announced takeovers.

There are two major forms of 'people issues' or cultural differences; differences in education and occupation, and differences in geographical and ethical culture. These differences are the result of us having been trained and brought up differently. Both considerations are equally important.

In a few cases, we have seen that it was more difficult to get engineers and sales people to work together, than engineers from two different countries. One of the reasons for this is that education is becoming ever more global. For example, engineering students all over the world are studying from many of the same books and receiving similar training.[69] In addition, young people today watch the same movies, listen to the same music, and even eat much of the same food. When they meet they have few problems touching base and getting familiar with each other, and that despite the Long Tail hypothesis.[70]

---

[69] E.g. engineering students all over the world are reading Kreyszig's classic, *Advanced Engineering Mathematics*.

[70] Chris Anderson in his book the Long Tail shows how mass customization and lower distribution cost is leading to larger product differentiation. Anderson, C. (2006).

The problem from the Company Analysis perspective is that we as employees cannot hope to perform objective cultural analysis on our own company. Therefore, a company which wants to merge with or acquire another cannot use its own company analysis to understand the combined value of our two companies. In other words, the question of finding the value of the two companies is not a simple question of adding data from the two companies' respective company analyses. The company analysis only says what we are worth by ourselves, as we are now, not how we will be together.

To perform a cultural analysis as a part of a company analysis we would be wise to employ an outside assistant, simply because it is so difficult to see one self clearly. It is the same situation for a company as for individuals; we are not always the best at saying what our strengths and weaknesses are. We typically exaggerate our good sides and downplay our weaker sides. This is not always deliberate, but often because we have difficulty distinguishing between what we can do and what we would like to be able to do. The same is true for companies.

Cultural analysis is an essential part of identifying the potential synergies which can be had with a merger or an acquisition, but it is also the most difficult one both to assess and to realize. Other synergies can be drawn from examining the two companies' company analyses. In a merger the two companies should not accept the analysis of the other company, but perform their own. Each company will want to initiate their own independent analysis of the other company. When performed appropriately, this will be to the advantage of the new company. A merger preparation then could include six separate elements of company analyses:

Company/ Type of analysis	Company A	Company B
Analysis of our selves	Company Analysis of A	Company Analysis of B
Analysis of the other part	Company Analysis of B	Company Analysis of A
Analysis of joint values	Analysis of Synergies	Analysis of Synergies

Table 4.6 Analyses at Mergers

In an acquisition, especially if it is hostile one, there will only be one company performing the analyses, and that company will not have an easy time gathering accurate information about the targeted company. Besides, employees do not like to be forced into new working constellations. Many employees will perform less well if they are being forced to work for a new boss, for someone they did not chose, for someone they may not trust or find competent. This is particularly the case for high-knowledge workers. This alone no doubt explains many of the failures in hostile acquisitions.

In any case, once the merger or acquisition is in place, the new company should implement comprehensive intercultural training programs for its entire staff to assess and tackle possible areas of inter-cultural conflicts before they occur.

Divestments

In some cases, we would like to sell a part of our assets. A company analysis could be initiated to find out what part of the company should be sold out, and the industry analysis could tell us who could be the potential buyers.

There are many reasons for divestments. It may be that the company feels it should focus on its core business, or that it needs the cash either to stay afloat or to invest in other activities. Divestments may also be undertaken for legal and political reasons. Sometimes a company may have to sell off certain activities to get another merger approved by the authorities. A company may also choose to withdraw from a country voluntarily or by pressure as in South Africa in the 1980s due to the apartheid regime. More recently a number of American organizations have been divesting from Sudan. In all these situations, a company analysis will help tell us about the consequences of the divestiture.

Divestments are not a one-time event in the history of companies, but a part of a continuous life of investment and divestment activities, both nationally and internationally. They are not always the result of wrong investments, but of changing strategies and circumstances as the companies evolve. It should therefore be expected that the number of divestments increase with the number of investments.

We see this in the retail industry, where the number of divestments has increased considerably over the past 10-15 years. In the period 1991-1995, 38 major retailers divested in international markets followed by 78 retailers in the later five-year period (1996-2000). Among them were British retailers such as Laura Ashley, Wickes, Boots, Virgin, Next and Marks & Spencer. French retailers included Carrefour, Promodes, Auchan and Sephora (Alexander, Quinn, Cairns, 2005).

Decisions to divest should be based on a thorough analysis of all of the company's activities. This is best done in a Company Analysis, in particular the financial part, where we should be able to see the ROI from each operation.

Analysis of Synergies

The corporate synergy is the result of expected financial benefits due to mergers and acquisitions. The key word here is "expected" and the expectation should of course be based on thorough analysis. The problem here is to know how the new company will function without starting it first.

When companies think about synergies they frequently forget that there is a flip side to the process, namely the extra expenses. A merger or an acquisition is likely to lead to savings in certain areas but to extra expenses in others. This is inevitable. It takes not only time and money to carry through a merger. Those resources also mean an opportunity cost, as we could have used those resources to start other projects instead. Using a great deal of energy to conduct a merger is likely to lead to a temporary loss in regular income as we will be spending less time with day-to-day business.

Company A	Savings	Expenses
Revenues	Increased revenues	Customers sensitive to merger (bad will)
		Reduced focus on day to day business
Costs	Reduced costs	Costs related to cultural frictions
		Time and resources used to close deal
		Opportunity costs (other new projects)

Table 4.7 Savings and Expenses in Synergy Analysis

There are basically two kinds of synergies; the possibilities to increase revenues, and those to reduce costs. The most common reasons cited are those to reduce costs. Actually, in many cases when management talks of "synergies" they mean reducing costs (Kuehn, 2006).

Direct revenues and costs are often much easier to calculate than the general and administrative expenses. This is certainly one reason why they are also underestimated or ignored. It is of course the net result of these calculations which will tell us if the merger or the acquisition is a good idea or not. Therefore we must calculate both effects to get a realistic assessment.

We have earlier talked about the cultural dimensions. Cultural friction in the new company can be reduced if management can show the potential synergies to its employees. This is a process in two parts; first to show the expected synergies before the merger, and then to measure and communicate the actual synergies when the deal is done.

Interpublic Group is one of the companies which have been feeling the expenses of mergers. The idea that clients would embrace one-stop shopping for advertising, packaging, and promotions has turned out to be a pipe dream. Although it sounds simple enough to have sister companies working in concert for clients, in reality, Interpublic Group's units have fought the idea tooth and nail (Khermouch, 2003).

Another example is the AOL-Time Warner merger. Michael Kelly, the AOL division's chief operating officer has been critical about the misuse of synergy. He refers to synergy as a 'big sandbox': "People are doing crazy stuff and wasting money. Someone has to set priorities." (Craine, 2002). These priorities should come in two phases: first, decide what kind of synergies should be investigated, as these studies are very resource-intensive. Then, based on the company analyses of the potential candidates, we must identify lucrative mergers and acquisitions.

A final note of advice from the authors; many poor business decisions have been made in the name of synergies; conceptually, appealing synergies are very difficult to enact in practice.

In the next chapter we will talk about intelligence analysis in general, independently of industry or company analysis.

REFERENCES

Alexander, N., Quinn, B., Cairns, P. (2005). International retail divestment activity. *International Journal of Retail & Distribution Management*, Vol. 33, Nr. 1, pp. 5-22.

Cartwright S., Cooper C.L. (1994). The human effects of mergers and acquisitions. *Journal of Organizational Behavior*, pp. 47-62.

Carin, R. (2002). Synergy's promised rewards big waste of executives' time. *Advertising Age*, Vol. 73, Nr. 22, p. 24.

Drucker, P. (1964). *Managing for results*. London: Heinemann.

Jenster, P., Hussey, D. (2001). *Company analysis: determining strategic capabilities*. Chicester: John Wiley & Sons, LTD.

Firstbrook, C. (2007). Transnational mergers and acquisitions: how to beat the odds of disaster. *The Journal of Business Strategy*, Vol. 28, Nr. 1, pp. 53-56.

Khermouch, G. (2003). Interpublic Group: synergy--or sinkhole? *Business Week*, Aril 21, pp. 76-77.

Kuehn, R. A. (2006). Will Carriers' Synergy Serve Their Customers? *Business Communications Review*, Vol. 36, Nr. 1, pp. 66.

Porter, M. (1987). From competitive advantage to Corporate Strategy. *Harvard Business Review*; May/June.

Porter, M. (1985). *Competitive advantage*. New York: Free Press.

Porter, M. (1980). *Competitive Strategy: Techniques for Analyzing Industries and Competitors*. New York: Free Press.

Short, R. (1996). Western Resources company analysis. *Management Quarterly* Vol. 37, Nr. 1, pp. 15-21.

CHAPTER 5

Intelligence Analysis

The Need for a Method

One of the pitfalls of competitor analysis is to arrive at a situation where there is a great deal of data but very little need-to-know information. This happens more frequently than might be expected, and the end product of the competitive analysis effort is a cabinet of files of press clippings, often obtained more or less at random, which may or may not have been circulated to managers in periodic bundles of cuttings or as e-files and internet links. Every so often there is a splurge of interest in a particular competitor, followed by a scurry of activity as someone tries to makes sense of the heaps of data. Typically these files do not include very important information contained in documents like market research reports or internally generated information such as customer analyses. Sometimes the files may include snippets of information sent in by sales people, but unless the system is carefully designed, there is an initial burst of enthusiasm when the sales force is asked for its support which often tails off over the next few months.

Of course, this bleak picture is not typical of every organization's competitive analysis activity, but more importantly here there is no reason why it should remain typical of any. What requires careful thought is how competitive information will be collected, organized, analysed, and disseminated. There are elements of structure, system, process and culture to be considered. This chapter is about ways of producing, using and presenting competitive information. It will be followed by some thought of how to build an effective Business Intelligence System in chapter 6.

What do we want from Competitor Analysis?

The most important part of a competitive analysis is the competitor analysis. Competitor analysis should deliver some specific advantages to the way strategic issues are considered, with possible side benefits for shorter-term operational activity, such as being able to brief the sales force on the benefits of the company's product offerings compared to those of our competitors. In order to achieve this, there is a need for up-to-date information that can be communicated and understood by those who are expected to use it. There may be several different requirements from competitor analysis. We suggest that these include:

1. *On-going knowledge of competitors.* This is to ensure that we are aware of what our competitors are doing that will affect us and what they might be considering doing. In addition, we need to turn the thinking around to how things we are doing will affect each of them and what the reactions of each competitor might be. Continuous knowledge of competitors calls for a method of recording information that is kept up to date, and which is always immediately accessible. The method we suggest is competitor profiling.

2. *Special studies.* From time to time every organization will need to produce a special report on a competitor which relates to a particular purpose. An obvious possibility is if a competitor is being considered as an acquisition candidate or as a partner in a strategic alliance. Another possibility is to answer a query that arises from an action observed from the on-going monitoring, such as what are they really doing in Southeast Asia, or why have they started to recruit so many scientists. To answer this sort of question quickly requires organization of the competitor information so that what is available in the system can be rapidly identified and retrieved. It may also require a willingness to commit resources to special surveys and investigations, and the competence to undertake or commission these.

3. *Performance comparisons.* A third use of competitor information is for performance comparisons across as many parameters as possible. The aim is to be better than competitors in areas of performance which are critical. Knowing their performance is a first step to this. We enlarge on one tool for performance improvement (benchmarking) later in this chapter.

A trap to avoid is the writing of reports on competitors which resemble a corporate history book. We are interested only in those aspects of the past that have a bearing on the future, so what we choose to find out and analyse about competitors should be selective and relevant. Managers do not need all the atmosphere and character development that takes place in a great Novel. We should ensure that they are not swamped with a mass of detail that cannot be interpreted.

Developing Competitor Profiles

Just as we did with industry analysis, we recommend a method which shows the key information about each significant competitor on one A3 sheet of paper or software equivalent. This will not be all the information we keep about the competitor, but it is the shorthand version that managers could consult regularly, and which should be updated on a continuous basis. We should also explain the one piece of paper target, and in stating this we are thinking of a competitor who is in one of our industries and in one country. If we compete with the competitor in two industries, we will need one profile for each, although some of the information will be duplicated. Where we compete in more than one country, we will need a profile for each country, plus a global summary: how we might organize to achieve this is a matter for Chapter 6.

A second point is that we describe a generic profile based on a sort of average industry. Experience in applying this in a variety of industries and countries have shown that there is always a need to modify the format of the profile slightly to fit the real life situation. Modification is always easier than developing the outline from a blank sheet, so we feel that the suggestions here are justified, even if in practice different needs mean that an exact copy is not workable in every situation. The outline given in Figure 5.1 is deliberately the same as that used in the case history of Harbridge Consulting Group Ltd mentioned later, where there is an example of what a completed profile might look like, but there have been very few examples in our experience where we have not found it necessary to adjust the outline to the specific situation. We probably do not need to add that the outline in this book is drawn to fit the page, and is not to scale. An A3 sheet gives scope for the boxes to be drawn to a size which allows space for information to be recorded.

Perhaps the best way is to think of the profile as a series of notepads on which information and assessments can be written. The headings, which are described below, sometimes cover hard fact, such as market share figures from an objective source. Often they are deduced from the evidence, such as the apparent strategy: Sometimes they are judgments, based on a mix of deduction and hard fact, such as the critical skills factor ratings.

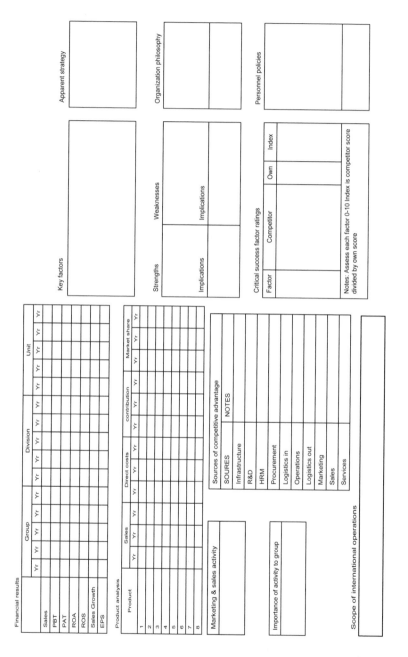

Figure 5.1 Outline Competitor Profile

- *Financial results.* The aim is to record a few meaningful figures that give a snapshot of the competitor's recent history. Unfortunately, few competitors are single-business companies and, even if they are, they may be multinational. The three sub-headings across the matrix reflect this. If the competitor were Otis Elevators, "group" would be changed to United Technologies, "division" to Otis' worldwide organization, and "unit" to the country company we were studying. In fact, in this example we may find it necessary to insert a sub-heading to cover the geographical region, or we may decide that the Otis organization is so big that we can miss out the parent company for our purposes. However, this would mean that some of the information suggested would not be appropriate, such as earnings per share (EPS). Let us also be clear that some of the information we need for the ideal profile may not be available, and cannot be reasonably estimated. Chapter 8 deals with the sources of information, and although there is frequently more available than may be believed at first, sometimes nothing can be entered in some of the boxes.
- *Product analysis.* Companies compete at the level of products and services. It is possible to argue that there is competition at the unit level for scarce resources, but for the most part we are concerned with product competition in relation to our industry. Thornton, for example, is a British manufacturer of chocolates. Among its competitors are Nestle and Cadbury-Schweppes. The resources that these giants can command, and the synergy between their activities, are of concern to Thornton because they affect how these competitors may behave. However, Thornton competes only with the chocolate confectionery activities, and would have no interest in the wide range of other products the other companies produce. And even within the chocolate confectionery market, Thornton has a niche position and would be more interested in the boxed chocolates products than in chocolate bars.

  As designed, the outline suggests analysis of up to eight products, although this can be extended, and records information under the headings sales, direct costs, contribution, and market share. In many cases what are recorded here will be estimates, based on evidence from sources such as market research and reverse engineering. For some types of products an additional column showing advertising expenditure may be of value, and there is also the option of a column showing growth trends.
- *Marketing and sales activity.* This notes key information about how

the competitor influences the market. It may include information about the size and organization of the sales force, and note promotional activities and their duration. Information about discounting may be of value. Other relevant information might be the number of outlets operated. For example, this would be important if Nestle were studying Thornton, because a feature of the latter organization is a network of tied retail outlets trading under the Thornton name. If analysing a professional services firm, it might be relevant to include the number of major organizations they serve, information which often appears in their marketing literature and in some journal surveys.

- *Sources of competitive advantage.* The thinking behind this box is derived from the value chain approach (Porter, 1985), which is discussed later in this chapter. It is an attempt to identify which of the particular activities of the competitor provide value to the customer, and are therefore a source of competitive advantage. The headings here are the generic descriptions used by Porter, and are useful as a reminder to the analysts, but are jargon to most managers. Replace them with a tighter everyday description of the actual source of advantage.

- *Importance of the activity to the whole group.* Our argument here is that a competitor is likely to be more aggressive, and to respond more fiercely to attack, if the activity is of importance to the company's overall results. This means that it is of value to try to establish just how important each activity is. There is no need to be pedantic. It does not need very much analysis to determine that the activities of the training department of a large multinational, which sells its services to other companies, are not particularly important to the overall strategy of the company, and would probably be abandoned if put under severe pressure. A division which has lost money over several years may not receive the same support as if it were a major contributor, and may be vulnerable in that it may not be able to match your modernization program, and so will fall further behind. However, a division which contributes most of the profits and cash to a multinational might be considered to carry an invisible sign: "Don't tread on me - I bite".

- *Scope of international operations.* At first sight this may not seem to be important to anyone studying competitors within a particular country. This would probably be a correct assumption if all that was recorded was the number of countries in which the competitor operates. There are two more important aspects. First, there is the competitive advantage given by multi-country operations, which may be economies in production because factories produce on a larger scale, the bigger base of revenue to support R&D, and in certain cases the ability to offer advantages that cannot be matched by all competitors. An example of the last is the business travel agency competitors, where only those that have established a global network can gain the volume business of global customers. Second, the way in which a competitor organizes its international operations will have a considerable impact on how it makes decisions. Hussey (1998) states that "The competitive reactions to your strategy will be very different if the competitor operates on an individual country basis, what has been termed 'multi-local', than if it manages globally through an integrated strategy. One Europe-wide grocery products company I studied operated at a disadvantage because each country's operation was treated as a separate business, and had to achieve its return on investment targets as its main priority. Its main competitor, who was winning all the battles in every country, treated Europe as one strategic area and would put resources into any country to beat off a competitive threat, regardless of the short-term impact on that subsidiary's bottom line. The virtually uncoordinated country strategies of my client meant that it could rarely win against the superior strategy of the competitor. Knowing how your competitor views global operations is a critical first step to understanding and predicting how it will behave in different circumstances" (p. 179).

- *Key factors.* There are always a number of facts about a competitor which helps our understanding, and which are either a manifestation of its strategy or suggests that a new strategy may emerge. Under this heading we would record facts such as the location and number of factories where R&D is undertaken, changes to the top management team, and any recent change in ownership. It is a notepad for whatever is important. What is worth noting will vary with the industry and the type of competitor.
- *Apparent strategy.* This is the heart of the profile and also the most difficult box to complete. The word "apparent" is used deliberately: it is what can be deduced about what the competitor is trying to do. Although a useful picture can be developed, it should never be forgotten that there is uncertainty, both in whether the deductions are correct and for how long they will remain correct. Continuous monitoring and analysis of the competitor is the best way of confirming the deductions, spotting inconsistencies, and observing when new strategies appear to be implemented.

- *Strengths and weaknesses.* This box does not need explanation but it does require a caution. Although the assessments of your own managers may be valid, where possible they should be backed up by an analysis of the hard evidence. There may be a temptation to mix wishful thinking about weaknesses you would like the competitor to have, with an overestimation of its strengths and infallibility. One American client had undertaken regular assessments of its competitors, and concluded that a number of them were on the verge of financial collapse. This assessment lost some of its impact when it was realized that identical conclusions had been reached every year over the previous five to ten years, and the competitors were still alive and kicking. Customer surveys can be used to reveal some strengths and weaknesses which might otherwise be seen only from an internal, and biased, perspective.
- *Organization philosophy.* How an organization runs itself will have an impact on its strategies and many operational issues. What role does its head office play in the running of the organization? Is the competitor a pawn in a much larger strategic game that the head office is playing? How is performance of the competitor judged by its head office? How does their accounting principle affect how the company views its costs at the product level? Such questions are not only matters for competitors who are subsidiaries of larger organizations. Even single-industry companies are affected by the structure and management style.
- *Personnel policies.* The personnel policies of an organization have an impact on its strategies and performance. A low reward policy may make it difficult for a competitor to attract and retain staff, affecting operational performance and the longer term success. The quality and qualifications of its employees, the career development opportunities open to them, and the training that is provided are all matters which may have strategic importance and are therefore worth recording.
- *Critical success factor ratings.* The concept and use of critical success factors need no further explanation. What is suggested here is a development from the previous discussion. The first task is to assess the critical success factors for the industry and to rate your own company against them (a 0-10 scale is suggested). This element would be a constant on the profile of each competitor. Next, rate the competitor in the same .manner. The index is created by dividing the competitor's score for each factor by your score. Making such judgments about a competitor forces deep consideration. Experience

shows that it is best undertaken by a panel of knowledgeable managers rather than by an individual acting alone.

Before moving on, we should spend a little time on the use of the profiles. First, they present a good way of ensuring that all information is analysed and recorded, so that the assessment is always up to date. Ideally they should be discussed regularly by a panel of interested managers, a matter we will return to in Chapter 6. When strategies are considered, they are an essential tool to use in conjunction with the industry charts discussed earlier. Finally, they enable comparisons to be made of what competitors actually do against what you thought they would do, so that there can be immediate reporting to management that something needs consideration. Essentially they are a tool for senior managers and analysts who are involved in strategic decisions. Because they show what you think a competitor is doing, they should be treated as confidential. If they moved into the hands of the competitors they could become a target for misinformation. For dissemination of regular competitor news across a wide number of people we recommend another approach, which will be discussed at the end of this chapter.

Marketing Diagrams

It is possible to be more imaginative in the way information is displayed on the profile, to substitute graphs for tables, and to include diagrams such as the three-dimensional approach of Abell (1980). Such diagrams can give a visual indication of the differences between competitors which can save lengthy narrative explanations. Market positioning diagrams have a much older pedigree than most of the techniques discussed so far, and offer another way of comparing competitors in a diagrammatic way. The concept is simple, and is not very different from the method used by Porter (1980) to map strategic groupings.

Again the idea is to create a matrix with two axes which show a view of how the competitor is positioned. A possible matrix might be constructed with axes for price (low to high) and perceived quality (low to high). Competitors offering a food product might be compared using convenience and nutritional value as the factors. For a car polish the factors might be speed of application and life of each application. A number of such diagrams, with all competitors plotted, can aid understanding of the market, and each individual competitor. The technique has been used in other marketing situations, such as a comparison of advertising campaigns. We have used it to look for gaps in a market, for example to identify possible journals that might be launched to meet the needs of specific segments of the market.

Portfolio Analysis

Another diagrammatic technique which has value in the examination of competitors is portfolio analysis. Like the market positioning diagrams, portfolio analysis was designed for a different purpose. A full description of the technique and its origins is beyond the scope of this book, but for those who want to probe deeper we recommend Hussey (1998), which provides scoring rules for one variant of the technique, and Segev (1995a, b). The books by Segev cover a wide range of variants in detail, one giving conceptual descriptions, and the other is in effect a detailed manual, including computer software to enable application of the various methods.

Here we will restrict ourselves to the bare bones of the technique, and then draw attention to the two ways in which it might be useful in competitor analysis.

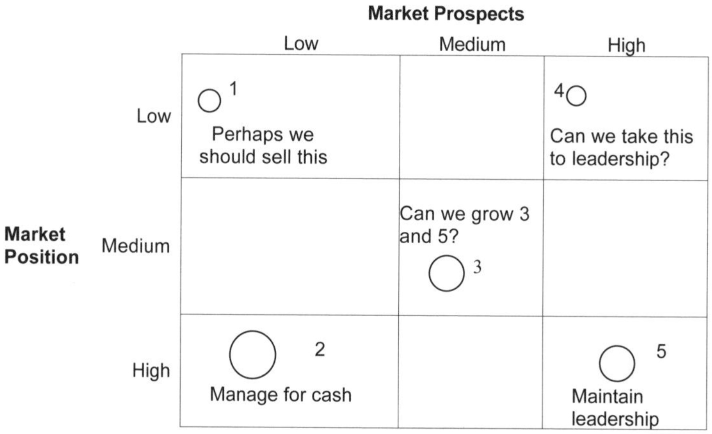

Figure 5.2 Example of Portfolio Chart. Each circle is one SBU, area is proportionate to revenue and comments are indications derived from the chart: more analysis is needed to reach a decision.

Figure 5.2 illustrates a typical portfolio chart onto which it is possible to plot strategic business units, or with some adaptation to the scoring rules, major product groupings: Each business activity plotted is typically represented by a circle, the area of which is proportionate to the importance to the company of that activity. There are several different ways of measuring this, and one which is the easiest to use in competitor analysis is revenue.

The basic purpose of portfolio analysis is to enable an organization to look at all its business activities in relation to each other, to help determine which activities to invest in, which to manage for cash, and which should be sold or closed down. In the example, the probability is that an activity with weak market prospects but a high market share should be run to generate as much cash as possible, with just enough investment to maintain the business. A weak share in a poor prospect market raises the question of whether the business can ever become successful, and, even if it could, whether this would be the optimum use of scarce resources, of talent and money. The indicative answer from the analysis is to consider disposal. At the other extreme, a high market share in a high prospect market implies a cash-hungry business that needs to invest to stay ahead, which should yield good returns. A weak share in a high prospect market is something the organization should either try to develop or drop altogether if it does not want to do this. Without a commitment to driving for a much higher market share, activities in this box will tend to get weaker over the long term as the leading contenders strive for more market share and higher market growth.

The remaining positions on the chart are interpreted as various degrees of intensity of the same three broad strategies. All indications are indicative, and other evidence should be examined before decisions are made. The main value of the portfolio chart is not to give dogmatic answers but to help the organization to choose between its activities; if it does not have the resources to back them all, to examine how a strategy such as acquisition or strategic alliance might change the position in the matrix, and to ensure that the number of cash-hungry activities chosen does not exceed the cash-generating/raising ability of the organization.

The chart also helps the consideration of timing. In a fast-growing, emerging industry, where a company has a strong position in one or two countries, it is tempting to think of an expansion plan that rolls out across the world, building on success and reducing apparent risk. However, the analysis behind the portfolio chart might show that this would be disastrous as it would allow other competitors to get ahead in the race, after which it may become impossible to catch up again. If the investment required is too great or too risky for the company, the indication would be either to sell the business now, while there are potential buyers, or to expand by other means, e.g. though strategic alliances.

One use of portfolio analysis in competitor analysis arises from this sort of situation. If we plot competitors on the company portfolio chart we can see which are better placed if we are to win such a global race. This may be most useful when we are looking at a global opportunity, at a stage when every competitor has a regional strength but no one has yet gained a truly global position, as there may not be full awareness of the other competitors who have not yet been encountered in the market-place.

A second use of the portfolio approach in competitor analysis is to try to think like the competitor when it is a multi-activity organization. We may compete with only one of its activities, but what it does in our industry is partly affected by the relative position of the activity in the competitor's portfolio. If they have an activity in the central box of the matrix, which has to operate as a cash generator to provide resources for more promising cash-hungry elements in the portfolio, while our choice is to develop that business because it is one of the best in our own portfolio, we may well have an advantage in that they may not wish to match our investment. The disadvantage of using portfolio analysis in this way is that it requires the collection of information on other industries in which the competitor operates but in which we have no direct interest. It is therefore a tool to be used sparingly, but it is nonetheless valuable when justified by the situation.

Sources of Customer Value: The Value Chain

In our discussion of the competitor profiles we touched on a list of headings which aimed to show how the competitor was delivering value to the customers. This was inspired by the value chain concept by Porter (1985). He argued, "To diagnose competitive advantage, it is necessary to define a firm's value chain for competing in a particular industry" (p. 45). He also maintained that "Competitive advantage cannot be understood by looking at a firm as a whole. It stems from the many discrete activities a firm performs in designing, producing, marketing, delivering, and supporting its product. Each of these activities can contribute to a firm's relative cost position and create a basis for differentiation" (p. 33).

Porter envisages an organization as having five broad operational areas: inbound logistics, operations, outbound logistics, marketing and sales, and service. Each and all of these are potentially capable of delivering unique value to the customer which, provided the economic equation is satisfactory, can create a competitive advantage. So the first step is to examine the processes which cluster under these broad headings, to establish where the costs are incurred, and which processes produce value to the customer.

Supporting these operational activities are procurement, technology, human resource management departments, and the infrastructure of the firm. These may not be visible to the customer, but nevertheless can create or destroy value. For example, the comprehensive training given by an airline to its cabin staff may create value not through the training itself but through what the customer experiences, the behaviour of the in-flight staff.

The idea is that a chain of value exists inside every organization, and understanding this and building on it is one way to build a strong competitive position. It follows that understanding a competitor's value chain, to the degree that it is possible to do this from the outside, is a useful step in determining an appropriate strategy.

Value is created, according to Johansson et al (1993), in four broad ways, alone or in combination: improved quality, service, reduced cost to customer and reduced cycle time. The starting point for an assessment of the value chain may be to establish what the organization believes are the processes which deliver value to the customer, but by itself this may be dangerous and inadequate. It is the customer who is the key, and to make any sense of the value chain there is a need to define what it is that the customer is looking for. However, there are limitations to this when the company is considering an innovation that has never been seen before, and therefore customers may have no experience or even understanding of it.

So although much of the value chain analysis is about self-inspection, it may become meaningless unless it has customer inputs. Market surveys may yield some of this information but greater depth may come from focus groups of current and potential customers. Such marketing research methods can yield valuable information about the value chains of competitors. A focus on these formal ways of obtaining information should not obscure the important information that is gained when the organization is always in close contact with its customers, enjoys good relations with them, and discusses their needs with them on a continuous basis. Unfortunately, comparatively few companies are close enough to their customers so that we can say that they are really in each others' confidence. In any case knowing a customer well may not help you understand why your competitors' customers do not buy from you.

Porter's thinking goes beyond the boundaries of the firm, and argues that the industry company is only one series of links in a much larger chain which stretches from raw materials to the ultimate buyer or end consumer. Many of the value improvements lie at the interfaces between the organizations which make up this chain. Therefore there is considerable merit in working closely with suppliers, customers and through them the customer's customers, to seek areas of overall improvement. Collaborative work of this kind is, of course, now a feature of modern approaches to quality management, and appears in much of the literature on business process re-engineering. It is no longer considered stupid to give up an activity which is not performed as well as it could be and instead to transfer it to a supplier.

Benchmarking

Using competitor analysis for performance improvement takes us to the topic of benchmarking. There is often confusion about what benchmarking really is, and some consider that they are benchmarking when they compare performance ratios. Although it is an important first step to use such ratios when they can be obtained, benchmarking is about understanding the processes through which someone else is achieving performance which is better than yours, and comparing them with your own. We may say that the elements in benchmarking are:

1. Decide what to benchmark, which may come about from a comparison of performance ratios of competitors or from a less specific indication that performance could be improved.
2. Decide who to benchmark against. This, of course, requires their agreement, as normally benchmarking is a reciprocal process.
3. Study your own processes in the area which is causing you concern.
4. Study the equivalent processes of your benchmarking partner(s).
5. Compare the results with what you are doing.
6. Develop an action plan to improve weak points.

There are of course many versions of this list. In a recent article it is suggested that outliers should receive special attention, not the least because it may be that the calculation has been conducted wrongly (anonymous, 2007).

Benchmarking as a whole has only limited use in competitor analysis, since it is unlikely that the necessary cooperation can be obtained. In any case, the normal code of practice in benchmarking is that information obtained from a reciprocal process is only used for the purpose agreed at the outset, which would make it unethical to use such information for a wider purpose. Only the first step, comparing as many aspects of performance as possible against your competitors, is often all that is possible, although this, of course, is most valuable. Performance indicators may be collected by trade associations and other external organizations. Although the names of the competitors are usually replaced by a code number, it is possible to compare your performance against others, even if you are not quite sure who has the best performance in that area. Other indicators can be developed from marketing research. It is possible, for example, to obtain information on how long it takes various competitors to deliver the goods from the time a customer makes an order, or to compare the performance of service engineers when called into a customer's premises. When a process is carried out in full view on premises which are open to the public it is possible to observe and record it. Things such as the length of customer queues at supermarket checkouts or bank counters and waiting times at peak periods could be obtained, although loitering too long in a bank may of cause result in the unwanted attention of the security staff!

Benchmarking can be a very useful tool in building competitive advantage, and is one of the tools that might be used to help achieve world-class performance. Xerox is recognized as being among the leaders in the use of benchmarking, and the methods this organization uses are described in Watson (1993). Bounds and Hewitt (1995) give a case history of Xerox's overall performance improvement activities over several years.

If you cannot easily benchmark yourself against a competitor, what can you do? There are two options.

- In many industries it is possible to find a firm in the same line of business with whom you do not compete. So an electricity-generating firm in Holland should be able to benchmark against a similar firm in Japan or the USA, or a chain of health shops in Hungary might find cooperation with a similar chain in the UK.
- As the interest is in processes, and these are common across wide swathes of economic activity, we may learn most from benchmarking against firms that are not in our industry but which operate with a particular process. Once this expansion of thinking takes place, it becomes possible to see that we may actually gain more through doing this than if we restricted the study to our own industry, because members of our industry may include the best in the world in one process but be well below world-class in another.

Benchmarking can be used totally internally where, for example, an organization has operations in several countries or has numerous branches which undertake the same tasks. Here it is possible to benchmark against the best with relative ease. This may bring an overall improvement, and build confidence in the process before going outside, but it is unlikely to help the organization jump ahead of the competition.

Finally we would add that the last stage of the process; developing and implementing the improvement, does not mean that the aim is just to copy someone else. Other people's solutions may have to be adapted to fit the circumstances of your organization, and in any case it may be possible to spot how those solutions can be improved to take you even further ahead.

Competitor Newsletters

Although it moves us a bit away from methods of analysis, we should like to suggest a way of disseminating information about competitors which can be used more widely than the profiles. This is a development from the common practice of sending out files of press articles, which has value but tends to be repetitive. Besides that, what is passed out is often not validated. Instead, it is worth considering the production of a periodic competitor newsletter, which can be produced in a confidential and a non-confidential version. In this way a summary can be provided of the facts gleaned from the various sources, so that there is an awareness of what the competitors are doing. The ideal would be to have only one version which incorporates information from various sources. This is particularly motivating when it can acknowledge the contribution of pieces of information provided by the sales force and others with their ears close to the general industry gossip. However, this depends on the trust management has in its employees, as the newsletter should not reach competitors. In any case, the newsletter should avoid any statements which are based on unsubstantiated rumours, which could cause problems if repeated to customers or if they became known to competitors.

Like so much in competitor analysis, the right answer requires a healthy dose of common sense. Only given this can sensible decisions be made.

Using Critical Success Factors in Planning

Leaving benchmarking we shall now take a look at some other analyses, first of all the use of Critical Success Factors (CSFs), also called Key Success Factors (KSF) and most often identical to Key Performance Indicators (KPIs) discussed in the next chapter.

This section introduces a strategy planning and strategic control process which is designed to aid directors and senior managers in executing and monitoring their strategies. On the basis of this research, the authors provides a detailed description of this method for developing, monitoring and integrating critical information into effective strategic management decision support. This design method incorporates nine steps:

1 Provide structure for design process
2 Determine general forces influencing strategy
3 Develop a strategic plan or review/modify the current plan
4 Identify a selected number of critical success factors (CSFs)
5 Determine who is responsible for which critical areas
6 Select the strategic performance indicators (SPIs)
7 Develop and integrate appropriate reporting procedures
8 Implement and initiate system use by the senior personnel
9 Establish evaluating process and procedures.

Through appropriate introduction, this approach can create an integrated strategic context within which top management and key personnel can execute the strategy and maintain a competitive advantage for their firm.

Successful strategy development and implementation relies on the quality of the available information. Further, this information is a vital resource which can make or break a firm's chance of success. The availability of information to senior managers, however, is usually not the problem. On the contrary, they are generally inundated with data (see Calingo et al, 1983).

Thus, in this increasingly complex and information-oriented world the main challenge confronting managers is the identification, selection and monitoring of information which is related to the strategic performance of the company. (Depending on the nature of the business, this methodology is appropriate for smaller to medium-sized firms.) Also, the right information requested and communicated by the managers will help shape the way in which other members of the organization define their tasks, interpret the firm's strategy, and determine what is important and what is not.

A leasing firm recently brought in a new president. The previous manager had received summary reports from several accounting systems which were considered state-of-the-art. The new president identified the firm's "spread" (i.e. the difference between the firm's cost of funds and the firm's yield on an annualized basis) as one of his primary

concerns. However, not only was this figure not available in current reporting, the data required to provide the "spread" figure resided in external as well as internal databases. Once the reporting was realigned, a
key measure replaced and/or supplemented multiple reports.

More important, consider the strategy implication of the new margin
figure, as compared to the previous segmented reporting. The single
measure provided the president with the "pulse" of the firm on a weekly
basis. Thus, he was able to have a generalized feel for the firm's exposure, its position vis-à-vis other firms, and trends indicating the need for
asset or liability repositioning. Additionally, he was no longer required
to analyse multiple reporting sources, except when conditions warranted
accessing the detailed information.

This section introduces an information-based approach to strategy
development and control which can aid managers in turning their strategies into action. The author provides a method for designing a planning
and control process whereby crucial information can be identified, organized, evaluated and communicated in a manner which supports execution of the strategic plan.

Information Focused on Factors Influencing Strategic Success

An increasingly popular approach for identifying strategically relevant
information is through the critical success factor method (Hise and
McDaniel, 1984; see also Daniel, 1961, 1966). Critical success factors
(CSFs) are events, conditions, circumstances or activities. Specifically,
they are "the limited number of areas in which results, if they are satisfactory, will ensure successful competitive performance for the organization" (Rockart, 1979). These factors may also result from:

- The outcome of external events when there is risk exposure (e.g.
  past political developments in South Africa)
- The achievements of one or more individuals, such as members of
  a particular engineering project
- The internal operating process (e.g. attaining better quality or decreasing the default rate).

Thus, CSFs relate to the basic internal or external conditions for the
firm's strategy (e.g. customer acceptance, competitive moves), or those
competencies or resources (e.g. human, financial) it must attain. Recent
research has expanded this notion into a more comprehensive and strategic concept, suggesting that the definition and monitoring of critical

118

success factors differs for various strategy types. A study of 128 firms in mature manufacturing industries found a number of interesting results (Jenster, 1984). In particular, this research indicates that the firms which had a higher return on equity:

1. Formally identified their CSFs
2. Used these factors to monitor their progress in the implementation of strategic changes
3. Benefited from formally integrated reporting and information systems.

Others have found that CSFs, when formally identified, implicitly communicate top management's priorities and thereby direct organizational efforts in the desired direction (Millar, 1984). More specifically, the desired direction is attained through the motivation of the organization's employees. Provided with a framework against which they can make sense of priorities, assumptions and environmental conditions, the employees are then able to better contribute to the execution of long-range plans.

Consider a company which views the introduction of new products as one of its CSFs. Beyond communicating that top management views the organization's future as hinging upon being a product innovator, this clearly conveys to individuals where their most significant contribution can be made. Most members of management are strongly motivated to excel in relation to the expectations of corporate leadership. They will adapt to meet those expectations provided that top management's wishes are clearly and consistently communicated. Effective leadership necessitates the clear definition of the success factors, the ideal organizational performance in relation to them, and the explicit communication of these factors to all appropriate levels of management in a structured manner.

In addition to providing a bridge between the firm's objectives and management's strategy, the isolation of critical factors also provides a vehicle for the design of an effective system of performance measurement and control. This way, the design of CSFs becomes more than just identifying the areas which must go right, but also assumes a powerful strategic role in which the specific efforts of top management and the employees are joined and aligned in a manner consistent with the firm's vision.

In summary, the factors identified as essential to the organization's success serve as the primary integrating mechanism between management's long-range goals and the channelling of resources and executive attention. Explicit recognition and use of such CSFs, provides, therefore, a planning process/system through which strategy formulation can be made operational and controlled within the firm, as depicted in Figure 5.3.

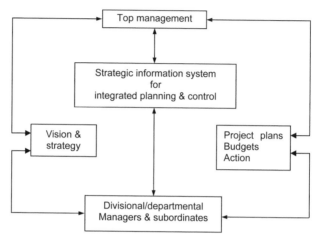

Figure 5.3 An Information "Bridge" for Making Strategy Operational

An Overview of the Design Process

The design procedures for a strategic process and information system for integrating planning and control are shown in Figure 5.4 and discussed over the following pages. This approach is based on the idea that the executive must focus on factors most vital to the organization's success and then manage by creating a context within which others are able to align their efforts accordingly. The method as suggested incorporates nine steps:

1. Provide structure for the design process
2. Determine general elements which will influence success
3. Develop a strategic plan or review/modify the current plan
4. Identify a selected number of CSFs
5. Determine who is going to be responsible for what
6. Select the strategic performance indicators (SPIs)
7. Develop and enact appropriate reporting procedures
8. Initiate use of procedures by managerial personnel
9. Establish evaluation procedure

Provide structure for design process
Determine general forces - audit of external and internal
factors Strategy formulation
Identify critical success factors
Determine who is responsible
Select strategic performance indicators
Develop and integrate reporting procedures for strategic
monitoring Implement and initiate system use
Evaluation of plans, process and system

Figure 5.4 Designing a Strategic Information System: Procedural Guide

The design method serves as the means for top management to create
and identify essential strategic elements, make use of information
relevant to success, align rewards and incentives, and reach strategic
goals. More importantly, however, it is the means for creating a strategic context for the firm.

On the surface, this design may not appear to be novel or unique.
After all, planning and control system design has not undergone any
major changes in the last 20 years or so. It is argued, however, that the
integration of the planning and control processes through the design of
an information-based context can better aid managers in defining and
interpreting environmental events and changes. In other words, we can
say that this approach enables top managers to provide a setting in
which others can interpret information and adapt their roles to meet the
objectives of the firm. Thus, the design philosophy is that the strategy
formulation and the plan execution cannot be treated as two separate
issues. Modern strategic management must view the strategic planning
process and the system facilitating implementation as interrelated.

Designing a Strategic Information System

This section consists of a detailed discussion of each of the nine steps
in the design and implementation process (see Figure 5.5).

Step 1: Structure the Design Process
Before engaging in the planning design process and the actual planning, it is important to determine who is responsible for overseeing the
specific steps and the planning outcome. In most cases, it is recom-
mended that the chairman/CEO designates a steering committee to
oversee the whole process. This should include selected members of
the board, the president, plus the vice-president of planning or any
equivalent positions. This primary committee must articulate the firm's
objectives and, in turn, oversee and receive reports from secondary

committees consisting of lower-level employees. The secondary committees will be selected to tackle the specific steps and issues in the design process outlined below.

Step 2: Determine the Elements Influencing Success
The second step in the planning process is to audit the forces which are relevant to the firm's present and future position. Strategic areas may include:

- *General environment.* Factors which influence the firm and over which it has no control. Included here may be issues such as general socio-demographic trends, interest rates, exchange rate fluctuations, etc.
- *Industry characteristics.* Features of the firm's industry and related industries. In general, it appears that each industry has a set of common dimensions to which individual firms need to adhere. For example, supermarket chains will have one set of dynamic factors and banks another.
- *Competitive forces.* Postures of competitors, suppliers, customers, potential new entrants as well as those elements to which firms following similar strategies in related industries need to be alert. These may include certain quality standards, product mix, cost control, etc.
- *Company-specific characteristics.* Factors derived from the unique aspects of a particular firm's competitive position (i.e. its strengths and weaknesses as well as its opportunities and threats), traits of the management team, and/or time elements.
- *Personal values of key players.* The demand, wishes, needs and capabilities of key players, executives and other personnel must be examined. For example, the personal preferences of the major stockholders should not be neglected.
- *Resource availability.* Availability of financial as well as physical and human resources will have an impact on the strategic success.

		Governmental issues (specific)	Competitor X (specific action)	Exchange etc. rate	
F U N C T I O N S	Marketing				
	Personnel				
	Production				
P R O J E C T S	Project 1				
	Project 2				
P R O D U C T S	Product 1				
	Product 2				
G O A L S	Goal 1				
	Goal 2				

Figure 5.5 Assessing a Firm's Vulnerability to Its Environment - Using an Impact Grid

These strategic characteristics may form the basis for defining the firm's sensitivity to the influences or changes along the various dimensions. Figure 5.6 shows how the firm's sensitivity can be examined using a weighting scheme where 1 equals no effect, to 10, which implies substantial or critical impact. The Impact Grid can also be used in the design/review and integration of a firm's strategic plans, as well as to assess reversibility of resource commitments. Moreover, this evaluation is used to create the list of potential elements from which management selects the firm's five to ten critical success factors.

The dimensions may also be used to develop alternative result scenarios and for the identification, achievement and evaluation of management's objectives, as well as in the subsequent transformation of ideas into action. This technical part of the strategy-formulation process has been described in numerous books and articles (see, for example, Grant and King, 1983).

Some of the identified factors affected by the various elements are strategic in nature, in that they relate directly to the way senior personnel interpret situations and carry out plans. Other success factors are operational and not necessarily directly useful to the tasks and activities of key personnel. While they are important to the way lower personnel define and integrate particular tasks, they may receive management attention on a less frequent, ad hoc or by-exception basis.

Step 3: Develop or Review the Strategic Plan
The third step is the formulation of alternatives and the choice of a strategy, or a thorough review of the current strategic plan. This step is concerned with the evaluation of the firm's strategic ends and means. That is, this step must address the organization's mission by asking questions such as:

- What type of firm do we want the organization to be?
- What type of activities do we want to engage in?
- What markets do we want to pursue?

Although these questions sound simple and straightforward, it is the authors' observations that it can be a long and tedious affair which is validated by the experience of managers who have actually gone through this process. In addition, the associated objectives must be clearly defined, the goals relevant and attainable, and a set of alternatives must be identified. In this step, the firm's current plans may also be reviewed to ensure consistency among anticipated environmental threats and opportunities and the firm's internal capabilities.

Example 5.1 Iowa Farmatics Inc.

Bill Sobek, founder of Iowa Farmatics Inc. (IFI), a distributor and manufacturer of fertilizer-spreading equipment, was proposing to withdraw from the day-to-day management of the firm. The last 15 years had been marked by a steady increase in sales averaging 23%. The success of the firm over the years had rested on a philosophy based on the primacy of customer service. Since the period for fertilizing fields is short, a disabled spreader can cost a customer a considerable amount of money. Although the firm inititially was a distributor and assembler of equipment, management realized that to ensure quick response to customer's needs for spare parts, the firm had branched out into the manufacturing and extensive stocking of spare parts. In order to fully satisfy customer needs, the firm also began designing and manufacturing customized liquid sprayers. Unlike the standardized dry spreaders, these liquid spreaders are made to customer specification. Because of the unique nature of liquid spreaders, these units take considerable amounts of time to design and manufacture.

   While most producers of farm machinery were hurting, the firm was straining capacity and planning for future growth became essential. The prospect of expanding sales of liquid sprayers into states outside the present market area looked very favorable. Although Bill Sobek desired growth for the firm, he recognized the need for any growth to be controlled. Additionally, he desired that even with future growth of the firm, his personal involvement would have to be significantly reduced. It was clear that the future growth strategy required an improved monitoring system and new management structure.

   The Impact Grid depicted in Table 5.6, exemplifies the relationships between developments in some of the critical success factors and elements of Sobek's strategy for IFI.

Step 4: Identify CSFs

Critical success factors (CSFs) are those limited number of factors important to strategic success. They are limited number of areas which must be monitored to ensure successful execution of the firm's strategic programs. These factors can be used to guide and motivate key employees to perform in the desired manner, in a way which will ensure successful performance throughout the strategy.

The use of these factors in discussions and planning within the firm will clearly and succinctly communicate critical elements of the strategy to members of the organization. More important, the CSFs direct the attention of key managers to focus on the basic premises of the firm's strategy. The selection of proper strategic dimensions is essential, in as much as they will serve as motivation for those whose performance is being measured.

Thus, the CSFs must:

1. Reflect the success of the defined strategy
2. Represent the foundation of this strategy
3. Be able to motivate and align the managers as well as other employees
4. Be very specific and/or measurable.

A manufacturer of cutting tools has as its major strategic theme "Shipping of orders within 24 hours". The board of directors subsequently identified timeliness of shipments, and industry market share as two of their CSFs.

Step 5: Determine who is Responsible
Most organizations rely on the actions of a relatively small number of key people whose functions are vital to the strategic plan's implementation. It is important, once the critical success factors have been determined, that these individuals be identified and properly motivated to achieve the targeted strategic ends.

The identification of key people is accomplished by analysing the critical success factors and selecting the individuals whose efforts apply to a particular factor. Key personnel include those employees ultimately responsible for achieving the particular strategic dimensions or goals, plus other individuals designated to undertake specific major steps to deal with the critical dimensions. The following simplified example illustrates how key personnel and CSFs were identified and matched by management of a manufacturing company attempting to implement a low-cost strategy:

- *OSHA standard*
  Legal council
  Vice President of Operations Plant
  Superintendent
  Service Engineer

- *Customer Services*
  Vice President of Sales & Marketing Manager of Distribution Managers of Production Planning
  Managers Service Department
- *Manufacturing costs - reduction by 22%*
  Vice President of Operations
  Chief Cost Accountant
  Plant Superintendents
  Managers of Production Planning
- *New low-priced products*
  Vice President of Sales & Marketing Senior
  Market Analyst
  Manager of Products Development
- *Sales growth of 17%*
  Vice President of Sales & Marketing Manager of Advertising
  Four Senior Salesmen
- *Work Force Development*
  Vice President of Personnel
  Manager of Training and Development
  Two Foremen
  Union Representative

It should be noted that because some critical factors are long range in nature, different key individuals may be identified over time as conditions change. While more than one individual may be designated as responsible for the achievement of a critical factor, each individual typically has appropriate strategic performance indicators or responsibilities assigned so that his or her performance can be monitored separately, as discussed in the following section.

This analysis of key individuals may also highlight certain organizational problems. For example, the individuals selected to fulfil certain responsibilities must have authority and resources to take the necessary steps required for the successful implementation of the strategy. This authority should be clearly articulated to match accountability. Any organizational problems which exist should be explicitly addressed.

CSF	Introduction of liquid spreader by competition	Disruption of parts supply	Securing distributors in new markets	Decentralization of management	Expansion of facilities
Marketing: Distribution	10	2	10	1	4
Promotion	10	8	2	1	1
Personnel: Design	10	2	1	1	5
Management	8	6	1	10	8
Production	8	4	1	1	8
Production: Assemble dry spreaders	1	10	1	1	10
Design liquid spreaders	10	1	1	1	10
Manufacture spare parts	1	10	6	1	10
Projects: Plant construction	7	1	6	1	10
Products: Dry spreaders	1	1	2	1	8
Liquid spreaders	10	1	8	1	8
Goals: Controlled growth	5	1	7	1	10
Reduced time commitment/ CEO	1	2	3	10	2
Customer service	1	10	3	3	7

Key: 1 = *Little or no impact* ... 10 = *Substantial or critical impact*

Table 5.6 An Impact Grid for Iowa Farmatics Inc.

Step 6: Select Strategic Performance Indicators

CSFs are also the basis for identifying the Strategic Performance Indicators (SPIs) used in measuring the short-term progress toward the long-term objectives. The SPIs are the indicators specifically used to measure and monitor key individuals' short-term progress toward achieving good performance along a critical dimension. SPIs provide motivational information which must be explicit enough to allow managers to understand how their actions influence strategic success, even though they may not have a full understanding of the underlying strategy. The indicators must ultimately be approved by the steering committee and the board, but designed with significant input from subordinates.

SPIs must strive to satisfy six specifications. They should be:

1. *Operational.* They must focus on action and provide information which can be used for control.
2. *Indicative of desired performance.* Indicators must be measured against a desired level of performance.
3. *Acceptable to subordinates.* Subordinates should have significant input into the determination of the indicators during the design/review process.
4. *Reliable.* Most phenomena cannot be measured with precision, but can be described only within a range or as a degree of magnitude. It is up to the steering committee to think through what kind of measurement is appropriate to the factor it is meant to measure.
5. *Timely.* This does not necessarily imply rapid reporting. The time dimension of controls should correspond to the time span of the event.
6. *Simple.* Complicated strategic performance measurement systems often do not work. They confuse the organization's members, and direct attention toward the mechanics and methods of control, rather that toward the targeted performance results.

After being selected, the indicators should be analysed in terms of the information required to measure their achievement. Performance indicators will generally require information from a wide variety of different sources, both internal and external, in order to enable management to monitor progress in the different functional areas of the organization.

Step 7: Development of Reporting Procedures
There are three basic steps for translating the information requirements of a modern business into a formalized reporting system:

1. *Strategic information planning.* This task addresses the development of an information plan for the management team. Remember that information can be a strategic resource to the firm. The first objective of the plan is to assess the gap between the available and required information to monitor the CSFs and measure actual performance. The second objective of the plan is to assess that availability of information related to the operating success factors

(OSFs). The strategic information plan must develop an approach for obtaining the information which is not immediately available from existing sources. Since information systems are not created in one day, an interim system may be installed using some surrogate information until the sources called for in the information plan are established and procedures completed.

2. *Preliminary system design plan.* The functional and technical requirements of the reporting system and of the necessary hardware/software are identified during the preliminary design phase. The primary objective is to bring to the surface all associated design issues prior to the installation of systems and the establishment of procedures. For example, "What constraints do the firm's existing data systems impose? Can the barriers be overcome or do we have to undertake major re-design?"

3. Procedure/systems installation plan. This phase involves the detailed design, installation and testing of procedures and systems. The technical part of the process for computerized systems includes developing programming specifications, developing logically structured programs and required procedures; training user personnel; and fully testing and converting the system. For manual procedures, it is worthwhile having the individuals involved in gathering and synthesizing information conduct a trial on old data. A simulation or case exercise can be successfully used.

In order for CSFs and SPIs to be of motivational as well as control value, they must be explicitly utilized by the senior managers. This makes subordinates aware that the measures are being used by management to track progress and performance. The competitive environment, the firm's size, the particular strategy, as well as the management style will determine when and how CSFs and SPIs are used.

For example, when Bob Russell of Golden Wheel Creations Inc. introduced the firm's new CSF-reporting system, he emphasized one-to-one meetings with subordinates. Moreover, the firm recognized high performance achievements on the bulletin board. Other executives went further and utilized a computerized information system that included a communication network for the management team, and direct information input from key customers. The system also allowed these customers limited access to the system.

Step 8: Implement System and Initiate System Use

Several criteria are important for successful implementation of plans and procedures. Top management support and involvement is essential. Lower-level employees may not take the plan or planning and control efforts seriously unless the firm's top management clearly demonstrates interest in the activity. Therefore, it is important that top management, whenever possible, actively guide and participate in the implementation. It is equally important to create commitment or a team spirit which will pull participants together.

A set of implementation recommendations is useful. These simple guidelines should be introduced by the CEO or the most senior manager at the "kick-off" meeting. The following recommendations are examples; others may be created to suit the particular situation:

1. This project and its success belong to all employees, with no one left out; thus, these game rules belong to all involved, let's all help to keep them.
2. Everyone involved must take responsibility and demonstrate team work.
3. Think positive - all negative and non-constructive statements undermine the project.
4. Excuses don't get the job done. If you can't complete a project assignment on time, the delay should be brought to the attention of the CEO/senior officer in advance of the due date.
5. Success is dependent on timely completion of all assignments. Any unsolved problems or emergencies must be reported to the CEO or senior manager within 24 hours of discovery. All problems and emergencies are to receive immediate attention.

We recommend that these implementation recommendations be handed out to all participants. The implementation must be presented to support team spirit, not to alienate employees.

It is also vital that members of the organization have a firm understanding of the different steps. Thus it is necessary to involve the right people as early as possible in the process and to provide the necessary training and education. From time to time, managers expect that the benefits of plans and procedures will be realized with little effort. Adequate input of time and resources must be used in both plan development and execution.

Step 9: Establish Evaluation Procedures

It is important to establish a review schedule for the strategic plan as well as a re-evaluation of the procedures and information systems. This part is often forgotten. Procedures and managerial habits tend to live a life of their own. As the competitive and organization conditions change, it becomes necessary to re-evaluate the strategy, the CSFs, and SPIs, as well as the procedures and systems which generate the needed information.

Conclusion

Intelligence analysis lies at the heart of any competitive organization. There are many ways to perform an analysis of internal and external factors which bear an influence on the strategy of a company. In this chapter we have suggested some approaches.

Strategies are formulated based on a number of assumptions. During strategy execution, however, these premises and other factors are likely to change as time passes. Therefore, getting the right information on developments in critical issues and the firm's strategic progress is essential to the directors and managers of any business. Furthermore, this specifically identified information is used in communicating and monitoring strategic progress, and to measure key personnel on vital aspects of the firm's strategy and provide powerful motivators for the firm as a whole.

Research suggests that relatively few firms are engaged in systematic monitoring of factors critical to the firm's strategic success. However, the firms which have adopted these more sophisticated methods for strategy formulation and monitoring of strategic progress seem to achieve better performance. The planning process and procedures described in this chapter provide a framework which firms can use to bridge the gap between the vision of top management and successful strategy execution.

With the method presented here, the directors and the top management team are able to clearly communicate the firm's strategy to the organization. Moreover, they have a method for receiving the right information as well as for measuring performance and ensuring that appropriate actions are taken. In addition, individual responsibilities in relation to strategy implementation can be identified and monitored to reach the intended goals. Given appropriately tailored procedures, firms can attain higher levels of achievement and motivation among employees as they are helped to recognize top management's expectations and their own responsibilities in the execution of the firm's strategy.

RERERENCES

Anonymous (2007). Follow these six steps to become a benchmarking process expert. *Hospitals Materials Management*, Vol. 32, Nr. 1, pp. 1-3.

Abell, D.F. (1980). *Defining the Business*, Prentice Hall, Englewood Cliffs, NJ. Bounds, G. & Hewitt, F. (1995). Xerox: Envisioning a corporate transformation, Strategic Change, 4, No. 1. (This appears also in Hussey, D.E. (ed.) (1996). The Implementation Challenge, Wiley, Chichester.)

Calingo, L., Camilus, J., Jenster, P. & Raghunathan T. (1983). Strategic management and organizational action: a conceptual synthesis, 43rd National Conference of the Academy of Management .

Grant, J.H. & King, W.R. (1983). Topics of Strategic Planning, Little, Brown, Boston.

Hise R. & McDaniel, S. (1984). CEOs' views on strategy: a survey, *The Journal of Business Strategy*, Winter. See also Daniel, D. (1961). Management information crisis, *Harvard Business Review*, November-December; and Daniel, D. (1966). Reorganizing for results, *Harvard Business Review*, March-April.

Jenster, P. (1984). *Divisional monitoring of critical success factors during strategy implementation*, Doctoral dissertation, University of Pittsburgh.

Hussey, D.E. (1998). *Strategic Management: From Theory to Implementation*, 4th edition, Butterworth-Heinemann, Oxford.

Johansson, H.J., McHugh, P., Pendlebury, A.J. & Wheeler, W.A. (1993). *Business Process Reengineering: Break point Strategies for Market Dominance*, Wiley, Chichester.

Porter, M.E. (1980). *Competitive Strategy*, The Free Press, New York.

Porter, M.E. (1985). *Competitive Advantage*, The Free Press, New York.

Millar, V. (1984). Decision-oriented information, *Datamation,* January.

Rockart, J.F. (1979). Chief executives define their own data needs, *Harvard Business Review*, March-April

Segev, E. (1995a). Corporate Strategy, Portfolio Models, International Thomson, London.

Segev, E. (1995b). *Navigating by Compass*, International Thomson, London.

Watson, G.H. (1993). *Strategic Benchmarking*, Wiley, New York.

Solberg Søilen, K. (2005). *Introduction to private and public intelligence.* Studentliteratur, Lund.

CHAPTER 6

Building an Effective Business Intelligence System: Technology and Organizational Structure

When we say Business Intelligence (BI) today, it usually means the technology that goes with intelligence analysis. As new technology is introduced to the market and adopted by ever more companies, the BI part is becoming more important. It is now hardly possible to give a full course in Intelligence Analysis or Competitive Intelligence without treating this topic in some depth. For instance, at the Blekinge Institute of Technology (Sweden), Business and Competitive Intelligence goes hand in hand as part of the same course.[71] Students are asked to take part in the process of improving the software and engage in simulations. Then there is the organizational question. So far much research has focused on why companies should get engaged with Business Intelligence (BI). Far less has been written on how to implement BI in organizations (see e.g. Jaworski, Macinnis, Kohli, 2002). In this chapter, we propose to start to do both.

BI is a relatively new organizational function, and most companies will have little or no experience in its implementation. Technology is important, but it gives nothing by itself if there is no competent and dedicated staff to use it. Another problem is that there is no single correct organizational solution for all companies. However, one observation that applies to most companies, is that the intelligence needs and ways of monitoring and handling intelligence are different at different levels in the organization. We can suggest a number of organizational models to choose from, for different levels in the organization, as depicted in the figure 6.1 below:

---

[71] See www.subsoft.se (2007-06-26).

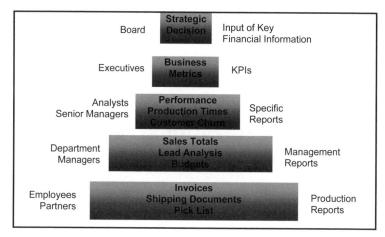

Figure 6.1 Different BI Needs in the Hierarchy

Some of the terms used in the figure require explanation. Executives tend to have less time to read long reports. Instead they often look for the essentials, the "executive summaries". For example, many enjoy following Key Performance Indicators (KPIs). As we saw in the previous chapter, KPI consists of financial and non-financial variables used to evaluate the performance of a company or a department. Today, these are often visible on an electronic dashboard. An e-dashboard is a business management tool used to get an overview of the organization's performance. At its best, it lies on the desktop of the PC and gives a signal whenever there is a change in figures. Most dashboards use simple graphical presentations, histograms, pies, and maps in different colours to indicate the score of different KPIs.

The example below is from Kramerica Industries, a web design company for non-profit organizations and small businesses, operating out of Flushing, NY.

This dashboard is based on SQL Server relational analysis services and Cognos data sources. It lets end users build their own views of OLAP data. On Line Analytical Processing (OLAP) is like a fast-calculating, online Excel spread sheet which many users can share simultaneously. We speak of databases configured for OLAP. As in Excel, we have different dimensions in the rows and columns, and different values at their intersections. The most common use of OLAP is to present sales figures, budgeting, forecasting and financial reports.

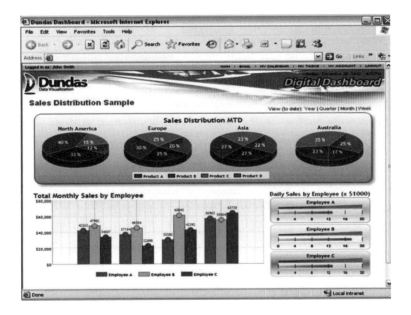

Figure 6.2 Dundas Digital Dashboard

The further we move down in the hierarchy in the figure above, the broader and more extensive the information. Thus, down at the specific department levels, we find the classic management reports, and at the lower levels, the production reports. Each form of information is suited to the performance at each level in the organization.

Strong Growth in BI Software Market

The BI Software market has experienced strong growth over the past few years, not the least in new and advanced technical solutions.

With the continuous development of efficient computer and software technology, more managers are implementing Marketing Decision Support Systems (MDSS). MDSS are formally structured computerized information systems that help managers make routine decisions. With current information systems technology this is possible.

An MDSS can vary from sophisticated expert systems to simple sales variance analysis. MDSS is usually best applied to repetitive and routine decision-making activities: for example, decisions related to order scheduling, field service, or order quantity discounts. MDSS is also used in sales reporting, customer service, and variance analysis related to product shipment. In general, the major portion of strategic marketing intelligence tends to be manual. It may be difficult to get good returns on very sophisticated MDSS in business marketing.

There seem to be four major categories of software which give support to business intelligence activities today: Intelligence software, Knowledge Management solutions, Search Engines/Agents and Data Warehouse/OLAP solutions. Only the first category actually supports information analysis from other Business Intelligence software. The other three present useful and valuable software solutions, but no real analytical support:

Support categories	Search engines/ agents	Intelligence software	Data Ware-House/OLAP[72]	Knowledge Management
Information gathering	Yes	Yes	No (from internal Databases only)	Yes
Analytical support	No	Yes	No (only numerical Quantitative analysis)	No
Information distribution and reporting	No	Yes	Yes	Yes
Examples of Software/Company	Autonomy	Brimstone Intelligence	Cognos, Business Objects	Comintell

Source: Primary research.

Table 6.1 A Selection of Business Intelligence Software and Characteristics

The major types of analysis presented in Intelligence software may be divided into three broad groups:

1. *Relationship analysis* helps the user analyse relationships between variables such as companies and people.
2. *Analysis of structured text* helps the user structure and find important information in unstructured text (such as text documents).
3. *Comparative analysis* helps the user compare information in the system and has a wide range of application areas. It can focus on quantitative data, qualitative data, or help use existing models such as SWOT analysis and Porter's Five Forces.

Together with the other phases in the intelligence cycle, these types of analyses give what we call degree of comprehensiveness in intelligence software. This is placed on the x-axis. Another important criterion for users of intelligence software is the degree of visualization,

---

[72] For more on OLAP, see http://www.olapreport.com/ (2007.12.22).

which is placed on the y-axis. This does not mean that a software program which scores poorly on both criteria is not worth buying. It may be good for a specific operation in the BI cycle, like data gathering from news sources. However, the quality of this kind of software will always depend on the quality of the data sources subscribed to, according to the formula garbage in, garbage out.

Degree of Visualizing

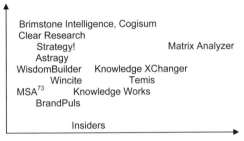

Figure 6.3 Degree of Support in Intelligence Software - Fuld Report and Primary research

Among the current top performers in BI Software, we find a list of 17 products published by Fuld & Company. The products have been selected for their explicit or inherent CI functionality.

One of the more interesting products presented at SCIP's European CI Summit 2007 in Bad Nauheim was Astragy's Competitor 2.0 which allows the customer to pre-connect a large selection of databases into the software. Within a year, Arent van't Spijker, the company's Managing Director, thinks it will be possible for the customer to do this himself, plugging in and out of databases very much at free will, given that the data is in the right format. When this happens, it will be a breakthrough in data mining ability. Also, Temis' Luxid surprises with its large capacity for knowledge extraction from unstructured data. And Reuter's business intelligence solutions, which give detailed information on companies, industries, economies and markets, have become more structured and easier to use. New and better solutions are continuously presented on the market. The above mentioned abilities will soon be yesterday's technology.

---

[73] Market Signal Analyzer.

	CI Tool Type						
	CI Tool	Text Mining	Visualization And Sharing tool	ERP (integration)	ASP	Custom Solutions	Market In-telligence
Autonomy		×					
Biz360		×	×		×	×	×
Brimstone	×			×			
Cipher	×	×	×	×	×	×	×
ClearForest		×	×				
Coemergence	×	×				×	×
Comintell	×			×			
Cymfony		×	×		×		×
FirstRain	×	×			×		
Intelliseek	×	×					×
Netro-City	×		×				
QL2 Software	×	×					
RocketInfo		×					×
Strategy Software	×						
TEMIS		×					
Traction Software	×	×					
Wincite	×				eWincite-version for low usage		

Sources: Intelligence software report 2006/2007, Fuld & Company (2006)

Table 6.2 BI Software and Tool Type

At the end of this software presentation, it may be worth giving a few words of warning. None of this software does the real intelligence work for you, but it can make your work much more effective. Executives want fast results, but it takes time to build and maintain a good database. The software is really just an empty shell. You have to fill it yourself, with need-to-know information and good analysis. Believing otherwise is much like buying a MS Word package and expecting it to turn out beautiful poetry!

Integrated Business Intelligence Systems

Business Intelligence has now become commonplace in many organizations. A decade ago, when we started our research in this field, business intelligence and competitive intelligence did not only have the same meaning, but attracted little interest among top management. Today it has been accepted that just to stay in touch with the market it is necessary to have timely information about financial operations, customers; in short, everything that influences your operations, and that these services are best kept and organized in electronic systems. What is happening today is business systems integration. Companies do not want a BI system as a stand-alone unit. They want a solution they can use together with their other business systems, a BI database that can communicate with other databases and share data.

Data-sharing is the order of the day. DHL's and UPS' customer system for tracking packages is one example mentioned earlier. Both company and customers are expecting to see where their package is at all times. In many Northern European countries, customers are so used to purchasing electronic devices over the Internet and having them shipped home that going to a regular store is starting to feel awkward. Other retailers are following close behind. Even men's clothing companies can sell online, assuming they can solve the "try-on" problem by using some innovative body-scanning device. Good bye, prêt-a-porter. Your tailor-made suit may as well be delivered to you directly from China. This demands advanced CRM and e-commerce solutions, which are tied up to Decision Support Systems (DSS), where your accounting system and the Business Intelligence function is an integrated part. Supermarket chains are just waiting to use all the data they have been collecting about us for years now on our bonus cards. As they know we buy sweets every Friday, they will soon start to send us an SMS/MMS offer with a 15% rebate on our next purchase Thursday afternoon! Market research today is trying to figure out how far is too far, i.e. when consumers start to get offended by too much advertising. Mobile CRM, or eCRM, is opening up as a new area of research. Preliminary market studies suggest that customers, especially young males, are welcoming certain offers from Trusted Stores through a system of Permission Marketing, but that unsolicited SMS are heavily rejected (Aamir Turk, M, 2007). The Business Intelligence system is not interested in our individual transactions at the supermarket, but wants to catch any piece of information which could influence the company's strategy. For example, the eCRM system could teach us more about what segment of customers shop when and what kind of other goods they buy as to help us make more attractive bundles of offers, but this will probably still be too detailed for the intelligence function. However, the success or failure of such bundled offers would be a piece of intelligence caught by the Business Intelligence system and vital information for decision makers. What this means is that specific pieces of information are transferred to the appropriate software. In the future, we are likely to go from integrated systems to complete business systems, where the BI function will only represent one module.

Gartner Inc., the very company which is accredited for having coined the term "business intelligence", reported in 2005 that 1,300 CIO's (Chief Information Officers) representing more than 57 billion USD in IT spending, cite business intelligence as the number two technology priority in their companies. Evidence of this drive is also found in the InfoWorld Business Intelligence Report 2005.

We could speak of an Information Turn, a paradigm shift in the way we run our organizations where technical solutions have become an integrated and natural part of the way we work and make decisions. The focus is no longer hardware, but software. More than that it is not isolated, but integrated, communicating and sharing; web based solutions before stand-alone applications. More than ever, we are aware that information or rather intelligence is the basis of all good decision making, and that decision-making is what business is really about. Consequently, organizations are going out of their way to build electronic systems to help them in this process (see e.g. Gangadharan, Swami, 2004).

Real Time Business Intelligence Systems

When an employee at the Gartner Group started to use the term "business intelligence" in the late 80s, supposedly he was thinking about what we today understand by "competitive intelligence" or "market intelligence". Ultimately, it is the use of a term which decides its meaning. There is nothing new or shocking about this. The meaning of many words change over time, some quicker than others. The jungle of abbreviations and acronyms is a way in which we try to understand the changing business environment.

The Business Intelligence System consists of an organizational structure and an infrastructure, predominantly IT related, with a combination of selected hardware and software. Decision Support Systems (DSS) is another, broader term. DSS makes no discrimination as to the nature of the data entered. It is helpful in sorting and organizing large amounts of quantitative data. Consequently, DSS technologies are used in all sorts of companies at all levels, from sales in IT companies to the status of patients in hospitals (see e.g. Sauter, Free, 2005).

The number of standardized systems is increasing. We see fewer BI systems being made in-house today. Instead, operational BI is increasingly bought by the big vendors, from companies such as the SAS Institute Inc., Information Builders Inc. and Cognos Inc. (Havenstein, Heather, 2005).

The big dream for these companies and their customers is to develop a real time business intelligence system (Watson, Wixom, Hoffer, Anderson-Lehman, Reynolds, 2006). For example: you want to know the sales figures in your store right now, how many customers have entered, if you are a bakery how much bread has been bought and therefore how much needs to be ordered. You want to know it now, because you want to make the call for a new order now, not at the end of the day, not tomorrow. In many cases, it is already a reality; especially for simple data manipulation where no further analysis is required. Real time BI today then works rather well for intelligence adhering to the Company Analysis, less for the Industry Analysis.

The more difficult the analysis, the more valuable the information, and the longer it will take to get the intelligence. Good analysis demands time for reflection. Computer ability will help in this process, but is not ready to replace the work of the intelligence analyst. Observations presented numerically e.g. from our stock of bread at the store are one thing, however, where historical synthesis is required, e.g. in some of the macro factors of the Industry Analysis (social, political, economic), we need more patience, at least if we are requesting useful and reliable conclusions.

Organizational Models of Intelligence

Where should the Intelligence function be placed in the organization? There are many opinions about this, and companies have been trying out different versions and collecting experience for a number of years. The list presented below is the joint summary of some of these experiences, most of which builds on primary research, and of the available theory in the field.

As the intelligence function sprang out of the marketing function, and more particularly from the marketing research function, it was common in the beginning to see this special function placed in the marketing department (see the single departmental model). As it was discovered that other departments in the company could profit just as well from the intelligence activities, managers started to experiment with other organizational possibilities, spreading the knowledge and know-how around. One of the suggestions was to form a special intelligence department, after the model of state and military intelligence services.

1. The Special Department Model of Intelligence

The main idea behind the special department model is that the intelligence function is placed in a separate department, much like in military and state intelligence organizations. The argument is that specialization leads to better performance and output. The major problem with this model is isolation of the competence from where it is most needed; i.e. elsewhere. Special intelligence departments tend to close themselves in, working alone on projects they think will be useful for the company. These self-initiated projects are only then useful to the extent that the special department know exactly what intelligence is needed. If they do not communicate well with the top managers, their work will be based too much on guesswork, and the output will be less relevant. In other cases, the department will have the report and the answer, but the results will never reach the manager who needs it, at least not in a timely fashion.

Ericsson struggled with exactly this type of problem in its first years of introducing the business intelligence function in the company. As a direct response to the problems with this model, it was thought that the intelligence function needed to be close to the major decision makers in the organization. Even more, it is often concluded that the person delivering the intelligence needs to have the full attention and the trust of the top managers.

2. The Advisory Model of Intelligence

The main idea behind the advisory model is to make a senior advisor to the CEO and to top management responsible for two functions in the intelligence cycle: taking down and formulating the questions to be answered, and delivering the results. The information gathering and analysis could be performed elsewhere, whether on the outside, as is suggested in Fahey (2007), or in different departments, according to their needs. The senior advisor often has neither the time, nor the skills to search for information himself, nor does he have time or skills to conduct thorough analyses. Instead, he will often compensate for this by his or her deep knowledge about the industry and by applying common sense much needed in this line of work, as it tends to tackle the multitude of hypothetical problems commonly encountered. Up until a point some years ago, the senior advisor rarely was a technological "wizard". Today's business intelligence projects have become increasingly technical. From now on, the senior advisor will probably be more technology-savvy, as a new generation of computer literates are entering top management.

In the advisory model, a senior advisor either has a designated number of people working for him, or he has the right to take up the time and resources of specific employees who possess the required intelligence skills. One problem with not having specific staff dedicated to intelligence work is that the outcomes, i.e. the intelligence reports, often become "left-hand" work. As the intelligence function is not the employee's main activity, he or she very often has inadequate training and understanding of the assignment, and so the intelligence work tends to receive low priority. Very often it is executed in haste. There is a need for someone who could dedicate more time and resources to intelligence work. This was the starting point for the development of the professional intelligence model.

3. The Professional Model of Intelligence

The professional model allows special personnel to go through the training needed to be able to make intelligence work their priority, i.e. university studies and practical training. Where they are then later placed in the organization, is another question. Some intelligence professionals will discover that they prefer field activities, including in-field intelligence gathering. Others discover that they are more comfortable with desk jobs such as intelligence analysis, reporting and presentation. This may later determine each person's specialty. The amount of field work required for intelligence work in private sector is still very restricted and mainly reduced to marketing research. Even marketing department staff members have become more used to desk jobs now, and prefer to hire outside help to perform market research, or they rely more on secondary data.

In the end, the professional model is often a question of resources. Few mid-and smaller-sized companies will find that they have the funds available to make investments in educated intelligence personnel. Instead, they continue to focus on what they see as their core activities; production and sales. Unfortunately, too few companies have understood the possibilities of what it means to be living in the Information Age and they are still not using the technology available to them.

Even among the companies who can afford it, there are often a number of misconceptions about the value of intelligence activities. Many managers believe that it is enough to rely on secondary sources, like trade magazines and special reports. They think that they themselves are able to bridge the gap between understanding the industry (secondary sources) and understanding their own company (personal experience). They think that it is enough that they as managers tell their employees what is important. This is sometimes referred to as the top-down model of intelligence.

4. The Top-down Model of Intelligence

The top-down model of intelligence is based on the idea that intelligence is gathered and communicated mostly from the top of the organization. It is a model that can work well for smaller companies. Top management receives or generates intelligence, which is spread throughout the organization on a need-to-know basis. This model is often found in production based organizations, where the majority of employees are low-skilled workers. The CEO and the top managers should be the best qualified for identifying what is important for the running of the firm. After all, that is why they have been selected to run the company. One of the dangers is that they become know-it-alls and stop listening to what others say. The feeling in such company cultures is often that intelligence is too important for regular employees. However, it is not necessary to be a manager to find a piece of vital information concerning the running of the company. A regular employee might come across an interesting article or see something noteworthy, like a large shipment of raw material on the way to a competitor's plant. Finding useful information can be a pure coincidence, a question of being in the right place at the right time.

5. The Integrated Intelligence Model

An intelligent company – not to be confused here with an intelligence company – is one which divides different areas of knowledge and competencies among its employees. In this way, some employees may be looking at local newspapers, others go to a specific trade show, etc. Together they will try to cover as many arenas as possible for potentially useful intelligence. This is referred to as the Integrated Intelligence Model. It has been advocated strongly e.g. by Sven Hamrefors (1999).

There are many advantages to this model, which has been used by many larger Japanese companies. It draws on the collective experience and effort of employees in the whole organization. An integrated intelligence model makes intelligence work seem less dangerous, less secretive. It is a sign of trust when all employees are told that they too can come across pieces of important information, which they are then encouraged to share. This trust can in turn create a better atmosphere in the organization and make people feel more useful.

Organizations that make much fuss about intelligence tend to create extra and unnecessary tension. This is often the risk with the departmental model. Such tension in turn can reduce productivity and creativity in the organization.

The less that is said about secrets the better. Companies need a system of information classification, but they also need to downplay its importance. One way to present the situation is with the allegory of the family: There are certain facts, certain incidents and stories which are no one else's business, and therefore best kept within the family. We do not talk about these facts as secrets. There are also secrets inside of the family. When you start to think about it, practically all fathers and mothers know things they will not tell their children. That it is so is a natural part of social life, not a biological error. It is the same in companies: all employees do not have to know everything for the organization to be harmonious and pull together. To think that man is moving towards a society of no more secrets is an illusion. Instead, having and guarding secrets is a part of human nature. There is no real reason why this notion should create more fury in an organization than it does at home.

6. The Bottom-Up Model of Intelligence

The opposite of the top-down model is the bottom-up model of intelligence. In some companies employees at the bottom of the organization tend to get access to especially important information. This model is often seen in sales- and marketing-driven organizations. The situation is often such that it is first of all the sales people who are seeing customers out in the field, who can bring the most valuable intelligence back to the company. CEOs and top management will often spend their days with each other, inside the office or away. When they are outside of the office, they will typically spend much time in airports, on planes and in hotels, which are not the kind of environments where one is likely to pick up specific news about the company's immediate surroundings.

When sales people get back to the offices, they can enter what they believe is valuable information into a database, which is then sorted, analysed and distributed by an intelligence function within the company. Much of this information may not have any value at all; it will be disregarded. In other cases, sales people will come home with changes to KPI's that will lead to immediate changes on the dashboard of top managers.

It is a good idea to have some sort of intelligence reward system for employees. The problem in most companies is that sales people and those who are out in the field do not bring intelligence home because they lack the incentives. Even worse, if looking for valuable information takes time away from their paid job, this eventually leads to decreased efficiency. That is, without an intelligence reward system they risk being punished for spending time gathering information even though they themselves recognize its importance. Such situations are common.

An efficient reward system should be a scaled system. For instance, information can be sorted by value into A, B, C, D, and E categories, each connected to a particular reward, or in the case of useless information (E), no reward at all. The actual evaluation is performed by intelligence professionals in the company. The financial results are seen on next month's pay check. Each employee can go into the company's intranet system and see how his or her intelligence is being classified. A and B may be secret information distributed only to specific employees on a need-to-know basis, while as C is open for anyone inside of the company, and D to all outside. As soon as a piece of information is deemed valuable to the company, we do not want to share it with other companies.

All competitive information is classified information, even if you think your competitors possess it. The intranet system helps the employees to know what they can talk about and to whom. This becomes increasingly important in a bottom-up intelligence organization where by necessity the amount of valuable information is spread over a large number of employees.

7. The Single Departmental Model of Intelligence
When the SEB bank in Stockholm developed its first intelligence capabilities almost a hundred years ago, it set it up as a "statistical department". In reality it was a pseudonym for what looked much like an intelligence department, with the objective of gathering information not only about customers, but on competitors and the surrounding environment. Since then, it has been a common practice to place the intelligence function in an already existing department, first of all in the Marketing Department, but also occasionally in Finance, Business Development or R&D. At SEB, this may have been done to hide the function, but later it was seen as more practical, and became a way to concentrate competencies. Top management was never convinced that Intelligence Analysis was worth the special attention and investment.

So it was placed as a secondary function tagged onto someone's job description.

Some may think that this was early for any organized form of business intelligence activity; after all, the CIA was built up after the Second World War and the British intelligence apparatus took shape in between the two World Wars. In fact, the art of intelligence gathering, both for commercial and political purposes is a century-old practice. The Wallenbergs were not the first to build an organized intelligence capability, but were continuing a tradition of serious information gathering about customers, competitors and market conditions that had been the practice in the world of banking and trade for centuries, with roots back to Renaissance Italy. The height of the art of Intelligence Analysis is seen in the writings of the Venetian ambassadors of the 16th and 17th century, but even centuries earlier the Medicis, whose motto was borrowed by the Wallenbergs - esse non videri, "to be [act] and not to be seen" - spent much time gathering intelligence from all major European trading cities and families, from places such as Bruges, Antwerp, and Augsburg.

The early Medicis knew that they were only as good as their network and the trust they enjoyed in the great markets. To build this invaluable resource, they needed fast and reliable information. This information had to be put down in writing, building substantial trade archives. Thus it is no coincidence that much of the accounting system we use today was invented in this city. It was all a part of the need to take accurate notes, in order to be able to make the right decisions.

In private companies, it is still uncommon to see outright intelligence departments. To the degree that companies have full-time intelligence officers or analysts, these often work in other departments or as a supporting function, often much like appendices, to top management. Much of the reason for this is that companies do not want to be perceived as overly secretive and are uncertain about what this might do to the organization internally, increasing the level of distrust among employees.

At the same time, with the increased focus on security and the development of new intelligence technology, it is likely that intelligence departments will become more popular among companies. The function could be a part of the security or IT departments. For the moment, the security department focuses primarily on securing the organization's physical premises and does not have intelligence know-how. The IT department limits its intelligence activities much to data security and checking employees' computer traffic. As BI systems become more complex, there will be a need for more cooperation between IT and Intelligence specialists. It is too early to predict what this might look like in the future. It is possible that we may even see an umbrella-like intelligence department, encompassing plant security, IT security, and intelligence activities.

8. The Omnipresent Model and Multiple Department Model of Intelligence

The model basically says that the organization already has the Intelligence Analysis skills and tasks incorporated into most of what they do already. It is more a question of finding out who possesses what knowledge and sharing it at the right moment. Organizations fitting into the Omnipresent model often have a well-developed and functioning technical platform already. They will often see the BI system as a small complement. It is more a question of fitting the systems together than about creating completely new and expensive solutions. On the other hand, they may be prepared to pay for it.

The model can be found in knowledge-intensive companies, who are already engaged in a large deal of analytical work, e.g. the consulting industry. Other companies are too proud to admit that they are not Intelligence experts and that they know little about it. There is always the risk that we exaggerate our own abilities. Writing reports does not mean we understand much of intelligence work. In many cases it would probably be better for the organization to leave the intelligence function to a few designated employees, in which case it would resemble the single department model. Alternatively the individuals could be dispersed among several departments, in which case it would resemble a Multiple Department Model.

So far it has not been possible to present one single "right" organizational solution for all organizations based on experience and empirical studies. However, we can make some careful suggestions given one or two assumptions.

9. The "Intelligence Amnesia" and the Ad-hoc Model of Intelligence

The name "Intelligence Amnesia" is taken from a survey completed by Fuld & Company in 2006 and published the year after. Their conclusion is that CI programs and functions tend to come and go within the company, and that as a consequence, many CI experts feel they are just starting to build some kind of CI capacity within the firm. Now, this is probably not a deliberate CI policy on the part of these companies, however it may present a more realistic picture than the ideal model. As long as we do not know more, we can only speculate as to the reasons for this. It may be that CI initiatives are very person-dependent, that they are closed down and reopened with new management. Another term used here is "the dissolved CI Unit". There seem to be a large number of failed or at least terminated CI units in companies. When the CI Unit does in fact function, it will work according to one or several of the models described above.

There may be one other reason why the CI Unit disappears and that is that the function initially was set up to answer some specific questions. When these questions or issues have been dealt with the "unit" may disappear. We may call this an Ad-hoc model of intelligence. The point is that it may be difficult for some employees to see why top management suddenly lost interest in the CI issue, or if they initially thought of it as a preliminary arrangement. This misunderstanding may in turn have a negative effect on trust and working morale within the organization.

It must also be noted that CI is still more of a working task and a function than a formal description of a position in most organizations. There are many CI assignments but very few CI positions. The view in most organizations is still that CI is something which is performed on the side and in addition to other assignments. Thus, the Shell Group today have several hundred marketing people, and many "futurists" but only 2,5 CI specialists.[74] ABB's CI unit is about the same size.[75] This does not mean that companies find the CI function to be unimportant, but that they still consider it an integrated function, e.g. with marketing, strategy and controlling. How this will be in the future we do not know, but it is quite possible that we are still finding ourselves in a time when CI units are still trying to convince top management of their added value.

Deciding on an Intelligence Model for Your Organization
In reality - when the CI Unit does exist - most companies will implement a combination of several different models, depending on the kind of industry they are in. At the same time, they will tend to adhere more to one model than to the other. This will be the intelligence model characteristics of the company.

---

[74] According to Manjula Nadarajah, Technology Strategy Advisor at Shell.
[75] According to Daniel Niederer, Head of Strategy Controlling & Operations, ABB Group.

Historically we see a development from the single departmental model, to more of a top-down advisory model. In the future, it is possible that this will be combined with a departmental model, either free-standing or as a part of the Security and/or IT department. In light of the fact that all kinds of security, intelligence and counterintelligence activities require the same type of expertise and training, it would be natural to place them all under one roof.

Another question which often comes up is, if Knowledge Management (KM) and BI should be placed in the same department. KM is the concern of top management, but is often carried out by the Human Resource Department (HRD) or function. That there is a clear synergy between them has been pointed out by several (e.g. most recently by Canongia, 2007). But to place BI in the HRD makes little sense. HR is good at what they do: looking for, hiring, looking after and laying off employees. This also includes assembling employees' knowledge and know-how, and of setting clear KM strategies for the company. But the HR department or function is no better or worse at handling information than any other department in the organization. Most importantly, it is people, not information, which is their primary focus. At the same time, the information gathered by the KM function is essential to the BI function. This could suggest a close cooperation.

We see that most CRM resides in the marketing department. Much Decision Support Database (DSD) funding is also allocated to this function. For many consultants, software producers as well as Business Intelligence System providers, CRM and Data Mining are the entry points. As the marketing department is the first point of entry for many business intelligence systems, it also becomes the place for the execution and handling of gathered intelligence. This is why the next chapter is dedicated to Marketing Intelligence.

Investment in Intelligence Competences and Infrastructure

The range of infrastructure depends on the intelligence ambitions of the organization and their budget to fulfil their goals. In intelligence investments we find everything from small Mom and Pop shops, which gather information about their customers using MS Excel, looking for patterns in purchasing behaviour, to, at the other extreme, the NSA (National Security Agency) and other governmental equivalents, which aim to tap into the world's electronic information, via satellites, and increasingly via cable.

It is largely a question of resources, and also accountability. Only nation-states have the resources and the legitimacy required to set up large scale intelligence infrastructures. To take an example, the NSA is estimated to have about 30,000 employees and a budget considerably larger than that of the CIA (Central Intelligence Agency).[76] In comparison the combined UK intelligence services had a budget of 900 million pounds as reported by the BBC in 2004.[77] No multinational company is currently able to invest anything close to these resources into intelligence infrastructure. Even if they did, they would not be able to justify the costs.

Small companies may invest a few hundred dollars in a standard BI application or software, like the "Brimstone Intelligence 2005". Mid-size companies may get a small tailor-made solution from Cognos for a few thousand dollars. Very seldom are BI investments comparable to the cost of employees in any department in the organization. Multinationals may have a small staff consisting of a handful of employees whose main job is information gathering and analysis. Even at its most lavish, this expenditure seldom reaches into the millions.

Most of the hardware, such as PCs, servers and the like, is shared with the IT department. What costs extra are specialized personnel such as intelligence analysts, plus their ongoing training and education, as well as industry reports and special studies. The number of spyshop devices on the market has increased considerably. Still, private companies are mostly focused on counter-intelligence equipment: anti-bugging devices, encrypted mobile telephones and hidden camera detectors, all of which have become relatively inexpensive, and which are only used in specific circumstances, like before a major negotiation (for cases of industrial espionage in negotiations, see Solberg Søilen, 2004).

Direct surveillance equipment is mostly reserved for certain industries and certain countries. Most small operation mini transmitters, recorders, listening devices, electric lockpickers, etc. are sold to private individuals and most are used to spy on spouses, not competitors. Private companies in industries marked by low trust between managers and staff are buying web watching programs and hidden cameras to observe their own employees, but also their customers. Known examples include retail stores and production facilities.

---

[76] Current US intelligence budgets are classified information. An estimated total intelligence budget for the US which has been used in different sources is more than 40 billion USD (Drew, 2003).

[77] http://news.bbc.co.uk/2/hi/uk_news/3460275.stm (2007-04-19).

Video surveillance is mostly used for security purposes, not for spying. As a consequence, security departments and IT security will often have larger budgets than any intelligence unit or function. Customer Relations Management, Data Mining and Knowledge Management still attract more funds than Competitive and Business Intelligence activities. Private organizations still make relatively small individual investments in training intelligence personnel and purchasing intelligence equipment.

A dramatic change over the past few years is the large number of companies which are now making small BI efforts, so that in sum, private intelligence investments have become a quite lucrative business segment. It is likely that the availability of security, intelligence and counterintelligence equipment is going to continue to increase in the years to come, but it is uncertain how we will react to these intrusions in the long run. For the moment, the spy-shop industry is riding on the fear created in the aftermath of 9-11, i.e. the "War on Terror". As time goes by and if the situation does not deteriorate, it should be expected that the question of personal privacy will play a larger role.

Shareholders and CEOs in general are very sceptical when it comes to making large intelligence infrastructure investments. One reason is the question mark surrounding the return on investment, a problem which state and military services hardly have to worry about, due to the nature of their activities, which are classified and thus not available to public scrutiny.

Private intelligence faces much the opposite situation. Most top managers will agree in principle that Competitive and Business Intelligence is vital to the company, but are sceptical when it comes to specific investments. Maybe there is a feeling that this is something which should already be there, and thus seems superfluous. As the perception is often that Competitive Intelligence is not likely to lead to any immediate or direct results on the bottom line, as its consequences are often difficult to trace back and measure, it is often considered more as a long term investment. Top managers are hesitant unless convinced by clearly demonstrated advantages.

Business Intelligence providers and software companies are only recently starting to convince private organizations that they can actually add real value to the companies' business processes. What has changed is the introduction of new and better-performing intelligence technology. Any CEO who sees and understands the blossoming of this new sector will recognize its value. These are just two examples, soon to be surpassed by others:

154

- By homogenizing wikis and blogs, applications, such as Atlassian Confluence, are letting workers organize and share knowledge and hold interactive discussions more freely. Better categorization in search products is expected in the coming years. This will continue to replace the static navigation of traditional Web sites (Heck, Mike, 2007).

- Fast Search & Transfer, a Norwegian company known for its enterprise search technology, is substituting a smart search system for the structured queries and data warehouses required by conventional business intelligence systems. Fast already launched its Adaptive Information Warehouse. While business intelligence generally relies on well-scrubbed, historical data loaded into data warehouses, Fast's Search functions more loosely and finds information more easily than other BI systems, tapping a wider variety of sources (Babcock, Charles, 2007).

Intelligence Implementation in Practice

We have discussed the intelligence needs at various levels in an organization. We have also considered where to place the intelligence function in the organization, and we have given some thought to the size and rationale of intelligence investments. Sooner or later, we are going to have to ask ourselves how to implement these ideas. Some suggestions were given in the previous chapter. Another is given in a case by Pettersson (2001), based on his experience with a project done for the department for Financial Administration Systems at The Swedish National Financial Management Authority (ESV). In this example, the clients shared their opinions about the organizational structure.

Looking at the internal IT system of the organization in cooperation with the client, the following objectives were identified for the project:

- Create a continuous flow of market signals
- Monitor news and market information
- Acquire methods and tools for structuring and analyzing market signals
- Store profiles on players in the market
- Use the Intranet for presenting the information
- Create a knowledge base to capture internal knowledge and experience
- Use the available information on the Internet in a more efficient way

- Create a network of people that monitor and report important market signals

At a later stage, the target group was given the opportunity to express their views on how intelligence analysis should be organized. The employees came up with the following suggestions:

- "It's important to stress that environmental information doesn't have to take a great deal of time."
- "Use the internal knowledge."
- "Create a knowledge database where it is easy to find individuals with specific knowledge and experiences."
- "Use the e-mail system for delivering information."
- "Use the intranet for presenting information."

ESV thus succeeded in developing an effective BI system, which combined the customers' specifications, their own employees' suggestions and the supplier's solutions. The solution is a case of the omnipresent model of Intelligence and fits well with its characteristics.

BI implementation experiences are very different in different kinds of organizations. The difference is closely related to the general level of competence within the organization and to the kind of external advice received. Experience suggests however, that to succeed, the implementation of intelligence systems requires high-knowledge workers. Smaller companies or branches frequently complain about the difficulties of implementing BI systems (e.g. Songini, 2007). It is also a challenge for BI suppliers. So far BI system providers are mostly used to handling larger and more knowledgeable customers. However, this is likely to change in the years to come as the understanding for and the acceptance of business intelligence systems increases. It is all a part of our development as users of ever more sophisticated technology.

Conclusion

Intelligence Analysis is pushed forward today first of all by the introduction of new and upgraded technology, most notably BI computer software. There have been important advancements in this field over the last couple of years.

Intelligence Analysis is predominantly a working process. There has been and is still a tendency among CI professionals, whether consultants or academics, to see BI as an advanced and exclusive field of theory and practice. In reality, BI shares its theoretical foundations with other working processes (like general scientific methodology and project management) and there is, as of yet, very few established CI departments even in larger companies, so that its practice is often related to that of other and larger business functions, such as marketing (CRM), production (Benchmarking) and HRM (Knowledge Management). Those CI departments that do function as separate entities continue to consist of a few employees and attract relatively small investments. We think this will change in the future as more companies realize the consequences and the potential of living in the Information Age, and as they find help and support in the implementation of new and more advanced technology.

Next, we must consider where most of our Intelligence activities still reside, and that is in the Marketing Department. This will be discussed in the next chapter.

REFERENCES

Aamir Turk, M. (2007). Data Mining and Mobile CRM (mCRM). *MBA Thesis.* Blekinge Institute of Technology, April.

Babcock, C. (2007). Outrunning Business Intelligence. *Information Week.* Nr. 1121, p. 19.

Canongia, C. (2007). Synergy between Competitive Intelligence (CI), Knowledge Management (KM) and Technological Foresight (TF) as a strategic model of prospecting - The use of biotechnology in the development of drugs against breast cancer. *Biotechnology Advances*, Vol. 25, nr. 1, pp. 57-74.

Drew, C. (2003). Intelligence reorganization spotlights fabled FBI-CIA rift. *National Journal's Technology Daily.* March 17.

Fahey, L. (2007). Connecting strategy and competitive intelligence: refocusing intelligence to produce critical strategy inputs. *Strategy & Leadership*, Vol 35, nr. 1, pp. 4-12.

Fuld & Company (2007). From stick feathers to World Class. *A world survey of Competitive Intelligence Programs.* Cambridge, MA.

Fuld & Company (2006). *Intelligence software report 2006/2007.* Cambridge, MA.

Gangadharan, G.R., Swami, S.N. (2004). Business intelligence systems: design and implementation strategies. *Information Technology Interfaces*, 2004. 26th International Conference on Vol. 1, pp. 139-144.

Hamrefors, S. (1999). *Spontaneous Environmental Scanning - Putting "putting into perspective" into perspective.* Dissertation Stockholm: Economic Research Institute, Stockholm School of Economics.

REFERENCES

Havenstein, H. (2005). Users Turn to Operational Business Intelligence Tools. *Computerworld*, Vol. 39, nr. 12, pp. 1-3.

Heck, M. (2007). WEB 2.0. Info World, Vol. 29, nr. 1, pp. 20-21.

Jaworski, B.J, Macinnis, D.J., Kohli, A.K (2002). Generating Competitive Intelligence in Organizations, *Journal of Market - Focused Management*, Vol 5, nr. 4, pp. 279-307.

Pettersson, U. (2001). Creating an intelligence system at the Swedish National Financial Management Authority. *Competitive Intelligence Review*, vol. 12, nr. 2, pp. 20-31.

Sauter, V.L., Free, D. (2005). Competitive Intelligence Systems: Qualitative DSS for Strategic Decision Making. *Database for Advances in Information Systems* Vol. 36, Nr. 2, pp. 43-57.

Songini, M.L. (2007) BI Helping Retailers Control Inventor, Manage Finances. *Computerworld* Vol. 41, nr. 4, p. 14.

Solberg Søilen, K. (2004). Wirtschaftsspionage in Verhandlungen aus Informationsökonomischer und Wirtschaftsethischer Perspektive - Eine Interdisziplinäre Analyse. *Dissertation*.
Wirtschaftswissenschaflichen Fakultät der Universität Leipzig, Deutschland.

Van de Wiel, M. (2005). Managing Large-scale Business Intelligence Solutions. *Business Intelligence Journal*, Vol. 10, nr. 4, pp. 28-34.

Watson H.J., Wixom B.H., Hoffer J.A., Anderson-Lehman R., Reynolds A. M. (2006). Real-Time Business Intelligence: Best Practices at Continental Airlines, *Information Systems Management*, Vol. 23, nr. 1, pp. 7-18.

CHAPTER 7

Marketing Intelligence

The Marketing department is still the most common place for Intelligence Analysis to be performed in private organizations. As we have seen in the previous chapter, Intelligence Analysis is first of all a working process used by existing departments in the company by employees who have other assignments.

This chapter discusses Business Marketing Intelligence (BMI), or simply Marketing Intelligence (MI), an important activity because it links an organization to its external environment and makes it possible for management to make informed and rational decisions about markets, competitors, and strategy. We first introduce MI and explain why it is important. We distinguish MI from marketing research and argue that MI is much more than traditional marketing research. We then discuss different types of marketing intelligence: continuous and problem-related.

We also address issues related to MI system design, benchmarking, and sources of intelligence. We highlight the impact of demand analysis, and we explain customer satisfaction analysis, customer requirements analysis, and sales forecasting. We conclude the chapter with discussions about how to organize and manage intelligence efforts in the marketing department.

Intelligence and Information
The Importance of Marketing Intelligence
Intelligence is one of the most important business marketing functions. The intelligence activities of collecting and analyzing internal and environmental conditions are important to strategy formulation and operational conduct. The literature on Private Intelligence (PI)[78] and

---

[78] We have proposed here to replace the old meaning of Business Intelligence with Private Intelligence, as BI has come to mean the technology involved in Intelligence Analysis. Thus the old term Business Marketing intelligence is also better replaced by Marketing Intelligence. Notice also that the old BI cycle is now more

Competitive Intelligence (CI) has increased tremendously over the past few years. Other terms used are Competitor Intelligence and Intelligence Analysis (IA). MI may be seen as the part of the larger CI activity that is limited to the concern of business marketing.

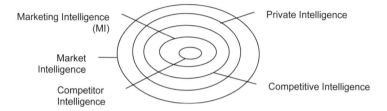

Figure 7.1 Types of Intelligence in a Company

We have depicted Market Intelligence as a broader area than MI, as there are many actors, especially public ones, who are active on different markets without engaging in any form of organization marketing activity. MI includes: the gathering and understanding of market trends, customer needs, perceptions, attitudes, beliefs, and behaviour; competitors' thinking, strengths and weaknesses, and all factors that influence business-to-business relationships. We view MI as a broad set of activities, because success as a business marketer requires understanding the broad context of the market and the customers' strategic and operating environment.

MI has three unique characteristics:

1. Business marketers usually deal with a smaller set of customers than consumer marketers do. Most business customers (and potential customers) are usually known to the business marketer. Therefore, intelligence activities often involve either the entire relevant customer population or much smaller samples than in consumer marketing.
2. Business marketing involves multiple buying influences, which impact the reliability of the intelligence obtained from customers. Business intelligence information is often dependent on who is talking to the customer and who in the customer organization re-

---

often called the CI cycle or simply Intelligence cycle. The underlying reason for all this is the increased importance of software in the CI function.

sponds. To get a response that depicts a customer's organizational viewpoint, several customer sample points may be required.

3. The business marketing sales force usually has a close relationship with customers. This relationship represents a tremendous source of information about both customers and competitors. A key issue in MI is how to capitalize on the information the sales force has or can get.

The globalization of business has increased the need for broad-based intelligence systems. Even companies that consider themselves primarily local or regional find that an intelligence system based on a much broader geographical base is necessary. Technology often forces organizations to do extensive intelligence. For example, when new laser technology is developed and announced in Colorado, it does not take many hours before competing firms in Japan have all publicly available information reported to them by local consultants.

Entrepreneurial firms and firms in early stages of a product life cycle often need entirely different types of intelligence than firms in mature stages of the life cycle. A young entrepreneurial firm often needs market, product, and customer intelligence, while a firm operating in a mature oligopoly may need price and cost intelligence.

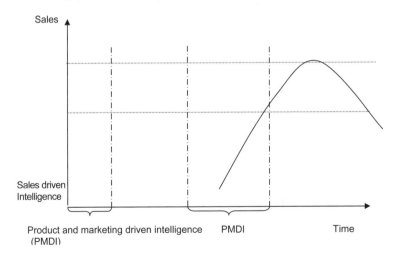

Figure 7.2 Types of Intelligence Focus over the Product Life Cycle

There may be said to be two different kinds of intelligence processes related to the product life cycle which demand quite different competencies. The first is intelligence related to the planning, production, and adjustment of products. The second is intelligence related to the phase when the product has conquered the market, whether on an upward or downward sales curve. The first type is often strategic and tactical in nature, the second operational.[79] The first kind of intelligence is more technical and market-related, whereas the second is more sales-related. For a company to be successful in its overall private intelligence efforts, it is important that the two different kinds of intelligence activities are synchronized so that the one knows when the other is taking over.

Marketing Intelligence Defined

Marketing intelligence is the collection, analysis, and interpretation of relevant internal and external marketing information. It is a process that makes it possible for a firm to learn about, understand, and deal with new challenges. Marketing intelligence is therefore a future-oriented activity that helps an organization cope in the market. It includes all ways an organization acquires and uses information. It is comprised of all kinds of market and marketing research; the collection and analysis of internal data, competitive analysis; analysis and reverse engineering of competitor's products; understanding how and where to add value for customers; and the process of synthesizing large amounts of informally gathered information about the industry and business environment. This environment can be divided into a number of areas of study; economic, political, social, technological, infrastructural, ecological, legal, and demographic, which together illustrates the interdisciplinary nature of the subject. Marketing intelligence can be as comprehensive or as narrow as a company may want it to be. The intelligence process is often illustrated by a number of specific intelligence tasks in a circle, where the company gains experience for each time a new intelligence process is started. In real life a company may be working on several assignments at the same time, or it may go back and forth between the specific working tasks in the circle. Whatever

---

[79] See also Figure 7.4: The Different Kinds of Intelligence Requested.

the case, the illustration is helpful. The Intelligence Cycle may be said to consist of five distinct tasks or phases:[80]

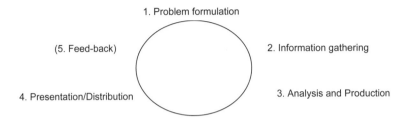

Figure 7.3 The Intelligence Cycle

From these tasks we see that MI consists of three important management activities. These activities are:

- Gathering internal and external data. The gathering of MI data is a comprehensive task that includes activities ranging from collecting objective empirical market research data to recording subjective statements from salespersons. It may include activities such as periodic, detailed analysis of current data about customer sales gains and losses; recording employees' attitudes towards a particular customer or competitor; and scanning the trade press to assess events in the industry.
- Coding and interpreting the data collected. It is often very difficult to code and to provide valid and reliable interpretation of the broader dimensions of MI. Over the last few decades, many firms have made substantial efforts to create centralized Marketing Information Systems (MIS). Most of these efforts have failed due to the variety of data usually collected through MI activities, the lack of appropriate technology required to handle the complexity, or a lack of commitment by higher management.
- Application of knowledge to produce useful information from data to be used in a developing marketing strategy. An essential ingredient of MI is the application of management knowledge and experience to marketing data. Only managers with the appropriate industry experience can assess the validity of MI, translate it into a proper strategic

---

[80] These five different intelligence activities are also used to describe the different working procedures for Figure 7.5: The Types of Competencies Related to the Five Phases in the Intelligence Cycle.

context, and convert the knowledge into appropriate operating activities.

Table 7.1 shows examples of marketing intelligence activities. MI includes continuous and problem-oriented activities. Continuous MI activities consist primarily of collection of data from secondary information sources and input from internal resources such as accounting, sales and cost data, technical standards, customer sales gains and loss data, and so on. Specific problem-related activities include market research, research related to product development, establishment of target customer profiles, and specific assessment of market potential.

Problem related	Continuous	Integrated
Market potential analysis	Sales forecasting	Scenario analysis
Concept testing	Competitor analysis	Trend analysis
Alpha-and beta testing	Market pricing analysis	Game theoretical approach
Focus groups	Customer satisfaction surveys	Industry analysis
Ratio analysis	Pro-con analysis	
SWOT analysis		
Benchmarking		
Cost analysis		
Delphi analysis		
Network analysis		

Table 7.1 Examples of Marketing Intelligence Analysis

A final activity is the integration of management inputs through informal observations, reports from meetings with external sources and management, opinions and experiences. Common to all this information is competitive data. The central component of the intelligence system is a function that conducts an analysis of the data collected and provides integration. This includes synthesizing the information and preparing reports and recommendations to management. The intelligence is then integrated into strategy, planning, and implementation.

The Society of Competitive Intelligence professionals (SCIP) asked its members a number of years ago what methods of analyzing CI information were most used, and which were rated most effective.

From the evaluations about the analytical methods used we see that it was often the simpler methods which were considered most effective.

From the evaluation of the role of competitor intelligence in support of sales and marketing we see that most importance was placed at the strategic level.

Tools for Analyzing Information [Percent using each tool]	Effectiveness of Analysis Tools [Percent rating each tool extremely or very effective]	CI Effectiveness in Support of Marketing [Percent Rating CI Extremely or Very Effective]	Objectives of Sales and Marketing Intelligence [Percent Rating Objective Extremely or Very Important]
Competitor profiles: 88.9%	SWOT analysis: 63.1%	Decision support: 67.4%	Develop marketing strategies: 76.2%
Financial analysis: 72.1%	Competitor profiles: 52.4%	Market monitoring: 66.7%	Anticipate change/ Market monitoring: 74.5%
SWOT analysis: 55.2%	Financial analysis: 45.5%	Identify market opportunities: 66.3%	Identify new opportunities: 67.2%
Scenario development: 53.8%	Win/loss analysis: 31.4%	Market plan development: 63%	Identify new sources of advantage: 64.8%
Win/loss analysis: 40.4%	War gaming: 21.9%	Market plan input: 57.4%	Help sales win business: 58.4%
War gaming: 27.5%	Scenario development: 19.2%	Investigating market rumors: 51.9%	Develop marketing programs: 43%
Cojoint analysis: 25.5%	Cojoint analysis: 15.8%	New product development: 50.3%	Prioritize R&D spending: 23.5%
Simulation/ modelling: 25%	Simulation/ modelling: 15.4%	Anticipating competitor initiatives: 48.1%	
		Identify alliance partners: 36.9%	
		Anticipating technology changes: 35.6%	
		Investment prioritization: 33.6%	
		Identifying competitor intangibles: 33.1%	
		Understanding competitor costs: 27.4%	
		Promotion/advertising changes: 26.4%	
		Anticipating changes in distribution: 15.1%	
		Anticipating supplier changes: 6.4%	

Source: The study was conducted for SCIP by The Pine Ridge Group, Inc. and the T.W. Powell Company, 1998. [81]

Table 7.2 Methods of Analyzing CI Information[82]

---

[81] See http://www.scip.org/ci/analysis.asp (2007.12.22).
[82] Percentage refers to population asked of firms.

The Value of Marketing Intelligence

Marketing intelligence and the information it produces tends to create change. Marketing intelligence is driven by the marketplace and by competitors. As competitors change strategy and introduce new products, customers respond to these changes by changing their preferences and purchase behavior. Competing firms must therefore engage in intelligence work to understand exactly what is happening.

As new intelligence emerges, competing firms find new ways of providing additional value to customers. They then deliver this new value to customers, which again produces change. This market- oriented information gathering is an ongoing process. Firms capable of learning by uncovering new information, and that can create knowledge through intelligence, are usually those that maintain their competitive position.

Marketing intelligence, like many other corporate functions, has changed dramatically over the last few years. Today marketing intelligence is global and very much influenced by changing customer behaviour and new technology. Not only large multinational corporations, but also small- and medium-size firms are sourcing goods and services to a much greater extent across borders.

The extent of sourcing varies from product to product and industry to industry. Sourcing is used extensively in the technology-related areas; for example, in electronics it is very common for smaller firms to establish alliances and source products, components, or assistance worldwide. This substantially increases the need for intelligence activities.

This system also influences the resources required to do intelligence work and the organization of such efforts. Even for small- and medium-sized firms there is substantial negative opportunity cost if such efforts are not conducted satisfactorily. Many small- and medium-size firms' existence is threatened by developments taking place thousands of miles away. Failure to know about such developments, and to act appropriately, can have serious consequences for business performance.

Often the benefits and the use of business intelligence are not recognized or fail because top management does not appreciate its value. Management often does not give this function the priority and/or resources that are required. The function is often staffed with low-level, inexperienced managers rather than experienced ones. Experienced managers who can help operating managers translate intelligence into strategy and implementations are often a scarce resource.

Culture and Marketing Intelligence

Culture influences the nature and role of marketing intelligence. For example, it is estimated that in Japan market research spending through agencies in 2000 was $1.206 billion. [83] This is a very small amount compared to the size of the Japanese economy and its economic and global success, despite difficulties which hit the country in 1997. CI Investments are not substantial in any particular culture or country. From recent figures we know that half of all companies spend less than 100.000 USD annually on CI. 12% of European respondents and only 6% of US/Canada spent more than 1.000.000 USD per year. By industry there is at least one surprise. 26% of pharmaceutical companies spend more than 1 mill USD annually, 16% of manufacturing companies. Pharmaceutical companies also top the list of industries that are best at reporting CI to senior management, followed by financial services industry. The legal industry comes out at the bottom here.[84] Thus there seems to be a difference in spending more based on industry than on culture and nationality.

This is not to say that culture does not play a role in CI. Market research often has a different role in Japanese firms than in U.S. or German firms. Japanese marketing intelligence is primarily an internal company function involving many employees at all levels. When a Japanese company wants to learn about a particular aspect of business in Europe or the United States, it often sends someone to live in that country for a period of time. Extensive, but often informal analysis is conducted, and all knowledge and raw data is forwarded to the main organization in Japan.

Much information on foreign companies and activities ends up at METI[85] (The Ministry of Economy, Trade and Industry) through JETRO[86] (METI's technology information collection service) who distribute the information to companies who they think may need it. This provides excellent insight and a broad base for the corporate staff to develop an effective marketing strategy.

Swedish managers approach marketing intelligence differently. A study of Swedish and Japanese subsidiary managers in the United

---

[83] More updated figures on this issue have been hard to find.

[84] Fuld & Company (2007). From stick feathers to World Class. A world survey of Competitive Intelligence Programs. Cambridge, MA.

[85] METI was founded in January 2001, incorporating the old MITI (Ministry of Japan's International Trade Industry). See http://www.meti.go.jp.

[86] For more information see http://www3.jetro.go.jp/ttppoas/index.html (2007.12.23).

States showed that the Swedish managers were more self-confident than Japanese managers. Swedish managers did not view MI with as much importance as Japanese managers did. Swedish managers also tended to screen information more, forwarding only those facts they believed their superiors needed. Swedish managers seemed to have a completely different approach to marketing intelligence and the dissemination of results from that of the Japanese managers. This implies that the focus, organization, and reliance on MI vary across cultures and that cultural norms may indicate management's use, willingness, and ability to use MI in business development.

Competitive Intelligence and Opportunity Cost

Marketing intelligence provides some firms with significantly potential market and competitive opportunities. But information is useless and the cost of collecting data is wasted if firms are not able to take advantage of intelligence. Few companies make conscious efforts to include systematic approaches to marketing intelligence. In many firms marketing intelligence is an ad hoc and occasional activity. Only when a particular problem arises or a plan needs to be developed does marketing intelligence become an issue.

Several Nordic companies have developed highly organized business intelligence systems over the past years. [87] Ericsson has an excellent approach to the issue with its EBIN network (Ericsson Business Intelligence Network), BIAP (Ericsson Business Analyst Program, a training program that all Ericsson analysts go through in order to get to know each other and to share methods) and the BIC (Business Information Centre: the information portal containing many thousands of industry reports and market studies.

The troublesome situation the company has encountered during the last couple of years has led to a reduction both in the number of analysts as well as the concepts described above, but the knowledge is still there. The portal at Ericsson is an excellent example of how to structure a large amount of information such as industry analysis, reports, newsfeeds, internally generated reports, and so on. The portal also provides the possibility to create individual newsfeeds about specific issues or companies that one needs to monitor.

Ericsson's Finnish counterpart, Nokia, has a more decentralized approach to business intelligence. Nokia is advocating a "virtual intelli-

---

[87] Examples provided by Hans Hedin, SCIP Scandinavia Chapter Coordinator.

gence approach", which means that they rely heavily on non-professional analysts such as product managers, marketing managers and other personnel. Nokia argues that this is a very powerful method since the intelligence issue is viewed from many perspectives and the brainpower of large groups of people can be utilized. Nokia's strong corporate culture is a key reason behind the success of the company. Nokia's employees are a part of a very successful and relatively young company, and possess a team spirit and curiosity that few companies can match.

Tetra Pak is another highly successful global company that has used business intelligence as a key issue regarding business development and market planning. "Intelligence activities are integrated in every part of the business development process", says Thomas Stridsberg, Business Intelligence manager at Tetra Pak.

Tetra Pak also tries to use the intelligence activities in customer activities. A new potential client often gets an intelligence briefing/market analysis concerning his major markets. This shows the potential client that Tetra Pak can also be a partner in future planning and that they have a thorough understanding of the clients markets. This, in addition to a very competitive product, can sometimes determine who gets the business.

Volvo has for a very long time had a coordinated approach to market analysis and competitor intelligence activities. Understanding today's and tomorrow's consumer trends as well as the potential manoeuvres of the competitors has always been an important part of the automotive industry. Other automotive players like SAAB and Scania are also very active in this area.

One of the companies in the insurance/finance sector that has reached very far is Länsförsäkringar ("county insurances"), a Swedish company. The company has taken a clear strategic approach to their intelligence activities. A number of internal intelligence networks have been established in a way so that each looks at a force in the business environment (e.g. customers, competitors, politics, technology, etc). Supported by intelligent agent technology as well as intelligence analysis software, their goal is to identify and foresee important events in their environment. This knowledge is then reported to the top management who are in charge of the intelligence activities at the corporate level.

Another insurance company, Alecta, is also active in developing business intelligence systems. In the words of the manager responsible for this system: "We have created Alecta Alert in order for all our employees to be aware of our situation". Alecta Alert is an intelligent agent that monitors selected information sources on the Internet and other sources. "Thus, it was possible for everyone to create his own agent in order to monitor exactly the things that are relevant". This is an activity that otherwise would take up a large portion of the time the intelligence function has to its disposition.

Many Nordic companies feel that decentralized models of business intelligence are less costly, and reduce the time for the information to reach the users. Many of these companies have learned the expensive lesson that the hardest part of the CI cycle can be to get the information out to the right person at the right time. This part of the intelligence process, which corresponds to stage 4 in the CI cycle[88] – presentation/ distribution – has as yet received little attention in the CI literature.

Types of Marketing Intelligence

Marketing intelligence can be divided into two broad categories: (1) continuous intelligence that picks up signals, symptoms, and the fact that can be used to assess performance or alert management to future problems, and (2) intelligence that focuses on solving a particular problem. Both types are important to a firm's total intelligence effort.

Continuous Marketing Intelligence

Continuous marketing intelligence efforts are broad activities often conducted by many people in the organization. This type of intelligence has an industry focus and often tries to identify unknown threats. The entire marketing, sales, and field service staff usually supports this effort in various ways. A market-oriented and inquisitive management culture often influences the effectiveness and quality of this type of intelligence and what can be done with it. In marketing oriented organizations, non-marketing employees are also involved in intelligence activity. This is particularly true for business organizations where engineers and R&D personnel are in frequent contact with customers.

Continuous MI efforts include market assessments and trend analysis, market potential analysis, customer gain-and-loss analysis, competitor assessment, competitive cost and pricing assessments, market share analysis, new technology assessment, and product and customer

---

[88] See Figure 7.3: The Intelligence Cycle.

satisfaction analysis. Table 7.2 lists a number of information items useful in conducting industry analysis.

Much of the data for ongoing intelligence usually comes from secondary sources. This activity, referred to as desk research, is overlooked in many companies. This type of MI is particularly useful due to systems such as the North American Industry Classification System (NAICS) and standardized electronic databases. The North American Industry Classification System (NAICS) replaced the U.S. Standard Industrial Classification (SIC) system and is updated every five years.[89]

The system divides economic activity into broad categories. The NAICS codes consist of up to 6 digits. The first two digits refer to a major product group such as "Food and Kindred Products" (Code 31). The next four digits refer to an industry subgroup. For example, the code for "Fruit and Vegetable Canning" is 311421. Over time these codes have become a consistent way of classifying data.

Many private industrial research and intelligence organizations use the NAICS code system. For example, American Business Information, Inc. in Omaha, Nebraska, provides prospect and mailing lists according to NAICS codes. One of the advantages of the NAICS system is that it has been developed in cooperation with Statistics Canada and Mexico's INEGI. NAICS also provides for comparable statistics among the three NAFTA trading partners.

Key sources of data for continuous marketing intelligence are financial reports, press releases, and trade magazines. Often firms subscribe to clipping services or newsletters that contain focused industry news or summaries of technological innovations, a large part of which are available electronically. Other data sources include electronic data bases and email, and services available over Dialog and Dun and Bradstreet; internal accounting information; trade shows; reports from sales and service field forces; suppliers and customers; multi-client industry studies; omnibus and syndicated research; and industry experts.

Marketing intelligence work may also include periodic customer satisfaction surveys and specific audit activities of suppliers and distributors. Availability and access to data vary from region to region. In Europe, multi-client industry studies, omnibus, and syndicated re-

---

[89] See http://www.census.gov/epcd/www/naicsind.htm (2007.06.20).

search are popular sources of information. In Latin America, on the other hand, multi-client studies are poorly developed.

Managing the continuous marketing intelligence effort is difficult. First, many managers do not understand the real value of this kind of intelligence work. Therefore, they tend to request it in spurts or when special projects require attention, requiring that employees and outside marketing intelligence effort is usually placed relatively low in the organizational hierarchy and is staffed with relatively young and inexperienced employees. Younger employees may know how to use the Internet, but often have a disadvantage in knowing what information is relevant. Analysis and interpretation of intelligence data often require extensive industry experience.

Problem-Related Intelligence

The second type of intelligence is problem-related. This type of intelligence is often initiated when a firm has a specific problem or need. The most common type of marketing intelligence is market research that collects primary data using qualitative or quantitative methods. Focus group and in-depth interviews are typical qualitative methods, and profiling target customers and defining the relative importance of product attributes are examples of quantitative intelligence. This ad hoc intelligence also includes such activities as benchmarking, reverse engineering, beta testing, and test marketing. Benchmarking is a systematic approach to comparing products and processes to the best firms in an industry.

Later in this chapter we discuss some of the issues related to benchmarking. Reverse engineering is a technical laboratory study of competitive products. Beta testing is the testing of a prototype product in a customer's operating environment.

Problem-related intelligence gathering is common and it is easier to manage for several reasons. First, it is related to a particular problem, the answer to which leads directly to some concrete action by management. It is therefore easier for a manager to assess the value of the research work.

Second, this kind of work is often perceived as essential and can therefore be more easily justified. It tends to reduce a manager's perceived risk, and reflects a "due diligence" approach to top managers. Many middle managers, therefore, use market research to cover their bases before a decision is made.

Third, this type of research is easier to manage because usually business firms hire a research manager who coordinates the work. This involves writing the research briefs, requesting bids, selecting a contractor, and presenting the results. Results from this ad hoc effort usually are produced quickly. If managers are satisfied with the turnaround, quality, and results, problem-related intelligence is often easy to justify.

Benchmarking

Benchmarking is a concept that has become popular during the past two decades and which has always been closely connected to the intelligence function. For industry companies it is not only a question of comparing products but also production capabilities. At Daimler-Chrysler AG today CI is mostly associated with Technical Competitive Benchmarking and led by a team connected to Competitive Analysis (Team TWA[90]). They use their own developed database, GoBench, where all divisions contribute with intelligence. What decides what is built into the new cars very much depends on customers' requests and a program of continuous marketing research. Technical Competitive Intelligence (CTI) is also part of the more important CI functions for companies such as Shell and Cisco.

In competitive benchmarking, a firm's performance is measured against that of "the best-in-class" companies to determine how to achieve desired performance levels. Business functions are analysed as processes that produce a product or service. Benchmarking can be applied to strategy, operations, and management support functions. Customers are the primary source for market and competitive benchmarking. Benchmarking should be a continuous process and should aim not just to match but to beat the competition.

Box 7.1 The AUTOBENCH case

Mavel is a French automotive consulting company and research firm which provides its members with quantitative and qualitative information, expert analysis and data on the global automotive industry by dismantling recent vehicles for benchmarking purposes. Its potential customers are part suppliers, car makers, material manufacturers, machine and tool makers, etc. The members, among them the French car manufacturer Renault, not only benefit from the analysis, but partici-

---

[90] TWA=Technische Wettbewerbsanalyse

pate actively in all steering committees deciding which cars are to be analysed and which criteria are to be used in the Benchmarking.

The company has two operational facilities, one in Lyon and the other in Detroit. Their AUTOBENCH program is devoted to the design analysis of vehicles that have recently been launched on to the automotive market. Twenty-seven vehicles have been fully torn down and analysed since the company started in 2000. In Europe one vehicle is dismantled per month.[91]

By outsourcing the Benchmarking function, the companies in the automotive industry can help each other, by splitting costs, gathering expertise, and trying to find objective criteria for Benchmarking analysis. Criteria selected are those which will likely have the greatest impact on sales on the global market.

In benchmarking, a firm compares its own performance with products and processes of world leaders. Nonetheless, many Western firms are wary of looking too closely at companies they admire, fearing accusations of plagiarism or using competitors' or other leading firms' proprietary information or processes. Most firms take apart the products of firms they admire in the hope of discovering their manufacturing secrets. To supplement reverse engineering, firms use benchmarking. The technique involves several stages:

1. Determine which aspects of products, technology, or marketing the company may need to improve.
2. Identify a firm that is a world leader in performing the process.
3. Contact the company to find out exactly why it performs so well.

Often the ideal benchmark is a company in a different industry. Unlike the process of gathering competitive intelligence, benchmarking often involves the sharing of information about internal processes and then improving the process. It is important to distinguish benchmarking, which is a formal and rigorous process, from competitive intelligence. The difference is that benchmarking is entirely based on mutual agreement between two firms. The information sharing is confidential and cooperative. For international companies, good benchmarking partners may or perhaps should be firms outside one's home market. For example, European and U.S. auto makers conduct exten-

---

[91] For more information see http://www.mavel.com and http://www.autobench.com (2007.12.22).

sive comparisons with Japanese auto makers to reduce their product development cycle time.

Some companies refuse benchmarking requests because their superb internal processes are sources of competitive advantage. As the popularity of benchmarking increases, obtaining good benchmarking data is becoming increasingly difficult. However, as indicated earlier in this chapter, there are legal and ethical ways to obtain non-confidential information that will enable effective benchmarks to be performed without the target company's direct knowledge. The objective of competitive benchmarking is to obtain as much valuable information as possible while giving away as little as possible about a company's own strengths and weaknesses.

If a company has not implemented its own Code of Ethics for gathering information, there are ready-made solutions. For instance, the Society of Competitive Intelligence Professionals (SCIP) presents one for its members, available at www.scip.org/ci/ethics.html. An advantage with ready-made Codes of Ethics is that competitors know what to expect, which again may increase confidence among competitors and the likelihood of cooperation.

Intelligence Sources

For organizations committed to establishing an intelligence system, there are many sources of information available. It is beyond the scope of this chapter to discuss each of these information sources. They are included merely as a checklist and to trigger thinking related to where firms may look to find symptoms of changes, competitive moves, price increases, or answers to specific questions. Each company has specific needs and may find that some sources work better than others.

One source of intelligence data that deserves some attention is related to the intellectual property or patents of another company. Gathering patent information is primarily used by companies as a defensive mechanism to determine a competitor's position with regards to technology and product development strategy. Searches of patent, trademark, and copyright databases are easy, and often help businesses avoid legal trouble due to violating a competitor's intellectual property rights.

Intelligence property files can also be used in a company's offensive strategy. The use of patent databases for competitive intelligence and other business applications is growing in importance. It is particularly easy for non-U.S. firms to access U.S. patent information. In contrast, it is more difficult (and expensive) for non-Japanese companies to access similar data in Japan. Creative uses of these files enable firms to analyse technology, identify new business licensing opportunities, establish what the competition is doing, identify potential new competitors, and protect one's own intellectual property. Some sources are listed in table below:

Internal sources:	Research related:	Periodical, Reports, Journals and Books:	Government and NPO Data:	Commercial Data:
Accounting records	Bankers	Business periodicals index	Census Data	Advertising agencies
E-mail hot-lines	Competitor's product	General Press	Country export councils	Advertising
Financial records	Competitor's customers	Handbooks	Country trade commissions	Annual reports
Intranet	Consultants	Industry reports	Court documents	Business intelligence agencies
Internet	Focus groups	Marketing journals	Federal Procurement Centers	Classified advertisements
	In-depth interviews	Moody's manuals	Government statistics	Corporate directories
	Industry gurus	Standard and Poor's Industry	International trade statistics	Country surveys
	Internet discussion groups	Trade directories	Patent and trademark office	Credit records
	Investment companies	University/academic case studies	State or country economic development offices	Industry associations
	Multi client studies'	Yellow Pages	Tax records	Industry surveys
	Original market research			Mailing list providers
	Own customers			Marketing research agencies
	Public activities			Security analyst research reports
	Stock market data			
	Suppliers			
	Unions			

Table 7.3 Varies Sources of Information.

Patents also have several advantages as a technology indicator. Patents provide a wealth of detailed information and comprehensive coverage of technologies. Some firms conduct statistical analysis of international records to assess and forecast technological activities of competitors. The results are often validated by comparison with expert opinion. Such analysis appears to be a valuable tool for corporate technology analysis and planning. Overall, results of patent analysis conform with the opinion of technology experts. This is particularly useful when such forecasts are combined with industry or product life cycle analysis.

Establishing an Intelligence and Information System

Much has been written about establishing marketing intelligence and marketing information systems. Proposals vary from formal computerized systems to informal manual systems. The system designed by Quest International described in Table 7.3 indicates that effective marketing intelligence should contain both formal and informal components.

Box 7.2 Management of MI and FMC Limited (a mini-case)

FCM Limited, a wholly owned subsidiary of Sherer International is one of the world's largest suppliers of flavors and fragrances. FMC consists of many business units that operate as profit centers and are responsible for their own strategies and plans, and regional organizations that interface with customers.

Customers range in size from small manufacturers of perfume to large manufacturers of detergent and food products. Some customers operate locally; other customers operate worldwide. Flavor and fragrance manufacturers are expected to work closely with customers to develop and supply flavors and fragrance that enhance customers' products. This requires active MI by FMC. The marketing research function is a corporate-level activity.

When FMC reviewed its approach to MI it identified a number of issues and obstacles that needed to be addressed:

- The business units felt that the centralized marketing research function was bureaucratic and excessively costly. Those in the function were perceived to feel that that they "owned" the data and that it was to be carefully doled out to the "less than bright" individuals in the business units.
- There was a "Kingdom of Information" attitude, as individuals used possession of information to achieve power in the organization.
- Timeliness was a problem, and in an effort to do all things, no one thing was done well.
- It was perceived that the system required the user to do all the work and that data was not available in the way the information needed to be used.
- Much of the research seemed to be interesting rather than relevant, raising the question of value added.

In broad terms it was felt that it was important to make MI data available to the business units and the regions in a standardized form, to continuously update the data, to offer tools and templates to facilitate its use by the business units and regions, and to restrict analysis done centrally for "big picture" issues. Specifically, FMC identified the following categories of MI data/information:

1. Competitive information, with data on more than 100 competitors.
2. Market information, with information on market volume growth rates, and so on.
3. Key customer information.

A key objective was to design a system that would accept data from many sources. The system, which is under development, also had to be designed to handle both structured and unstructured data. Structured data would include market, competitor, and financial information. Unstructured data would include a variety of information, including "comments" and input by members of the sales force and other employees.

A major source of the structured market data would be a market research firm in the United Kingdom, which agreed to provide information on volume and growth rates of food and other household products in some 40 categories from some 140 countries, together with population and gross domestic product figures. By applying appropriate conversion factors, FMC can translate these numbers into market potential for FMC products, calculate market share by country, and identify potential opportunities. The contract provided that the research company would bill FMC £120,000 per year for three years, and for this amount the company would continually update the information. Other structured data would come from company reports, industry reports, market research reports, and so on.

FMC would use special software to access the various data bases. Several members of the FMC's central marketing staff had been trained in writing computer software, and they had started a major effort to develop a comprehensive and user-friendly system. It is estimated that the users of the system would be able to generate some 600,000 tables of analysis. In addition, the system would provide for ways to search for the "comments" section using key words.

As with any MI system of this kind that contains proprietary information, there is the risk that the data may be used inappropriately. Restricting the access to the data however, would limit its use and seem to defeat the purpose of the system. The present plan, therefore, would allow essentially unlimited access, but patterns of use would be monitored for possible abuse.

Source: Company records. Company name and some data have been disguised.

The creation of a marketing intelligence system can be viewed as a strategic institutional change tool. Strategic and competitive intelligence systems should include management information systems, conventional decision support systems, and knowledge-based systems. The literature known as Knowledge Management may be taken to mean the comparison of information collected about employees with information about the external environment.

Many companies have such systems and substantial amounts of internal intelligence information. What makes MI a significant competitor at the beginning of the 21st century is the continuous development of easy-to-use database tools. Most firms have the necessary operating functions to integrate their own intelligence activities. In such cases, all that is needed is to organize the effort following a well-designed set of information- and intelligence-handling procedures. This requires a company culture that supports marketing intelligence as well as broad-based management commitment that can best be accomplished through senior management example and leadership.

The nature of and need for intelligence varies by company, market, and industry. Therefore, characteristics of intelligence systems also vary. Some factors that influence the design of the intelligence system include:

- The complexity of the environment.
- Organizational environment and culture.
- The complexity of the business (products/markets).
- Cultural transportability of products across international markets.
- The rate of technological change.
- Stage in the product life cycle and growth rates.
- Competitive structure and market share.

The lesson corporate leaders must heed from the history of intelligence in business organizations is that, as the complexity of the environment and their own organizations increases, their current intelligence activities may no longer suffice. With high business and environmental uncertainty, complexity increases and a marketing intelligence system becomes vital.

Changing customer demographics, industry innovation, the potential availability of product substitutes, the availability and new uses of technology, value changes, political instability, and shifts in public policy are factors that increase complexity and thus require marketing intelligence. Also, firms with many different products and markets must design their intelligence systems in such a way that relevant data are collected for each product/market combination.

Organizational structure impacts how and to what degree an organization conducts intelligence. Information flows from one organizational level to another and across organizational units. The organizational hierarchy and structure tend to influence the quality of intelligence and how intelligence information flows and is used throughout the organization. For example, in functionally organized companies, the integration and use of intelligence may be difficult across functions such as production, finance, and marketing because of entrenched cultures. This can particularly be true when marketing, rather than top management, initiates the intelligence efforts.

On the other hand, when each function gathers and interprets intelligence data from different perspectives, the quality of the information gathered and how it is interpreted and converted into intelligence can be enhanced. Consequently, intelligence based on functional specialization provides a depth of knowledge not found in organizations where all intelligence gathering and interpretation is conducted exclusively within the marketing department.

Different levels in the organization need different kinds of intelligence. Strategic decisions are first of all the concern of top-level management. The company is in need of tactics at the middle level of management, smaller steps that will lead the company to any defined strategy. To make tactical moves the company is in the need of information, but of another kind. A third kind is operative intelligence, information to secure the day-to-day operations among frontline managers. All three kinds of intelligence depend on each other for their combined success.

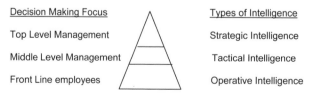

Decision Making Focus		Types of Intelligence
Top Level Management		Strategic Intelligence
Middle Level Management		Tactical Intelligence
Front Line employees		Operative Intelligence

Figure 7.4 The Different Kinds of Intelligence Requested

The aim of strategic intelligence in a sales and marketing department is to review budgets, make forecasts, and decide on market penetration and resource allocation. The aim of tactical intelligence is to implement strategic objectives, manage and analyse large quantities of data and managing sales employees. Operative intelligence is concerned with developing propositions, negotiations with customers and customer relationship.

Organizing Intelligence Work

One of the most important but difficult aspects of marketing intelligence is organizing and managing MI. Often this important function receives only half-hearted commitment by senior executives and becomes a periodic task in the marketing organization. The lack of commitment from senior management is often seen as the single most important reason for why intelligence work fails. Other reasons for failure include trying to serve too many employees with too many intelligence topics, creating databases before the intelligence process and procedures have been proven, not establishing legal and ethical guidelines or separating the analysis from the collection unit.

In this era of globalization, organizations need to incorporate new approaches in managing their intelligence processes. Several important factors include:

1. All key managers must agree that marketing intelligence is important and be committed to it. Managers must provide key strategic questions to guide the intelligence efforts and sufficient resources to accomplish required intelligence tasks.
2. Management must develop a company culture that encourages employees to search for intelligence and to question the validity and reliability of facts, assumptions, and conclusions in the spirit of organizational learning. In some of the companies most successful at implementing marketing intelligence systems (many of which are Japanese), all employees have an understanding for and contribute to the information-gathering effort.
3. Management must assign the intelligence function to a visible position in the organization. By doing so it signals the importance of MI to all managers. Management must also require the MI function to produce and widely distribute useful documents.
4. Management must provide a communication climate that facilitates horizontal and vertical dissemination of intelligence. This flow should be from the bottom up and from the top down.

5. Management must select executives with substantial industry experience. This provides maturity and credibility to intelligence interpretation tasks. Good intelligence briefings require positioning to organizational context. Senior managers are more likely to listen to a manager they know has significant experience than to a manager with little industry experience. This prevents irrelevant recommendations and predictions sometimes provided by inexperienced employees.

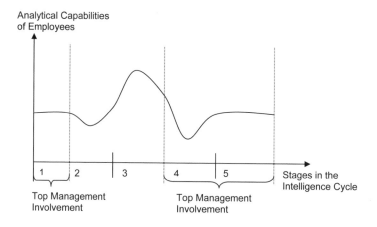

Figure 7.5 The Types of Competencies Related to the Five Stages of the Intelligence Cycle

The Figure illustrates the degree of analytical thinking involved in the five different processes or phases of the Intelligence Cycle. Analytical thinking is not only important in the analytical phase of the Intelligence process, but also in the planning and evaluation phase. It also illustrates in which parts of the process top management involvement is most important, i.e. in the planning, presentation and evaluation phases.

Information gathering involves less analytical thinking and is often delegated. This does not mean that analytical work is the only critical part in the CI cycle. As the Nordic cases presented earlier in the chapter showed, distribution and presentation is often where companies fail, either because they don't know who needs the information, information is produced for people who don't need it or the information arrives too late.

It is difficult to recommend exactly how the marketing intelligence function should be organized and where it should be located. However, the function commonly reports to a marketing manager or vice president of marketing. The advantage of this approach is that the marketing function has this resource at its immediate disposal. Market and customer data can easily be collected and interpreted.

The disadvantage of this approach is that it is often viewed as an exclusive tool for the marketing function. Other functions or departments may receive intelligence only on a need-to-know basis. This makes it difficult for other functions to become equal partners in intelligence gathering. As we stated previously, other functions such as research and development, engineering, filed service, and manufacturing should be included as essential players in the intelligence gathering activities.

Another approach that appears to work is to disassociate the MI activities somewhat from the day-to-day marketing operative activities. This can be done by establishing a marketing service organization that provides information and intelligence services to all departments. In practice this means that all functions receive intelligence and can request intelligence from this unit. Often when the marketing intelligence unit has such independent status, it also works closely with corporate and business management.

The broader intelligence effort of which MI is a part may be linked to Business Intelligence which not only includes information gathering about competitors and the narrower markets, but also technical competencies, possible partners, all kinds of influencers/organizations and individuals—all laws and regulations that define and limit business activities- in one term all that goes into keeping or making a business organization competitive.

Demand Analysis
Defining the Market Potential and Its Components
One of the most common CI activities is the determination of a company's potential in a particular market segment for a specific product. Figure 5.9 shows the various components of market potential. By understanding the nature and the size of these components, it is possible to determine market potential in a company-specific context.

The top line in Figure 7.6 represents the total theoretical potential market according to a Trajectory Forecasting, where there is a definite trend upwards or downwards and we assume the curve will continue in the same direction for the period of the forecast. A similar potential can also be mapped by other types of forecasts, like Cyclic Forecasting which is based on the assumption that history repeats itself.

The theoretical market size is the size of the market if all customers would purchase a specific solution to solve their functional needs. For example, consider the business office market for personal computers. One could argue that all employees could use a personal computer. However, it is not realistic to expect that this will happen in all offices worldwide as there will always be those companies who cannot afford to buy a personal computer for all employees or where all do not need one. Therefore, the number we get by counting all office workers is just a theoretical number. This theoretical number is the theoretical market size for personal computers. Therefore, the question we need to answer is how many firms are likely to purchase personal computers within a given period?

Industry Sales

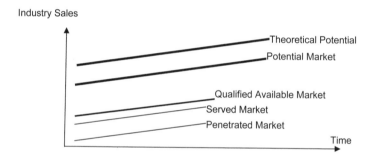

Figure 7.6 What is Market Potential?

The answer to this question helps determine the size of the potential market, which needs to be broken down into smaller components. The next question is what proportion of the potential market is available. Even though the market potential exists, the market infrastructure may be such that all potential customers may not be reachable. Many countries may have limited distribution or communications channels that restrict market penetration. Therefore, only a certain proportion of the potential market is available. This proportion is the available market or the level of likely penetration. The available market can be broken down into several components: the qualified market, the served market, and the penetrated market. The qualified market is the portion of the market for which a company with a given technology can qualify to compete. The served market is the portion of the market that the firm specifically targets. The penetrated market is that portion of the served market that the firm expects to reach with a particular marketing program.

It is very important for firms to go through an exercise similar to the one described above. It helps define what portion of the market is potential for the company. It may also reveal when a market potential represents an opportunity for a specific firm with a given solution.

Using Satisfaction Surveys to Understand Current Market Position

Many firms, particularly small and medium-size companies, do not have a good understanding of their market position. In many international markets, market shares and market share growth figures are crude and inaccurate, which limits a firm's ability to accurately determine its competitive position. It is particularly important to obtain relative figures because they are the true measures of performance. A firm can have substantial aggregate growth but experience loss of its relative market position.

For this reason, some business marketing firms conduct regular customer satisfaction studies. For example, the Diagnostics Division of Abbott Laboratories tracks customer satisfaction in 46 countries, a complex task that requires commitment and resources. To convince management that this was the appropriate intelligence approach, the MI group at Abbott used the arguments shown in Table 7.4.

If you do not measure it, you cannot improve it.
Do not mistake silence for satisfaction.
If you are not keeping score, you are only practicing.
It costs five times more to get a new customer than it costs to keep a current customer.
Increase in customer satisfaction = $ XXX increase in sales = $ XXX in company profits.
More than 90% of unsatisfied customers do not complain.
Satisfied customers tend to buy more and are more willing to pay premium prices.
Satisfied customers are loyal customers, less likely to switch to competitive products.
Companies can boost profits by 100% by retaining just 5 percent more of their customers.

Table 7.4 Arguments for Customer Satisfaction Research

For many of the reasons listed in the table, customer satisfaction measurement has become a popular intelligence activity. Although international customer satisfaction research is difficult to do, firms that can link satisfaction data to performance and evaluation may design customer satisfaction into their reward systems.

Understanding Customer Requirements

Another essential MI activity is gaining an understanding of customer needs. Many firms give lip service to this requirement: they push what they know best (i.e. they are product-oriented) without attempting to understand what the customer really needs. Business marketers that are market-oriented know the customer requirements better than the customer. In such situations, selling is less important and persuasion becomes unnecessary. In chapter 3 we discussed in detail the needs and motivation of business customers. Below are some of the key marketing intelligence aspects of customer requirements:

- Know the customer's operations and product in detail.
- Understand the customer's cost structure.
- Identify how the initial purchase enhances the customer's value versus its customers and how it impact cost.
- Understand operating implications related to installation and start up.
- Understand the role of operating costs versus up-front investment.
- Find out how important product life cycle costs or cost of ownership are to the customer.
- Identify the customer's understanding of your product's relative benefits and the impact on the customer's cost structure and performance.

To determine customer requirements, business marketers must communicate directly with their clients. Much of the responsibility for intelligence gathering in many companies is given to the sales force. If used extensively, this can be an ineffective approach unless it is properly managed. Because salespeople may be biased toward the sale, they may not be objective assessors of what is in the best interest of the customer and the company in the long run. Consequently, it is important that other company employees such as marketing staff, product managers, engineers, researchers, and planners, communicate with the client organization.

It is also common to use objective third parties, such as consultants and market research firms, to assist in the evaluation. Formal, problem-oriented market research is commonly used to identify customer requirements in addition to sales force recommendations. The nature of the research may vary from a survey to in-depth executive interviews.

Knowledge of the end consumer's needs is often overlooked in business-to-business marketing. The idea of derived demand explains how vulnerable an end supplier can be to actual consumer demand in today's world market. A producer of steel pipes to the shipping industry is affected by the changes in demand in the cruise industry through a series of links:

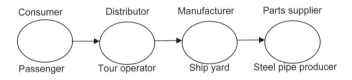

Figure 7.7 Derived Demand in the Shipping Industry

Assessing Market Demand

In Chapter 3 we discussed how aggregate business market behaviour often is a result of events in consumer or government markets. Business market behaviour can therefore often be traced directly to changed behaviour in these markets. Business market demand is often a derived demand. There is often a lag factor between changes in consumer demand and the impact that it has on business demand. Thus an extremely important intelligence activity for business marketers is to identify and monitor factors that influence changes and periodic fluctuations in demand.

Another important factor in analyzing demand for business products is demand elasticity. Commonly discussed in relationship to pricing, it reflects the positive and negative changes in demand as prices are reduced or increased. In some markets and situations, selling a substitute product can result in quick changes in a firm's demand. However, it is not always that simple. In business marketing, relationships are important, and there may be substantial resistance to change even though there are economic incentives to use alternative suppliers. Personal relationships, service level, loyalty, and organizational culture are other important influences.

Product characteristics are another factor that influences demand fluctuations. Firms may use simple but effective guidelines: From the customer's point of view, does the product we provide contain attributes that are "like-to-haves" or are they "must-haves"? If the firm provides a product with many of "like-to-have" features, it would expect that demand would fall as price increased. If the firm provides a product that has many "must-haves", it could expect demand to remain stable with price increases.

From a marketing intelligence point of view, it is essential to determine the "must have" criteria. Failure to understand the difference between the two may have serious consequences. Many international companies through product development and delivery have incorporated a large number of "like-to-haves". But these efforts have had no influence on demand. They have only increased the firm's product and delivery costs.

Sales Forecasting

One of the primary objectives of MI is to provide the basis for the forecast. It is thus directly linked to intelligence efforts. The better the market intelligence, the better the forecast. We include a description of forecasting here because it is essential to the economic performance of any business organization. Forecasts are directly linked to company budgets and plans. Figure 7.8 shows the relationships between the forecast and various company budgets. The forecast requires extensive external input, and most of the activities conducted by MI are directly linked to the quality of the forecast.

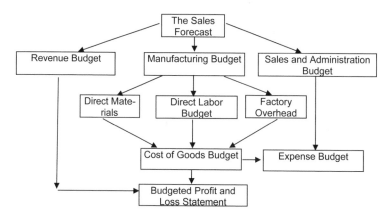

Figure 7.8 Why the Sales Forecast is so Important

Forecasting is important because it directs the planning, allocation, and use of a business organization's resources. If a forecast is too high, a firm has over-allocated resources and must go through the painful process of making cuts. If the forecast is too low, the firm usually has not allocated enough resources to satisfy the demand. This, of course, is also a problem, but a more pleasant one, because the firm may have to rush order materials, hire more labour, and do on. Forecasts should be on target. Therefore, many business-to-business marketers use rolling forecasts that are updated monthly. A forecast is not an objective or wishful thinking. A forecast is a commitment. It reflects what will be delivered in terms of sales. It is better to underestimate than to overestimate the sales forecast. Firms can choose from an extensive pool of methods and approaches developed to forecast sales. Below we describe some common approaches to forecasting.[92]

Forecasting techniques are often divided into two categories – qualitative and quantitative methods. The key qualitative methods are:

- *In-depth interviews* with customers regarding their buying intentions and purchase requirements. Due to the open-ended nature of this approach, it can contain significant bias. It is an excellent way of getting detailed information from important customers, and it allows for two-way interaction between the interviewer and the interviewee.
- *Jury of executive opinion* combines the average estimates of senior executives and knowledgeable individuals within the organization. The weakness of this method is that it strictly depends on the knowledge of executives. But because this method consolidates the knowledge of several people, it is less biased than the in-depth interview.
- *Sales force composites* are forecasts developed by salespersons for their respective territories. Salespeople may be biased. They may be either too optimistic, or, if they are paid a commission, salespersons may manipulate forecasts to plan their income stream. In spite of this weakness, this is still the most frequent used forecasting method in business marketing. It is easy to implement.
- *The Delphi method* is an extension of the jury of executive opinion approach. It is a group forecasting method that incorporates anonymity, forecasting revisions, feedback to other forecasters, and consensus. It is time-consuming but usually unbiased due to the anonymity.

[92] For a good assessment of forecasting, see Georgoff, D. M., Murdick, R. G. (1986). A Manager's Guide to Forecasting. Harvard Business Review, January.

Some quantitative forecasting methods are:

- *Survey of user needs* is similar to the in-depth interview, except that the customer fills out a questionnaire about buying needs and intentions. Because of ongoing negotiations, bias is likely to exist.
- *Time-series analysis* includes several methods – moving averages, trend fitting, exponential smoothening, least squares, and Box-Jenkins time-series analysis. All of these methods require historical data. Moving average techniques use the average of recent periods to predict the next forecast period. Trend fitting and exponential smoothening tries to fit past data with a particular curve or adjusts the forecasting with some proportional weight to predict sales for the next period. Box-Jenkins forecasting is a sophisticated computer model that allows the computer to pick a statistical time-series model that fits the data.
- *Regression analysis* involves identifying the variables that influence sales and building a model that can then be applied to historical data to determine the effect of each variable on sales. For maximum effectiveness, regression analysis requires a large number of past observations and it is limited in its ability to identify major turning points. It is most useful for products in the mature stage of the product life cycle and for products where a constant set of variables, which can be accurately measured, have been identified.
- *Diffusion analysis* is very difficult to use, but it may work when a firm is trying to forecast sales for an entire product class. This category of forecasting models is also useful for forecasting sales of new products. It is quite problematic because it is a form of market simulation and requires significant market research to estimate parameters used in the analysis.
- *Input-output analysis* is an econometric technique that establishes links between sectors of one industry with sectors of another industry. This technique is complex and time-consuming.
- Product life cycle analysis can be used when it is possible to estimate the parameters of the life cycle s-curve. Using this approach for forecasting requires knowledge of product acceptance rates.

By themselves, none of these methods may give an accurate forecast. A combination of methods integrated with sound intelligence and experience usually gives the best result. The Swedish telecom company Telia AB does not use any particular method of analysis in their intelligence process, but try to find a process that is efficient from case to case both for the users and the analysts. The company conducts several different types of analysis on the same questions to see if the answers differ. If they do, more analysis will be conducted.[93] For mature businesses with relatively stable patterns of competitive market shares, forecasting overall industry demand may be the most critical requirement. Still, estimates also need to be made of the relative marketing effort of competitors.

For firms introducing new products, forecasting becomes more uncertain. Sales patterns during previous introductions of similar products may provide guidance, as can intelligence gathered from customers by the sales force. Regardless of the forecasting situation, it needs to be recognized that even the best forecasts deal with the future and so are inherently uncertain. However, the better management is able to estimate the future, the better it is prepared to deal with it. Good forecasts, therefore, require both management attention and resources.

How to use Marketing Intelligence

Companies able to build intelligence and use systems that are better than their competitors often derive sustainable competitive advantage. It is the use of intelligence that represents an important asset. If the intelligence is not used, it is only a wasteful expense. How can companies incorporate market intelligence? Below are a few suggestions about how intelligence can be used:

- Publish internally the objectives of the marketing intelligence unit and explain who is responsible for what activity. Encourage managers to use the MI resource.
- Periodically develop a presumed competitor business strategy document. Circulate this document to all managers and productively solicit updates and revisions.
- Provide periodic status reports on competitor and customer activities.
- Provide all managers with periodic technology updates.

---

[93] See, Bertelsen, L., Mathison, M. (2000). Competitor Intelligence Process–A Case Study of Telia AB. Unpublished paper. Luleå University of Technology, Sweden.

- Provide an overview catalogue or database of available intelligence material on the Intranet. This might consist of a list of electronic databases available, research reports on file, market statistics, e-mail groups, and secondary resources.

How to Protect Intelligence and Business Secrets

There may be said to be two main kinds of intelligence strategies, one active and one passive. The passive is known as counterintelligence. Some companies may find out that their need for marketing intelligence is limited to marketing research, but all companies should make sure they have an efficient counterintelligence capability. Information that is vital for the company's existence must be protected. Examples of counterintelligence measures can be everything from making copies of the content of a server to full Technical Surveillance Counter Measures (TSCM).

TSCM is concerned with the prevention or detection of attempted theft of sensitive information. It typically involves an inspection by a technician or engineer (TSCM specialist) of a physical item or place. The TSCM specialist will do a sweep of the location, detecting any surveillance devices (bugs) and any technical security weaknesses. It was estimated in 1997 that $2.2 billion of illegal eavesdropping equipment was sold per year within the United States.[94]

For 2002 sales of security and surveillance equipment has grown to a $5 billion industry, up 30% to 60% since last year at spy-gear stores across the United States.[95] Some of this increase in sales is no doubt caused by the growing fear after the terrorist attack known as 9-11 and is not business-related. Still, even though the figures are rough estimates, they show that companies are more willing to consider alternative ways of gathering information with the development of new surveillance technology.

Another reason may be that the economic consequences of being detected are not sufficiently severe to prevent these methods from being used. As a result TSCM services are becoming increasingly necessary, even though general caution in many cases will be enough to prevent any serious damage from the loss of information. Managers should know when they are at risk and for what. Confidential meetings

---

[94] Source: U.S. State Department/DCI (Bureau of Intelligence and Research), March 1997.
[95] Source: Brooks Barnes Staff Reporter of The Wall Street Journal, February 13, 2002.

and bids are very popular targets for corporate spies. Other situations may be related to specific events like negotiations, litigation, lawsuit and layoffs. If your company is involved in the fashion, automotive, advertising, or marketing industry you are considered to be at continuous risk. According the FBI, the following types of businesses are under continuous and special risk: Materials, Manufacturing, Information and Communications, Biotechnology and Life Sciences, Transportation, Energy and Environment.

It is essential that business intelligence is kept inside of the organization. Intelligence should be treated as sensitive information and considered a trade secret. Such information is usually lost in three ways:

1. Accidental exposure by an employee entrusted with its possession.
2. Intentional theft by an unauthorized outside agent.
3. Internal theft by an ex-employee or a disgruntled worker who has access to the information.

Since there is no possible way to keep all information secret, management must create an awareness and responsibility program that informs and requires employees who work with MI that it should not be disclosed to outsiders. Employees should be required to sign a statement related to disclosure of information. For example, throughout IBM, during its period of unparalleled success, a responsible and consistent approach existed among employees. Few employees divulged confidential information to outsiders. Internally IBM was very open, while to an outsider it appeared closed, with little market intelligence available to non-employees. Above all, talk of secrecy should not be exaggerated and it should not be allowed to hamper the organizations ability to work efficiently.

Summary

Marketing intelligence is an important business marketing function. It represents a broad set of activities that supports strategy formulation and implementation. MI is broader than marketing research and is conducted continuously by employees from a variety of company functions. Globalization of business has increased the importance of MI, making it more complex and more taxing. New technologies like the growing use of Internet, have worked in the opposite direction, making MI faster and less expensive.

The MI function is often ignored, poorly resourced and inadequately staffed. This chapter distinguishes between problem-oriented and continuous MI. Companies that conduct both well are often leaders in their field. Their managers are willing to change strategy as MI requires.

Furthermore, we are convinced, and the content of these chapters will hopefully illustrate this, that Intelligence Analysis or CI has much to gain from being incorporated with the discipline of Management Strategy. After all, it is the strategy which decides what is need-to-know information as opposed to only nice-to-know. It all starts with the need to make better decisions.

Further Reading

Ashton, W.B., Klavans, R.A. (1997). *Keeping abreast of Science and Technology*. Columbus, OH.: Battelle Press.

Burwell, H.P. (1999). *Online Competitive Intelligence: increase your profits using cyber-intelligence*. Tempe, AZ.: Facts on demand.

Cook, M., Cook, C.W. (2000). *Competitive Intelligence: Create an Intelligent Organization and Compete to Win*. London: Kogan Page.

Delmater, R. (2001). *Data Mining Explained: A Manager's Guide to Customer-Centric Business Intelligence*. Boston, MA.: Oxford University Press.

De Ville, B. (2001). *Microsoft Data Mining: Integrated Business Intelligence for e-Commerce & Knowledge*. Butterworth-Heinemann.

Dutka, A. (1999). *Competitive Intelligence for the Competitive Edge*. Lincolnwood, Ill.: NTC Business Books.

Fialka, J. J. (1997). *War by other Means*. New York, N.Y.: W.W. Norton & Co.

Fahey, L. (1999). *Competitors*. New York, N.Y.: John Wiley & Sons.

Fleisher, C., S., Bensoussan, B. (2002). *Strategic and Competitive Analysis: Methods and Techniques for Analyzing Business Competition*. Prentice Hall.

Fuld, L.M. (1994). *The New Competitor Intelligence: The Complete Resource for Finding, Analyzing, and Using Information about Your Competitors*. New York, N.Y.: John Wiley & Sons.

Gordon, I.H. (2001). *Competitor Targeting: Winning the Battle for Market and Customer Share*. New York, N.Y.: John Wiley & Sons.

Halliman, C. (2001). *Business Intelligence Using Smart Techniques: Environmental Scanning Using Text Mining and Competitor Analysis Using Scenarios and Manual Simulation*. Houston, TX.: Information Uncover.

Hussey, D., Jenster, P. (1999). *Competitor Intelligence*. Chichester, England: John Wiley & Sons, Inc.

Pollard, A. (1999). *Competitor Intelligence*. London, England: Financial Times Professional Limited.

Platt, W. (1957). *Strategic Intelligence Production*. New York, N.Y.: F. A. Praeger.

Prescott, J.E., Miller, S.H. (2001). *Proven Strategies in Competitive Intelligence.* New York, N.Y.: John Wiley & Sons, Inc.

Kahaner, L. (1997). *Competitive Intelligence.* New York, N.Y.: Simon & Schuster.

Krizan, L. (1999). *Intelligence Essentials for Everyone.* Washington, D.C.: Government Printing Office.

Liautaud, B. (2000). *E-Business Intelligence: Turning Information into Knowledge into Profit.* New York, N.Y.:McGraw-Hill Education Group.

McGonagle, J.J., Vella, C.M. (1999). *The Internet age of competitive intelligence.* London: Quorum.

Miller, J.P. (2000). *Millennium Intelligence: Understanding & Conducting Competitive Intelligence in the Digital Age.* Medford, NJ.: Information Today, Incorporated.

Rasmussen, N. et al. (2002). *Financial Business Intelligence.* Wiley & Sons.

Rustmann, F.W. (2002). *CIA, Inc.: Espionage & the Craft of Business Intelligence.* Brassey's, Incorporated.

Simon, A.R. Shaffer, Steven L. (2001). *Data warehousing and business intelligence for e-commerce.* San Francisco, CA.: Morgan Kaufmann.

Underwood, J. (2002). *Competitor Intelligence.* Capstone Ltd.

Vella, C.M. (1999). *The Internet Age of Competitive Intelligence. Westport,* CT.: Quorum Books.

Vibert, C. (2000). *Web-based Analysis for Competitive Intelligence.* Westport, CT.: Quorum Books

Vine, D. (2000). *Internet Business Intelligence.* New Jersey, Medford: Cyber-Age Books.

Walle, A.H. (2001). *Qualitative research in intelligence and marketing: the new strategic convergence.* Westport, CT.: Quorum Books.

JOURNALS

Marketing Intelligence and Planning (MIP)

The Competitive Intelligence Review (CIR), edited by SCIP and published by Wiley, came out between 1995-2001.

A new journal, the Journal of Competitive Intelligence and Management (JCIM) has replaced CIR.

The Business Intelligence Journal.

International Journal of Research in Marketing (IJRM).

Information & Management and the Journal of Public Policy and Marketing (JPPM).

CHAPTER 8

The Strategic Perspective to Intelligence Analysis

Begin with a Decision

The competitor analysis is normally the most important intelligence report and therefore deserves some special attention. As we have shown in earlier chapters, most organizations will give some thought to competitors, although this may be a piecemeal, functional approach. In almost every organization there will be some people who obtain information about one or more aspects of the activities of the main competitors.

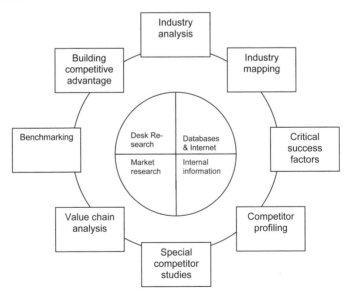

Figure 8.1 Approach to Competitor Analysis

To move from a piecemeal approach to something that is more systematic, thorough, and continuous requires a dedication of corporate effort. Therefore, it should begin with a top-level decision that this is the way the organization wishes to go, and the recognition that such an effort will require some expenditure of time and money. Without high-level commitment, a competitive analysis will yield little more than snippets of raw information which are called for only on occasions when something requires urgent analysis.

There are several elements to consider once the organization has decided to pursue this analysis. Figure 8.1 summarizes the elements of an approach to a competitor analysis which have been described in this book. The centre of the diagram shows the sources of information, and the essential elements. The boxes illustrate approaches which may be important for some organizations, or for any organization at some time, but will not be universally useful.

Using this figure as a guide, it is possible to distinguish among a number of tasks which need to be undertaken to ensure that the competitor analysis is effective. Starting from the centre of the figure and working outwards, we can identify the following:

- Collection, assessment and storage of regular external sources of information: databases, press clippings, abstract services, company annual reports, directories, competitors' literature and the like
- Marketing research, covering primary sources, and numerous secondary sources in addition to those mentioned above
- Collation and coordination of internal sources of information, which will vary from information from formal company records, such as sales analyses, to the harnessing of informal sources which may be tapped by many levels in the organization
- The task of regular analysis of the information
- Decisions and strategies which arise from the analysis
- Overall coordination of the competitor analysis activity of sources that should be tapped, and the organization of special external studies, such as additional marketing research.

One difficulty in describing how to organize for competitor analysis is that it is easier to identify what needs doing than how to ensure it gets done. This is because organizations are of different shapes and sizes, and may span over several industries. In this first part of our presentation we are assuming that the organization is a local business, of sufficient size to already have the various specialist functions we mentioned. Later, we will look at the complexities of the organization with many business units operating in many countries. All the initial discussion will be relevant to the more complex companies. The issue is how to deal with their additional complexities.

None of this means that smaller organizations cannot undertake competitive analysis. It simply indicates that the specialist support functions will not exist to the same extent, and that the tasks will have to be divided differently.

In one case whose specific identity must remain hidden, the managing director undertook competitor analysis as part of the strategic planning activity. Various people in the organization were involved in the special studies mentioned in Figure 8.1. At the time the case was written, the firm also employed a research assistant, who collected much of the intelligence, helped with some of the studies, and also fulfilled a general library and desk research role in support of client work. Because good employees are ambitious, and might be expected to seek promotion which the organization could not provide at this level, an arrangement was made with a university that the organization would annually recruit one business student for the industrial placement year of the degree. Although this meant regular replacement of the assistant, it also meant that a highly capable person was always available. As this was the most popular placement in the university, there was no difficulty in recruiting an appropriate person for the task. At no time did the organization in the case employ more than 20 full-time people in its UK office. This demonstrates that small size is not a barrier as long as the organization believes in the importance of seeking competitive advantage through market intelligence.

The Coordinator
Because of its importance, we will start with the last task on the list, and discuss the others in order. Typically this task requires a person of considerable seniority. Frequently the activity is part of the strategic management directorate, with the ultimate responsibility falling on the director in charge. This fits well with overall strategic planning responsibilities, and ensures a measure of integration with strategic thinking. Sometimes there is a designated competitor analysis unit within this directorate, although this does not necessarily imply a large staff, or even the full-time commitment of one person.

It would be a mistake to try to centralize every one of the tasks on the list, but the role is more than one of coordinating the work of other departments and functions of the organization. There has to be a proactive element, with adequate authority to be able to insist that certain things are done. Such tasks can include extending the press clippings service to take in new sources, or using a cross-functional team from research and development, manufacturing, purchasing, and accounts to make regular estimates of competitor product costs. If the organization wishes to undertake value chain analysis, the coordinator must have the power to pull together a multi-functional team to perform the work. The role should also become a centre where all sources are pulled together and cross-validation is undertaken of one source against another, much like a journalist using two independent sources for a story to be printed.

One task when establishing a competitive analysis unit should be an audit of the information that currently comes into the organization and the analysis currently undertaken. This should be compared to the needs of the organization, as discussed in earlier chapters. One suggested questionnaire for a strategic information unit will be found in Stanat (1990). This book also contains helpful advice on managing a strategic information unit.

Regular External Information

Many organizations have an information department, which frequently has grown out of the old corporate library. Where this exists, it is not sensible to establish a duplicate organization to access similar sources. Such departments are frequently very competent at accessing and distributing information. Few, however, deliver intelligence rather than data. Depending on the capabilities and ambitions of the people staffing the unit, it may be better to use this department as a first point of contact for regular information, and for periodic scans of databases, and to leave the evaluation to the analytical stage.

However, as implied earlier, it is vital to ensure adequate collection of the information sources needed for competitor analysis. There are now numerous clipping, briefing and abstract services, but the scope of these should be carefully studied and the gaps filled. Unless special arrangements are made, an ordinary clipping service would be most unlikely to cover recruitment advertisements. A balance must be determined between reliance on external services, periodic searches of library sources, and in-house scanning of journals and other material.

Marketing Research

Much marketing research will take place at the brand and product levels. Materials include surveys, subscriptions to marketing audit service purchase of published reports, and so on. Other research may be carried out at the instigation of the public affairs department, usually to provide data on the image of the organization compared with other organizations. Most organizations have specialist staff in the area of marketing research.

Competitor analysis requires access to all such research. It may be possible to reduce costs by adding questions which are needed for competitive intelligence purposes to a survey which is planned to meet a marketing need.

It would be sensible to use the skills of any specialist market research staff to undertake particular surveys of customers or suppliers to provide information for competitive analysis purposes. Using an in-house unit to undertake research on the strengths and weaknesses of the various players in the market may give biased results. However, the unit's experience in commissioning research might reduce costs and improve the survey.

Internal Information

The mobilization of internal information presents one of the biggest organizational problems, because it must tap into every area of the organization and access both formal and informal systems. Information which comes out of the internal routine management information system, such as sales analysis, usually presents few problems, as it is produced to a routine and can easily be accessed by the appropriate managers. As with the external information, it is prudent to audit what is available, because the priorities of competitive analysis may indicate a requirement to change the internal data that is collected. It would be wrong to assume that only that which is currently produced is available. Accessing informal knowledge is much harder. For example, sales personnel often obtain useful information from customers about the activities of competitors. They may be the first to know that a competitor has launched a new product, that special deals are being offered, or that some aspect of customer service has been dramatically improved by a competitor. This information may come from clients, customers and even from conversations with the sales people from other organizations. What typically happens when competitive analysis starts is an appeal to the sales people to pass on the snippets of information they pick up, and in the first few weeks a flood of useful information may result. Very soon this becomes a trickle, and then runs dry. To ensure a continued flow means establishing the importance of this source, and making it easy for information to be passed upwards.

This requires that during their meetings with subordinates, managers of all ranks discuss competitor information, both asking for information and passing on relevant information from other sources. What is passed on should be tailored to the interests of the recipients, which in most cases will be tactical and related to their jobs. Although it is possible to use these meetings to pass information upwards, their main purpose is to help create a culture of competitive awareness. E-mail and voicemail systems are a more immediate way of reaching the competitive analysis unit. The competitor newsletter that some organizations use to disseminate information may be useful. This has the advantage of passing back something to those who provide information, although the emphasis is again more likely to be tactical than strategic.

The above example was chosen because the sales force is one of the units of an organization that has regular contact with customers and the surrounding world of everyday business. However, it is not the only part of the company that can pick up competitive information. Many other functions also have such opportunities. Manufacturing personnel may meet competitors at conferences, local business association meetings or may hear gossip from suppliers. Service engineers may note customer comments on the reliability and quality of competitors' products. Research and development departments may read papers delivered by employees of competitors, or may note changes in the disciplines of a competitor's R&D personnel. All this has the advantage that all parts of the organization use the information as well as contribute to its collection.

Regular Analysis of Intelligence Information

Here we are concerned with strategic analysis, the regular updating of the industry and competitor analysis through the methods emphasized in this book and shown in Figure 8.1, and any additional special studies which may be required. Analysis covers the task of industry mapping, competitor profiling, and the initial interpretation. It is a question of turning information into various forms of useable intelligence, initiating action to validate suspect data or to plug essential gaps of information, and ensuring that the results are in a form which can be easily communicated to those involved in the strategic decision process. It should not be a passive activity, merely dealing with input, but a very active process which seeks to provide information and interpretation which is of strategic value to the organization. It is possible for the co-ordinator to fill this role, and certainly he or she should have responsibility for it. The scale of the task, however, may require the establishment of a competitor analysis unit within the coordinator's department.

The end products of the analysis stage should be something more than clever interpretation. If the results are to be used, there must be corporate ownership of them. Although part of this comes through the strategic decision process, the way in which the competitive analysis unit works can help to build this ownership and improve the validity of the interpretation of the figures. For example, regular discussions with key functional managers, emphasizing those parts of the analysis that relate to their areas, may both avoid misinterpretation and make the whole process more participative.

Decisions and Strategies

None of this effort will have much value to the organization unless the information is used to build competitive advantage, to seek out new opportunities, or to lead to ways of changing the structure of the industry. In most organizations, "strategy" is not something that happens once a year when a strategic plan is prepared, however helpful such a plan may be. Strategic management is a continuing process, which should react to and anticipate the various changes taking place and the opportunities which emerge. The more turbulent the business environment, the more need there is for rapid strategic response methods.

Organizations vary in the processes by which strategic decisions are made. Our assumption here is that the chief executive exercises strategic leadership, but that his top executives, at a minimum, are heavily involved in the process. This is neither a universal pattern, nor is it the only route to a successful strategy, but it is common enough to make it a reasonable assumption. Many of the top executives will be responsible for a function, and will bring to the table their views of the issues and opportunities facing the organization. Corporate strategy should be more dynamic than merely adding up what everyone wants to do. It is not our task to debate the entire process of strategic management, so we have limited ourselves to four suggestions for ensuring that industry analysis and competitor information are properly considered in the decision process:

● *Dissemination of hard information.* The obvious task is to ensure that the industry maps and profiles and the results of other analyses reach the decision makers at times when strategy is being considered, and that they are updated when significant changes are observed. This gives a sound foundation, and the shape of such a reporting service might well be an annual book containing up-to-date versions of the various analyses, regular information on major matters of importance as they occur, and updates of individual pages of the reports when this is worthwhile (as, for example, when there is another year of data to add to a competitor profile). Additional consolidated updates might be provided for any special needs that emerge during the year. This assumes a paper-based system. Of course, it is possible to go one better and always to be up-to-date by establishing an online competitor information system and passing on significant specific information by e-mail.

Unfortunately, this does no more than provide the opportunity for managers to use the information. It may not ensure that they use it, nor will it be enough to create a culture which makes everyone in the organization relate to the importance of competitor analysis. So we need something like the next actions as well.

- *Strategy workshops.* At least once a year, it is worth holding a strategy workshop as part of the strategy process. We have used this term instead of "meeting" because it implies a less formal, more participative approach. Competitors would be a key part of this workshop, which among other things should encourage discussion of the implications of the competitive environment, ways of changing it, the strategies that competitors appear to be pursuing, and the likely reactions of competitors to the strategic options that are on the agenda. Of course, there is much more to strategy than just competitor analysis, and the workshop should cover all elements. The process should be designed to improve the quality of strategic thinking by getting top managers to internalize and use competitor and other relevant data, and to facilitate creative thinking.

- *Regular management meetings.* Time should be allowed at every regular executive management meeting to review the competitive arena and the actions of competitors. This is to ensure that key information is shared, and to help create a situation where strategies are regularly reviewed in the context of competitor behaviour. Such a discussion should be of equal importance with the comparison of results against budget, which is normally a feature of such meetings.

- *Periodic meetings to discuss competitors.* It is worthwhile to hold periodic meetings to discuss competitors. Some companies do this by allocating a competitor to each member of the team, with a view to becoming expert on that organization. Each manager would role-play a competitor at that meeting, with the aim of building a better understanding of the competitor and its strategic behaviour.

These methods can be modified and carried down to levels of management below the top group.

More Complex Organizations

We mentioned earlier that our description was based on a relatively simple organization in terms of industry and geographical spread. Now is the time to discuss some of the complications that must be considered in organizations with higher geographic or industry complexity. We will first change our basic assumption somewhat, and assume that our organization is not operating in only one country and operates in many countries but still in related industries. What was described above would be appropriate for each country operation, particularly if the business was run as a multi-local operation, but the terms chief executive and top management group would mean "of the subsidiary".

This leads us to a consideration of the role of the centre. This is a very important role, because even if country strategy is largely delegated to the country level, the group chief executive has an overall responsibility. He or she should be concerned about the overall shaping of the industry, and must balance risk and investments, and make decisions about entering areas of the world where the organization does not currently operate. In addition, many of the competitors might be multinationals, and can only be fully understood when all their operations are studied. In these circumstances there is a role for a central competitor analysis unit. This unit will ensure that competitor analysis does take place across the whole organization, coordinate information on multinational competitors, and ensure that they are considered in the overall corporate strategy.

Much of the collection of information about and analysis of local competitors would take place at local level, so the corporate role would be somewhat different from our first example. Coordination would require multinational meetings to share methods and information. If our organization took a global view, with more centralization of the strategic task, there would be some further modification of the roles of the central and subsidiary competitor analysis units. Under any organizational concept, it would be criminal not to use the local operations as a source of information about competitor activity.

The role of the centre changes somewhat when the organization is a conglomerate, because although each business unit has industry competitors, customers and suppliers, the corporate office does not. Who were the competitors of Hanson,[96] for example, before the decision was taken to focus on a core of activities? At that time the company activities included tobacco, bricks, and batteries, as well as many other unrelated products. The corporate office of such an organization could have little direct interest in any competitors, except as an acquisition strategy, but might have a very deep interest in ensuring that each business studied their own competitors and were taken into consideration in strategic decisions

This different role of the head office applies when actions are in totally unrelated activities, which can never become related. No stretch of the imagination could envisage the merging of markets of cigarettes and dry cell batteries. Not so with the various components of the financial service industries, where industries are merging. An insurance company may indeed be of considerable strategic interest to a banking corporation. So it is not just the number of industries which dictates whether there are corporate-level competitors, but the degree to which they are related or have the potential to become related in the future.

Building Competence in Competitor Analysis

No organization will become effective in competitive analysis just because top management says it is a good thing to do. Something more than an initiating memo is needed, and this chapter has dealt with some of the things that will help create the right climate for competitive analysis within an organization (See also Hussey, 1998).

One common assumption is that managers and their staff will immediately be competent at competitive analysis once the organization has decided to undertake it. This is by no means correct, and a manager who fails to understand the reasons for and the concepts of the approach may not only make poor decisions but may also demonstrate an attitude which makes it harder to gain the support of his or her subordinates.

---

[96] Hanson Trust plc owned, among others, the Imperial Tobacco Group PLC, the largest tobacco manufacturer in the UK.

Our suggestion is to arrange appropriate training. An example of the scale of effort made by one organization is given in Hussey (1985):

One of the world's largest multinational companies, always seen as one of the best managed, identified that more attention had to be placed on competitor analysis both at the top level and in the development of marketing plans by each operating unit. This was after careful self-analysis had revealed that much of the company's growth was without profit, because of weaknesses in the market place where competitors were proving more aggressive than the assumptions on which past plans had been based.

Many companies would have issued an edict that future strategies were to be formulated after more competitor analysis, and many would have failed to cause any changes whatsoever. In this company, the chief executive personally directed a world-wide educational initiative to bring the new thinking to life. He led top managers in a week long introduction to the theme of "What about Competition?", and insisted that several hundred senior managers should spend two weeks on a strategic planning workshop. He also introduced an 8-hour audio-visual presentation to thousands more managers as a basis for discussion of and commitment to real strategic thinking. Many implementation workshops have been held throughout the world with practical training in competitor analysis, leading to the implementation of more realistic strategies.

The precise training solutions should be tailored to suit the organization, but a workshop mode, which includes the analysis of the participants' own industries and actual competitors, can be very effective. The cases in this book have been proven very effective in providing training in industry analysis.

Competitive analysis can take strategic thinking a long way forward, but making it happen in an organization requires thought and effort. Our own experiences have convinced us of the value of thinking in this way. The concepts described here are comparatively recent, and much of the methodology for applying the concepts has been developed from experience. What is not new is the idea that in any conflict situation, the agent who has the most intelligence about the competitors and is able to use this in strategic thinking will emerge victorious. The endurance of this idea should be very comforting to its users. We in management must use it well.

Obtaining the Information

Eventually, we are going to have to get down to the specifics of finding the actual information. None of the analysis mentioned here would have been possible without pertinent information. In the beginning, this task was somewhat daunting and it would have been easy to decide that nothing could be done as the information was too sparse. In the early years, desk research yielded very little, because little was published at that time. This meant that we had to consider primary research if we were to obtain any valuable information at all. The following exposé is an historical development of our own work with competitive analysis to illustrate what has changed over the past few decades.

Our first major competitive study, undertaken in 1985, set a foundation which helped us make sense of information from other sources. After that time, there was an increase in the number of published research studies, which meant that our information was becoming more complete.

Our first piece of research into the market was completed in 1983. This was not at that time intended to help us follow the sort of competitive analysis described in this chapter, but was the first of a series of reports that we had carried out into management development and training to increase our knowledge of the state of the art and to gain marketing information. Since most of these reports are published, they can be shared with other interested parties. Although they have contributed greatly to our understanding of buyer behaviour and awareness of changing needs and responses, they are not primarily market research reports.

In 1985, we undertook two interrelated pieces of research. We wanted to find out if the market for our type of training was expanding. Were we getting our fair share of the growth? What were the factors that the buyers considered when choosing a supplier?

We knew many of our competitors, but did we know them all? There was a great gap between the ones we could identify and the columns of names shown in directories. Who were the competitors who might be most critical to our future? Who did the buyers think were our competitors, and who did our competitors think were their most serious rivals? We wanted to know if we were competitive in price, quality, speed of response to the client, and in our overall philosophies; and we wanted to answer the same questions for each major competitor. Therefore, our first intention was to prepare a market-related assessment of our strengths and weaknesses relative to those of competitors.

A sample survey was conducted by telephone of 43 buyers of our type of training service, exploring aspects of all the research objectives. We made personal interviews at nine major competitors, building up our list of real competitors from information supplied by buyers and competitors. We were able to check much of the information provided by competitors from the interviews with buyers.

Date Published	Unpublished
1983 Management training in UK companies	
1984 MBA and UK industry	
1985	Competitor study
1986 Tailored management education	
1986 Distance learning	
1987	Competitor information project
1988	Innovation training
1988	Management skills
1989 Consortium/company MBAs	
1989	Management training Europe part 1
1989	Management training Europe part 2
1989	Hotels/study centers
1990	Competitor update
1991 Management training in UK companies	
1992 Competency assessment	
1993 Company MBA	
1993 Management training in UK businesses	
1993	Competitor update
1994	
1995	
1996	
1997	
1998	
1999	
2000	
2001 BI education in Sweden, MAH	
2002	Competitor update
2003	
2004	
2005	
2006 The "Business" of Management Education: An Analysis of the Industry, CEIBS	
2007	Nordic MBA programs

Table 8.1 Primary Research Undertaken for the Analysis

The information from this survey provided the base from which we could build and develop on the lines already discussed, and led to immediate tactical and strategic decisions. Meanwhile, we continued to add more valuable data from our research for publication, and focused some of this on areas of the industry map which were hitherto blank. For example, in 1986 we published a report on distance learning and another in late 1989 on consortium and company MBAs. Although not part of the published report, this survey enabled us to quantify the size of this sector of the market. As Table 8.2 shows, many of the earlier studies have been regularly updated and expanded, so that we are able to note trends and changes in the market.

In 1987, we had an MBA student help us build up the files of competitor information which we had started to compile. This involved collecting brochures from competitors, annual reports (where available), and press cuttings. In addition, we established our first database, using an earlier format of competitor profiles. We did the usual searches at Companies House, and probably bored the Charity Commissioners with our complaints about competitors who were registered as charities and who had not lodged their returns for several years.

Most of this activity is generally typical of competitive analysis. Three activities which yielded useful information were:

- Continued direct contact with competitors, including the exchange of the sort of information which would be in the annual report had we all been private limited companies. The competitor analysis system we have built up means that there is somewhere to put the results of all these formal and informal comments, as well as information that comes to us about a competitor from elsewhere in the industry.
- Obtaining feedback from clients when there is a pre-qualifying exercise or a competitive bid (whether we win or lose). This has been an invaluable source of information. On occasion, buyers have prepared an analysis of all the bidders which they have been willing to share.
- Helping journalists to write about the industry, and suggesting who to approach for the collection of data for league tables. In this way we filled in a number of gaps in our own information, especially as a few firms who had refused to exchange information with us on grounds of confidentiality did not feel the same inhibitions when it was a question of gaining publicity.

Published information and market intelligence have become much more important since 1987. A number of studies have been completed which when supplemented by our own studies have enabled us to quantify the sectors on our industry map. There is still no sound statistical base for the industry, but the combination of all our sources means that we believe that our estimates are as accurate as they need to be for the type of decisions that have to be made.

In 1989, we reworked our competitor database, and stored information in a form similar to the profiles in this chapter. We had hopes of creating a dynamic database that enabled us to update the industry map automatically every time a competitor profile was updated. This was not economical then, but it would be today. In 2007 an attempt was made to recapitulate on some of the collective experience we have had over the past decade with running MBA programs in Denmark, Sweden and China.

What, then, are the main changes in the way we perform a competitive analysis today as compared to then? First it should be said that the way of thinking is much the same. It is primarily the tools which have changed. Changes are basically related to the evolution of our techno-society.

- *Less expensive software.* The dynamic databases we wanted in the late 80s are here, which allow us to change and distribute variables in real time. The price of this software is decreasing constantly, making it available to companies of all sizes.
- *Faster PCs, bigger data storages.* The PC has become a fast and efficient working tool. Combined with large data banks there are now few limits to storage of large amounts of competitive data.
- *The explosion of internet use.* In the early 80s it was difficult to find reliable secondary data on markets and competitors. With the explosion in internet use this has changed dramatically. We no longer have to rely only on homepages. Everyone is sharing information about everyone. This raises a question of quality and reliability which we will discuss, but the advantages far surpass the disadvantages.
- *More mobile communication and availability.* We no longer need to be at the office to send and receive information. This means that we can work more and be more flexible as to our way of working, e.g. from the car, from home or from a hotel room in another country.
- *Awareness of the value of Competitive Intelligence.* The Information Turn has been acknowledged, and with the emphasis on decision making and human capital before machinery. Competitive Intelligence is on the lips of CIOs and is offered as separate courses at many business schools.

In a few decades we have gone from information scarcity to information overload. This has increased the importance of critical thinking.

Much information provided online is false, which means that the analyst must learn what sources are more reliable and he or she must seek different sources for the same information. As an example, wikis like the Wikipedia contains a great deal of useful information, but also many errors, as it builds on the idea that everyone can contribute with useful knowledge and much information is not critically reviewed by peers. Most valuable analysis in the form of reports is still not free, but can be sought, bought and downloaded on the net. A few decades ago we started our research in the library catalogue (at the library). Today it is normal to begin a quest for information with a Google search. Libraries provide most scientific articles on line, and we order books by email directly from the library. Sometimes we can even get the books delivered directly to our office by special mail delivery. Everything is done without ever setting foot in the library. This means that we as analysts can perform much more of work in front of the PC.

What is going to happen in the decades to come? We are most likely to see a continuous development of new software and hardware technology to be used in competitive analysis. This will make more data available faster, to all kinds of mobile appliances. Our systems will communicate and exchange information, turning out ready-to-read reports and summaries in ever-greater numbers.

A few conclusions stem from our work. First, a competitor analysis system will improve over time with the continuous application of effort. Second, even small pieces of information can be coordinated and used. Finally, the lack of published information about an industry and competitors may make analysis more difficult, but need not prevent it.

We have begun to extend the scope of our study to other countries in Europe, and have spent more effort on identifying organizations with whom we can build alliances rather than undertaking a complete competitive analysis.

Building Competitive Advantage

None of the analysis presented is worthwhile unless it leads to action. The sort of strategic and tactical actions which we took may give an indication to readers of benefits they might obtain from competitor analysis:

- We clearly identified market segments where we could gain advantage and differentiation.
- As a result, one of the things we did was to build our geographic and language capability, so that, through our own resources or al-

liances with other organizations, we are able to run the same course for a multinational company in every Western European language. This is especially important when the course is intended to support a Europe-wide strategy by the client.

- We developed strategies for operations in other countries in Europe.
- We started many new initiatives to build image and awareness, including our regular publication *Management Update* (10 issues per year, free to management development and human resources personnel).
- We redesigned all our stationery and literature to achieve a common, recognisable image.
- We developed a number of different products and concepts. The growth of in-company MBA schemes made us seek to become better informed about what was happening.
- In certain circumstances, we sought ways in which our work could gain academic accreditation, without in any way trading our commercial image for that of a pseudo-business school.
- We identified private-sector competitors who operated in our sector of the market, and began to establish a trade association among those with whom we shared common concerns.

At the tactical level we were able to more accurately identify our competitors' respective strengths and weaknesses. Even when we did not know who else had been asked to bid, this helped us plan our own proposals and presentation in a way that emphasized our advantages.

We redesigned our basic approach to proposal writing, to present strengths pertaining to a project in such a way as to invite favourable comparison with our competitors. Our research had shown significant areas where we knew that many of the competitors likely to be asked to bid did not possess similar strengths. Almost immediately after completing our competitor study we had opportunities to apply these tactical concepts, and won two major assignments on competitive bids in quick succession. We developed strong long-term relationships with both clients.

Our strategy has helped us to grow faster than the market since the mid-1980s, and our concepts of industry and competitive analysis have helped us to develop these strategies. Add this to the benefits which our clients gained from similar approaches, and the value of our competitive analysis becomes clear.

This progress is not without cost. Anyone thinking of undertaking a similar exercise needs to decide whether they are looking for a one-off injection of competitive data into their strategy formulation or to set up an on-going system. Either choice requires dedicated effort.

Whether the aim of competitive analysis is tactical or strategic, the only justification for the costs and effort is the action that results from the new knowledge. We hope that this case presentation has given some indication of the benefits and methodology of competitor analysis. Furthermore, we hope it shows that an initial lack of competitive information can sometimes be overcome though systematic intelligence work.

At this point, we are back to where we started with the question of Competitive Advantage. Modern corporations are gaining competitive advantage according to how they handle information. In the last chapter, we ask at what price this advantage is obtained. What are the moral and ethical considerations in private and public intelligence work?

REFERENCES

Abell, D. (1980). *Defining the Business*, Prentice Hall.

Englewood Cliffs, N.J. McGee, J. & Thomas, H. (1992). Strategic groups and intra-industry competition. In Hussey, D.E. (ed.), *International Review of Strategic Management*, Vol. 3, Wiley, Chichester.

Hussey, D.E. (1985). *Implementing corporate strategy: using management education and training*, Long Range Planning, 18, 5.

Hussey, D.E. (1998). *How to be Better at Managing Change*, Kogan Page, London.

Stanat, R. (1990). *The Intelligent Corporation, American Management Association*, New York.

McNamee, P. (1990). The group competitive intensity map: a means of displaying competitive position. In Hussey, D.E. (ed.), *International Review of Strategic Management*, Vol. 1, Wiley, Chichester.

Porter, M. (1980). *Competitive Strategy*, The Free Press, New York.

Porter, M. (1985). *Competitive Advantage*, The Free Press, New York.

CHAPTER 9

Information Gathering and Intelligence Ethics

Not Black or White, but Shades of Grey

All human actions have an ethical component attached. In everything we do, there is a question of whether it is predominantly good or bad; for ourselves, for other people and for the environment. This is especially relevant for certain economic and social activities. Competitive intelligence, and in particular information gathering, is one of these areas. For this reason it is impossible to teach and practice competitive intelligence in a responsible manner without paying close attention to the ethical component. To illustrate with some examples:

1. An employee wants to visit the booth of a competitor and wonders how he should present himself, as a competitor or as someone else? (lying)
2. An employee of a company has personal contacts with a journalist and thinks he can get some good publicity in the paper if the journalist was added to the media list of those invited to the company's new product launch in Hawaii. (oiling, or "bribery light")
3. An employee of a company wonders whether or not he can use students who are working on a thesis at the university to gather information about competitors without letting the company know. (deception)

The difficult ethical questions are not those which imply breaking the law, but those which belong to the Grey Zone of intelligence ethics, where we are called upon to make use of our individual ethical judgment. This may look simple, but it is not. The real problem is that the Grey Zone is not homogenous, but consists of lighter and darker distinctions of grey. In one way we might say that the lighter the grey, the bigger the ethical problem is, because the decision is more difficult to make. Every individual and every company will have its own definitions, and there will always be these small moral dilemmas. Which one should the company follow, or who should decide what is right?

In theory, it is practically impossible to find one set of rules that will cover all events or ethical concerns. In reality we will have to use a set of rules of thumb and encourage discussions. The rules may be formally written down or simply implied in the organizational culture. The ethical standard of the organization will depend on factors such as the national culture of the company, the industry which it is in, and the ethical concern and standpoints of its owners and higher management. For instance, although bribery is prohibited by law, it is widely used in large parts of the developing world. This is because in such places it is practically impossible to win contracts without bribery. This puts the business man in a continuous moral dilemma. If he does not bribe he may not get the contract, if he does, he will feel he has done something wrong.

With increased attention on ethical issues in business, organizations are working out clever schemes to avoid being caught. To take a simple example, many companies use an agent instead of paying out a bribe directly. When caught, the company ends the cooperation with the agent, saying in public that such conduct is ethically unacceptable to the company. As we shall see, this may be explained theoretically.

The Theory of Diversification of Moral Risk

Ethical problems studied within Economics are sometimes presented from a bargaining, or a Principle-Agent Model (hereon, PAM) perspective. We can use PAM and some basic notions from financial economics, to present a model showing how moral risk may be reduced or diversified.

Within a company a manager offers a subordinate a contract to do part of a job which contains a moral dilemma. If he wants to keep the task, the subordinate, can perform the action himself. Or, he or she can diversify the risk by engaging a subordinate. This subordinate in turn faces the same choices, etc. The more sets we get in the model, the more difficult the job of finding the person responsible for the initial order. If an agent refuses, the principal can always ask some one else or he can sanction his subordinate.

Diversification to agents outside of the organization reduces the risk considerably. We may define this as a diversification of second degree. Now the major question is, when will the action be performed, i.e. after how many sets? This will depend on the nature of the ethical dilemma. The problem may be modelled as follows:[97]

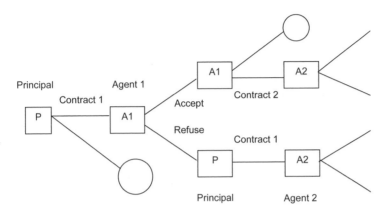

Figure 9.1 A model for the theory of Diversification of Moral Risk

Where,
  P= Principal
  A=Agent

P = The point where the Principal decides whether to bear the ethical risk himself or to diversify it. If he decides to diversify, he has to decide how much he wants to transfer. The circles are the end nodes. Each end node is equivalent to a specific quantity of risk, which may even be defined by the expected financial penalty, or its expected financial consequences. The more actors involved, the lower the risk.

A1 = The contract goes to the first Agent, who can accept or refuse it. If A1 accepts the contract, he will in turn make the same decision as the principal: whether or not to perform the action, how much risk to take on himself and how much to diversify.

---

[97] See Solberg Søilen, Klaus (2004), pp. 85-86. Moralisches Risiko durch einen unmoralischen "Principal". The idea was first introduced in an unpublished working paper at the University of Oslo, and has been modified here. See Solberg Søilen, Klaus (1995).

A2 = If A1 refuses P can give a contract to another agent, A2, who will then accept or reject, etc.

The theory continues to find support empirically in discoveries by the media. Only this spring, it was made clear that SAAB Aerospace in Sweden had used British BAE (A1), who again used a local agent (A2) to bribe politicians in The Czech Republic to persuade their national government to accept the hire of 14 SAAB Jas 39 Gripen air fighters in 2004.

Related research indicates that an agent will gladly lie about his product's quality (Akerlof 1970), that the agent will lie about his firm's output (Diamond, 1984), the value of shares (Myers, Majluf; 1984), about his proneness when about to be insured (Rasmussen, 1989), or as someone who "tries to shirk and steal by excessive perk consumption" (Jensen, Meckling; 1976). Dasgupta (1988) suggests that an agent may appear to be ethical because he is investing in a reputation for trust (which he may later destroy for some future, larger gain). Other researchers have shown ethical concern on behalf of their profession. Brennan (1994) makes the point that if PAM is taught as a theory where the Principal and Agent try to outsmart each other; with no ethical considerations, the theory may become descriptively true. This is not the intention of the authors by presenting the above mentioned model. On the contrary, we hope that its introduction may help detect and describe rather than encourage such schemes.

Legality and Ethics

Competitor intelligence is legal; industrial espionage is not. The rest of this chapter is about activities which are legitimate, and do not involve theft, trespass, electronic bugging, or the bribery of a competitor's employees. We want to show many sources of information which are available to all actors.

Ethics are personal, and our views may not be the same as those of all readers. One test to perform when uncertain about a potential ethical dilemma is to ask whether you would be happy for your competitor and all your customers to know how you obtained a piece of information: if you feel that your methods should be hidden, they are probably not all that ethical.

In our own code we would rule out lying to a competitor when making a direct approach for information. Thus we might employ a student to visit competitors to obtain information, but would not allow the request to be disguised as an academic project. Our involvement would be declared at the outset. This includes not hiding behind a partial truth (the academic assignment is genuine, but the information is for us as well as the project).

Similarly we believe it is unethical to press an employee who joins us from a competitor to reveal confidential information about that competitor. It is also unacceptable to have someone apply for a job advertised by a competitor to obtain information about the company, or any of the similar dubious activities which we are expected to applaud in private detective novels and television series. The end does not justify the means.

How Competitive Information Arises

Competitive information arises in four different ways:

1. The evidence left by its activities
2. The organization's own need to communicate with actual and potential stakeholders
3. Legal or association obligations, which make certain information public
4. Activities of outsiders, which may not be welcomed by the organization.

None of the information that can be gathered as a result of this activity should be treated in isolation. The same facts may appear under more than one heading, and even an apparently trivial snippet of information can sometimes provide the key which enables another piece of information to be interpreted more accurately. This means that all four of the broad sources should be examined in more detail.

One of the better examples that have been published of a comprehensive competitive analysis appears in Gulliver (1990). The motivation was acquisition, and the study was that of Distillers by the Argyll Group. Guinness became notorious for the way they won control of Distillers against Argyll (those who do not know the background will find a brief summary in another part of the quoted article):

My team went back 15 years with the Distillers accounts and up to 10 years with their principal trading subsidiaries. With a total of about 80 trading subsidiaries we were able to prepare a group consolidation which gave us a good feel for the contribution of individual profit centres. In addition, we scrutinized analysts' reports and trade and financial press cuttings back to the 1960s. We obtained drinks industry reports, and commissioned independent

*market research on Distillers' products and markets. We also
looked at its industrial relations.*

*Finally we made a pavement inspection of Distillers' properties.
After checking trade directories and the Yellow Pages, a small
team photographed and produced a report on every Distiller's
property we could find.* (Gulliver, 1990)

The bid for Distillers by Argyll was an enormously complex exercise
including research, analysis, and the development of a strategy for the
bid, and ultimately, the merger.

Evidence left by a Company's Activities

Much of a company's commercial activity leaves some trace: what we
might term the forensics and witness statements. Products offered for
sale may be observable, the sales measured, and market shares established. Buyers may be asked to give their opinion of a product or organization. Aerial photographs may be taken of an extensive plant.
Today, such information is even available for purchase over the internet. Observers can assess lorry traffic at warehouses. The only questions are whether the activity is legal and ethical, and whether the
likely costs exceed the expected benefits.

Imagine that you are standing on the bank of the river Zambezi in
Zimbabwe, facing upstream. On your right-hand side the Devil's
Cataract tumbles noisily into the gorge below. On your left hand there
is a statue of David Livingstone. You start to walk upstream, and soon
the well-groomed tourist path stops, although it continues as a narrow,
winding path, made by people or game. You notice some elephant
droppings. A little further on you realize that the droppings look very
fresh. As someone with no expertise in animal tracking you can make
one deduction. An elephant has passed this way recently, but you do
not know its direction of travel, or how long ago. As a sensible person
you turn back, hoping that the elephant was going in the other direction.

If you had a tracker with you with the required expertise, you might
increase the amount of information that you could gain. First, the
tracker would be able to judge when the elephant passed from an expert assessment of the droppings; second, he could ascertain the direction of travel from the signs on the ground; third, the tracker would establish whether multiple elephants had just walked past.

If you persuaded the tracker to put in additional effort even more
could be discovered. By moving around the area it might be possible to

establish whether the path is frequently used by elephants, and whether others were travelling through the bush on a parallel route.

You can use a similar combination of observation, expertise, and effort to discover what is probably the most valuable information you can gain about a competitor. It is often also the most relevant, since companies compete at the level of products and services, and may not be directly interested in non-competing activities of a competitor.

Information from the Market

As all businesses succeed or fail in the marketplace, this is where we should start. The richness of the seam of information that can be mined here varies with the market and the measurement services that have been established by market research organizations. These tend to be strongest for fast-moving grocery products and weakest for professional services and industrial capital products and consumables.

• *Market-measurement services.* There are organizations in many countries, such as A.C. Nielsen, which offer an accurate way of measuring sales of all the competitors through various types of outlets. This is achieved through regular audits of a sample of retail outlets, which record sales over the period, quantities in the retail area and in the stock room, and prices.

From this information it is possible to calculate the total sales in each measured product category passing through this type of outlet and the brand shares. In some countries, organizations such as Nielsen and SAMI/Burke offer data collected from supermarket scanners at checkouts. Other providers include the firms which analyse doctors' prescriptions to provide information on the market size and brand shares of various pharmaceuticals.

It is also possible to measure market movements and brand shares at the level of the consumer. The most consistent information comes from carefully controlled panels of consumers who keep diaries of their purchases in the product areas being measured. These are aggregated to produce comprehensive reports, which, although they may have more opportunity for error than the audit approaches, have the immense advantage that they cover all purchases from all types of retail audit. There may be published or syndicated surveys of various types which estimate market size and brand shares. These may be available from a variety of sources, covering a large range of consumer and industrial products, and, it has to be said, with varying degrees of efficiency and effectiveness.

- *Market Surveys.* As we all know, thousands of serious market surveys are undertaken every year. Many of these are specifically related to a product that a company either has on the market or hopes to launch, or to the advertising that promotes it. Consumers are asked what they think of a product, why they buy it, where they buy, if they buy, how often, who makes the buying decision, what newspapers they read. The list is almost endless. Surveys can be a very useful tool for probing a competitor's strengths and weaknesses.

Such surveys have to be related to the perceptions of the customer. A shopper may have views about certain retail companies, but these will be related to the outlets he or she deals with. Few consumers will have a view about Unilever, but they may have a very clear appreciation of the strengths of a particular detergent against others they have tried. The retail buyers, who deal with all the competitors, have a more complete view of a supplier. Their views, however, relate to the subsidiary or division which they deal with, and not usually to the entire organization.

Where the survey method really comes into its own in helping to assess strengths and weaknesses is with industrial goods and services. Here the respondents should be well informed, may deal frequently with competing companies, and are exposed to an entire unit of a supplier organization. Often their experience is based on a close relationship with the whole supplier organization, and their views of the various suppliers may have great usefulness. The patterns that emerge of who each buying organization in the sample knows of, and deals with, can give insight into the segmentation strategy of a supplier. When the market is fragmented, and has many niches, as in the provision of management training, surveys can help to establish which of the firms in the market are real competitors of each other.

Although many organizations undertake regular surveys of their markets, these are not always designed to answer the questions that increase understanding of competitors. Any organization serious about competitor analysis should consider additional surveys.

- *Bid analysis.* There are some industries where competitive bids are very common. Examples include civil engineering, building, some plant and machinery, lifts and escalators, and professional services such as management consulting, engineering consulting, and management training. The proportion of work that is subject to such bids varies with industries, and is higher with construction-related products like lifts than with a professional service such as management consulting, where buyers do not always solicit bids from competitors.

Wherever there is a competitive bid situation, there is information to be gained, no matter whether the contract is won or lost. To obtain this information means contacting the buyer to ask for information. This should be done tactfully. It is just as important to know why your organization won a contract as why they lost it. Our experience of this sort of follow-up is that buyers are usually cooperative, and in some cases have prepared an analysis of the strengths and weaknesses of the various bids which they are willing to share with all the bidders.

An example can be found in Hussey (1988, Chapter 9), which shows part of the analysis which Coopers & Lybrand were willing to share when seven proposals when they considered bids for a new management development program. The published reference hides the individual details of bidders, but in the actual situation full information was disclosed by agreement with the bidders.

When competitors in an industry bid for a high proportion of all contracts, post-bid intelligence can provide extensive and accurate information about the players. From your own proposal you know the technical specifications, the geographical details, the buyer, the purpose, and other information. If you win the bid, you know the price. If you lose, you need only ask the buyer for the name of the winning firm and the price to have all the information you need to complete the picture. The buyer is unlikely to withhold the name of the successful competitor, although some buyers may not give out the price of the winning bid. However, in these cases it may be possible to estimate the winning bid price from your own price and what the buyer tells you about the reason you lost. Put all this together in a database, and you have the ability to look at your strengths and weaknesses against each competitor. Overall market shares may hide the fact that competitors do better in certain segments, geographical areas, or with certain buyers.

For the appropriate types of business, a systematic and continuous follow-up of all competitive bids can be very rewarding. The key words are "systematic" and "continuous".

Product Analysis
Once a product is on the market, it can be purchased by any competitor and examined. Of course, this dictum applies does not apply to services, and may not be practical when dealing with huge products such as multi-million-pound paper-making machines.

Still, examination of a competitor's product can be a valuable source of information. For an engineered product, like a photocopier or video recorder, it provides an opportunity for the company to compare performance with its own similar product(s). It enables reverse engineering to understand particular functions of the product.

Both of these techniques were used with good competitive effect by Ashbrook Simon Hartley (ASH), an industry leader in liquid/solid separation technologies and a manufacturer of belt presses. A belt press is a machine for squeezing out liquids, and may have a number of purposes. With this company it was in sewage treatment, and the separation of liquids and solids for processing. ASH had found that winning competitive bids from the municipal buyers was a matter of chance, since the order always went to the lowest-priced bid that met the minimum specifications. They examined their competitor's machines and were convinced that their product offered superior operating performance. In order to convince buyers of this, they persuaded them to arrange side-by-side tests on-site before a vendor was chosen. Each supplier brought a truck-mounted machine to the site. They then coupled it up alongside the competitors' machines and processed sewage under controlled conditions. ASH always outperformed the competitors, which not only increased its proportion of wins but also led to a gradual increase in the performance requirements specified for the machines in future invitations to propose. A side-benefit was that the need to maintain a number of truck-mounted machines, and have trained teams to operate them, raised the entry barriers for newcomers. Much more had to be invested before a sale could be made.

The ability to analyse a product such as canned dog food, or to reverse engineer a computer, will often enable an estimate of the costs of production. This requires considerable effort and expertise, and is likely to be more accurate if there is an awareness of the competitor's manufacturing processes, and if the market information permits good estimates of the volume of product the competitor makes. It is unlikely to achieve that accuracy without combining product analysis with other competitive information. In combination with market audits or other information on a competitor's sales volumes, and other information from annual reports and other sources, it may be possible to estimate the sources of a competitor's profits in fine detail.

Although in some instances (such as the aforementioned Argyll whisky case) the analysis is straightforward, there can be a danger in assuming that competitors follow the same production methods as your own company. This was one of the factors that led the British motorcycle companies to misread the situation when Honda made its first attacks on the British market.

When it is not possible to buy a competitor's product it may be possible to arrange to see it on the premises of a buyer. Although this does not give an opportunity to see how it is made, it will provide opportunities to see it working and to obtain information from the buying organization of its performance capabilities.

Sometimes detailed knowledge of the competitor's product is needed to avoid patent infringements (patents are discussed briefly under another heading). Canon successfully developed a copier that did not infringe Xerox's 600 patents. It is hard to see how this could be done without comprehensive knowledge of the Xerox products.

Other Types of Survey

Surveys can also collect other types of data on certain industries which provide capacity or sales information that is not otherwise published. Journals and specialized economic monitoring services tend to be the major source. For example, it is possible to obtain regular information on the revenue of many consulting firms, their number of partners and the number of other employees, and sometimes similar information on specific segments from the pages of *Management Consulting*. Capacity information on a large part of the petrochemical industry is available from regular reports in journals such as *European Chemical News*.

Other Information from Observation

The Argyll example quoted earlier shows how information on properties was gained from a pavement inspection. Although the amount of effort spent should be related to the use to which the information will be put, particularly as many of the possible approaches are expensive, there are situations where direct observation can be extremely useful and are ethically acceptable to most:

● The best way for one supermarket to monitor its competitors is with regular visits on a controlled basis to a sample of their stores to observe prices, new products, and layout changes.
● Where dealers store equipment such as excavators and similar mobile plants in open yards, a regular observation on a controlled basis will allow observation of stock levels. This method is used regularly by one manufacturer of such products in the USA. The information is used to predict changes in discounting and other promotional actions.
● Market Planning Systems Inc. of Phoenix, Arizona offers a sophisticated approach to modelling area demand for retail petrol. This

technique permits the modelling of the total distribution system of a local area and the estimation of sales volumes of every retail outlet in the system. Using what it calls "tactics", the company asks "what-if" questions to study the impact of competitor actions such as price change, promotions or modernization. The data sources for these models built for specific clients include: the client's own statistics, observations taken of all competitor sites (either read directly on meters or to estimate the number of customers; aerial photographs which enable traffic volumes to be estimated around each filling station, and maps.

● There are usually opportunities to visit the factories of competitors, which can give clues to processes, the age of plant, efficiency, and the culture.

The Organization's Own Need to Communicate

Much information which is useful in competitive analysis is not considered by the competitor to be confidential and may be made available. This is because the modern company, particularly the quoted company, has a need to communicate with its current and potential stakeholders, and sometimes even with its competitors. The latter is a rather special case and we do not refer here to illegal actions such as price collusion.

Porter (1980, 1985) discusses market signalling, and shows how a company may wish to signal to competitors that it either will or will not take a particular action, or to indicate that an apparent opportunity is not likely to be viable. This may be a very good reason why chemical companies frequently disclose plant capacities or announce plans to expand capacity. Signalling is normally done through company press statements, speeches, and interviews with journalists that the company has engineered. There is also a school of thought that argues that all competitors will make fewer decisions which damage the whole industry if good market information is available to all, and that there is value in sharing certain information about the market.

But the main bulk of information that a company issues of its own volition is intended to inform and/or influence stakeholders or those who may become stakeholders. The company's own publications and circulars may be targeted at particular groups, like investors, customers or employees, but few can be contained within those groups, and some are multi-purpose. Much of this material goes into wide circulation, and will yield useful and accurate information. Statements to the media, and interviews by journalists, result in articles and broadcasts that are available to all who seek them out.

Investors: Present and Potential Shareholders

Private companies and partnerships may not have much motivation to ensure that investors are aware of the reasons for actions, the strengths of the organization, its values, and its vision, and may be able to treat anything that they do produce as secret. This is not so with public companies or those that need the support of the financial institutions, or believe that they will need such support in the future. For these organizations the annual report is expanded beyond the minimum legal requirements, and is made available to shareholders, stockbrokers, customers, candidates for employment, and anyone else who cares to ask. In most countries it is lodged within the annual return and is open for inspection by the public. The quickest way to obtain this information is to get on the competitor's mailing list, which can be done by making a straightforward request, and if this is denied, by rights through the purchase of a single share.

Because the annual report is a focused document, within a legal framework, some companies also produce company brochures and annual fact books, which are available to anyone with a legitimate interest in the organization, and which are often available on a help-yourself basis in company offices and other places. The fact book of ICI (a British company in the formulation sciences and a producer of paint) is used as an example, and our copy was picked up in the careers centre of a British university, although it is not a recruitment brochure.

The ICI fact book consists of factual information, some of which might have been obtainable from press cuttings, statistical publications, and the annual report, but much would otherwise have been difficult to discover. The fact book explains what the ICI Group does, how it is organized, who runs it, where it operates, and what its major products are, and it does this very well. It describes the overall organization in terms of the financials, vision, structure, and the pattern of share ownership. Each business sector is described, with financials, much capacity information, summaries of recent acquisitions and alliances, and a great deal more. There is a listing of worldwide locations and their activities.

ICI is not the only organization that issues regular fact books or similar publications. However, it is true that most public companies do not go into this amount of detail. For them, the main ways of reaching the investors are either through the media or meetings with investment analysts who write briefings for investors and may publish assessments of the prospects of all players in an industry. It is possible, but may be difficult, to research newspaper articles more than a few months in arrears. Journal articles are often retained in libraries for longer periods, but it is generally more effective to organize collection of cuttings and articles on a continuous basis. There are organizations which can provide such a service, in the form of either copies or abstracts: the latter may be particularly helpful for items that are in foreign languages, since the abstracts may be provided in your own language. Database services may be useful, particularly those which include stockbroker reports. Much of this is today available over the internet.

However, it is worth stressing that abstract and cutting services and database services only go to some of the sources, and it should not be assumed that there is total global coverage of all media. Check that the service is looking in the places you wish searched (this issue will come up again later in the context of case histories).

So far much of the discussion has taken single-country views of competitors, which may be relevant for some things but not for others. If you want to understand the local subsidiary of a multi-national company it is really necessary to study the parent as well. And if you are interested in a multinational, it is worth remembering that what the chairman says about the global strategy when opening a new complex in South Africa, and which is only reported in that country, may include information that would be invaluable if only you had known about it.

Customers

The type of communication a competitor produces will vary with the industry, and any product which flows through a distribution channel may require different communication media to the intermediary than to the end user:

- *Advertising.* An analysis of advertising may be useful for two purposes. First, it may help you to see how the competitor is trying to differentiate the product. Second, it may enable you to establish which market segments the competitor is targeting. The task may be relatively easy for industrial products, where advertising is not usually the key element of the marketing mix. It may be very complex with fast-moving consumer goods, where the media may extend from press and direct mail to television, radio, and cinema. The scale of advertising spending is often critical to success.

- *Product brochures.* Product brochures may be produced for persuasive purposes or to convey complex technical information. Both can provide useful information, and this source of information may be particularly important for industrial plant and machinery or for major consumer products like motor cars or computers. The brochures can give a better understanding of the competitor's product range, identify what the competitor feels are the strong points of the product, and may also yield price information. It is easier to pick up brochures for consumer products, which are often in the retail outlets for the taking, but it is not difficult to find ways of obtaining brochures for industrial products: sometimes the easiest way is the most successful - just telephone the competitor and ask for a copy.

- *Company brochures.* Not all industries produce company brochures aimed at customers, although the fact books described earlier may also be used for this purpose. However, for professional service companies, such as engineering consultants, market research agencies, management consultants, management training colleges and the like, the brochure may be the key document in the promotional armoury. Such firms sell intangibles, and usually concentrate on approaches, values, philosophies and skills, rather than specific products. Brochures struggle to build an image to counteract the basic problems of marketing intangible products. Analysis of these brochures will often reveal what the competitor believes to be its strengths, details of its main area of focus, and the type of market it is aiming for. The cynic might argue that relative fee rates can be judged by the relative thickness and quality of the paper.

- *Customer newsletters, journals, and related material.* These take many forms. The nature and style of the publication may sometimes reveal more than its content. Contrast, for example, the regular publications of various management consultancies. McKinsey produces a quarterly journal consisting of very high quality papers, which helps to sustain an image of quality and relevance. Harbridge Consulting Group LCC published a brief article nine times a year in its Management Development Update, which brought new ideas, case histories, and research findings to the attention of clients. The purpose was image building, establishing the expert nature of the firm, a soft sell of capability, and to give something of interest and professional value to the market. Other firms issue a newsletter, which describes their recent activities. Not all such publications are useful in competitive analysis. It is doubtful that much could be gained from some of the magazines issued by life insurance companies to their clients.

- *Public relations.* PR activity may take a variety of forms, but the most obvious are press statements and interviews which are designed to speak to customers. The trade or specialist consumer press is often the target, although when the issue is important enough it will make the main newspapers and other journals, and may lead to broadcast material on television or radio. Such material may announce new products, give notice of price changes, discuss new distribution arrangements, describe a plant expansion, stress a commitment to quality, or show how a problem has been overcome. These are just a few of the things that may be learnt about competitors in this way. Journalists may initiate interviews and company statements, and may undertake surveys which provide statistical information about the firms in an industry. Accounting and management consultancy journals may be among the few sources that reveal turnover and levels of employment of partnerships. We discussed earlier how to monitor the media for competitor information.
- *Directories.* Some information appears in directories, although often these reveal less than is obtainable from other sources. In a fragmented market, directories may help to establish the number of competitors. Occasionally a directory incorporates some form of survey, giving information not easily available from other sources. However, it should be remembered that numerical information provided to directories is not subject to audit and may be optimistically rounded upwards. The best place to consult directories is often a specialist library, where many can be accessed at the same time.
- *The Internet.* The internet has become a considerable source of information for all competitive needs through the past years, and its importance is continuously increasing. There are the company sites, the news articles and wikis all for free. We can attract customers to our sites and ask them questions (e-surveys). Then there are the commercial sources, special reports, satellite products, which can be purchased and delivered directly over the net. Just bear in mind that it is easy for anyone to put out anything on the

net. Using the internet as a source of competitive information puts even greater demands on our critical abilities.

Employees and Potential Employees

Communication with employees is critical for effective management, particularly in times of change. This means making much more information available to employees, to explain what the company is doing and where it is trying to go to. Some, but not all, of this information will appear in shareholder and customer publications.

We have already mentioned that ideas of what information should be kept confidential have changed, and in this section we are discussing information that is freely given and widely disseminated. We do not include confidential discussions which take place inside a company and which can only be discovered by illegal or unethical methods.

Employee Newspapers and Journals

Although intended for employees, these are often made much more widely available, and may be sent to pensioners, suppliers and customers, as well as interested parties like competitors. They are often exchanged between company HR departments. Some libraries maintain collections of them.

Anyone with experience of several companies will know that there are great differences between employee publications of companies: Some are mainly concerned with social news about employees, and are almost neutral about anything the company is doing. Others contain information about company successes, which may or may not be interesting to a competitor. The real value comes when the journal explains something the company is doing and the direction it is taking. One of our clients obtained considerable information on a competitor's information systems strategy by reading copies of the competitor's internal journal, which had been lodged with a London library. This caused it to examine what a competitor might have gleaned from its own journal, also in the library, and they were surprised to find that most of their Asia-Pacific strategy could have been deduced from a series of articles they themselves had published.

Case Histories and Case Studies

A company may cooperate with an author or academic to enable a the writing of a case history article about the company, or to allow an academic case study to be written for use in a university, and which may be available through the case clearing house or in an academic textbook.[98] Managers inside a company may find it valuable to write a case history themselves for publication in a book or journal. All will disclose information about the subject organization, which may not otherwise have become available. This may appear as written, video or audio material.

The reasons for doing this are varied and are generally in the company's interest. Generally it fits with the need to communicate to employees and customers, and gives reinforcement to the things the company is trying to achieve. British Petroleum went as far as to invite a journalist to attend some of its board meetings and to write up some articles based on the decisions taken to implement its Project 1990, a major business process re-engineering initiative. This action helped pass the change message to employees, and showed customers that the company was in the forefront of good management practice.

In addition to helping to put over a message or a particular aspect of the corporate image, such material is also useful internally to confirm the quality of managers and management actions, and as materials in internal training activities. Undoubtedly, some companies also feel that by cooperating with universities they are establishing goodwill with potential graduate recruits, and giving something back to the community.

Such case studies and case history articles are unlikely to disclose a competitor's strategic plan but they may provide many facts and figures about aspects of the competitor's business, an indication of problems the competitor is grappling with, and some of the actions being implemented which will have an effect on the competitiveness of the competitor. They may give insight into the way the competitor "thinks" and behaves.

Surprisingly this is one of the sources of potential information that we have found is often overlooked. Undoubtedly it is a matter of luck whether a case study or case history has been written about your competitor, but as several thousand are published in the world every year it is at least worth looking. Second, not everyone is aware that academic case studies can be accessed at universities, or often in the case clearing house (which in the UK is in the Business School at Cranfield). Harvard has its directory of case studies on CD-ROM to facilitate searching. Articles appear in many different journals and newspapers,

---

[98] See e.g. Solberg Søilen, Klaus, Huber, Stefan (2006). The book is the largest single collection of cases on Swedish SMCs to have been published.

many of which may be outside the normal press scanning activity. For example, the journals *Long Range Planning* and *Strategic Change* both publish some six to eight case history articles every year, and there are many management and functional journals that have similar philosophies.

It is one of the many sources which become more accessible as more journal abstracts are published on the Internet.

Recruitment Advertisements as a Source of Competitive Information

One potential source of information about competitors is the advertisements they place to recruit employees. Advertisements for senior management positions may provide the most information, but this is not definite.

Nevertheless the source should not be ignored, as information does appear that may fill in a piece of the jigsaw puzzle or confirm something already expected. The value may come from the existence of the advertisement itself: a batch of new jobs in a particular area of research and development may give a strong clue to the competitor's strategic thinking, for example. It may be useful to know the rates at which jobs are being advertised, although the salaries quoted are not a perfect indication of what is actually paid to the successful applicant. Information about the organization's strategy or operations may be included, and sometimes this may be the only source of such information: but be aware that figures in advertisements are probably and legitimately rounded.

The best way to illustrate the sort of information that can be gained is to look at the strategic information we found in the recruitment pages of one issue of a major British Sunday newspaper.

Of course, information obtained from advertisements has to be compared with what has been found out from other sources. You will rarely find all the crown jewels on display in an advertisement, but you may gain knowledge which helps you to understand more about a competitor and make sense of some of the other things they appear to be doing. And you may find nothing of value at all, which would have been the case in most of the other advertisements in this particular Sunday newspaper.

Graduate Recruitment Activity

Many companies have a focused recruitment activity aimed at newly qualified graduates, working directly with the universities. The visible output of this, as far as competitor information is concerned, is in details/ advertisements in specialist recruitment directories and in company recruitment brochures. The crown jewels are not left carelessly around in either of these activities. But, as with advertisements for specific jobs, some information may be gained. These sources may be of particular value when the competitor is a partnership which does not lodge annual reports with the registrar of companies, or for limited companies which have opted to restrict their annual returns to the legal minimum.

- *Company brochures.* Many of these give background about the company, and may include details of internal organization which is not always easily available from other sources, although, of course, it may be. A typical example of what may be in a recruitment brochure is provided by that published by Cegelec Projects Ltd, a Marine, Offshore, Oil, Gas company operating out of Aberdeen and reunited as Alstom in 1998. The brochure explains that this is a subsidiary of what today is the global company Alcatel-Lucent, information which a competitor will already know. After this, the brochure concentrates on the Cegelec Projects, giving a description of the activities and the number of employees. This is followed by a two-page spread describing the activities of the eight trading divisions of the company. The rest of the brochure deals with what the graduate can expect from the company. Brochures of this type frequently reflect the culture of the organization, although some companies may say only what the potential recruit is expected to want to hear and not what the true situation is.
- *Recruitment directory entries.* An example comes from Prospects Directory, published by CSU Publications. (Central Survey Unit (CSU) provides survey research to Northern Ireland Government Departments and the wider public sector in Northern Ireland). Only a low proportion of entries reveal competitive information of possible value. However, this is a feature of many sources of competitive information, and the source is worth checking. The entry for Smurfit UK is one example of hard information that may expand what can be discovered from other sources. The size of the Irish parent company is given in turnover and employment, and in the number of countries in which it operates. It also states that growth

has been obtained by acquisition. Within the overall company, Smurfit UK is part of the UK and Ireland region. Details for The Smurfit Kappa Group are found on the company's internet site. Such information includes financial statistics for 2006: total net sales of about 7 billion euros, up from 4.4 billion in the previous year.

Unfocused Communication

Some organizations also communicate in a less focused way, either because they have a feeling of social duty or sometimes as a matter of what could be understood as management egotism. Books have been written about many of the major organizations, sometimes as a corporate venture and sometimes giving cooperation to the author. As with some of the royal biographies, this cooperation is regretted from time to time when the resultant publication does not please the management. Such books may contain information that helps one understand the ethos of a competitor, but are often of limited value in competitive analysis.

Legal or Association Obligations

All organizations face legal requirements to provide information, and many have similar obligations through membership of a trade or other association. Although much of what is disclosed rightly remains confidential, there may also be requirements to disclose information to the public. Some examples of sources arising through legal requirements are given below.

- *Annual returns of limited companies.* We have already mentioned that in many countries limited liability companies are required by law to make an annual return in a specified form, and this document is available for public consultation. In the UK the return is lodged with the Registrar of Companies, and the disclosure requirement is most stringent for public limited companies (PLCs). The annual report, which forms part of the return, is, as we have seen, a vehicle of communication to stake-holders, and often contains more information than the minimum legal requirement. It is an obvious first piece of information to obtain when the competitor is a PLC. If the company is not a PLC, the annual report may give no more than the minimum legal requirement. For a company with many subsidiary companies it is often possible to obtain extra information, which does not appear in the annual report of the holding company, by turning up the records of each subsidiary in each country of operation.

An illustration of this activity was given in the Argyll example discussed earlier. In the USA, a useful source for listed companies is the 10K form which has to be filed with the Securities and Exchange Commission. In the UK registered charities have to make similar returns to the Charity Commissioners. While this may be of little interest to most industries, there are a few where competitors are charities. There are no requirements in the UK for disclosure on partnerships and organizations which do not have limited liability.

- *Monopolies and mergers.* Many countries have anti-monopoly legislation which will put into the public domain information that would not otherwise be disclosed. Enquiries are initiated by the relevant government body from time to time. In addition, an intention of an organization to acquire another can be referred for investigation when this might lead to an uncompetitive situation. Member countries of the European Union are also subject to EC rules on monopolies.

- *Court cases and legal enquiries.* Information may come into the public domain through court cases, such as prosecutions for infringements of health and safety legislation, or claims for compensation for injury, or discrimination in employment. There may be conflicts over a contract, which results in one party taking action against the other. Industrial tribunal headings may cover a variety of employment law issues. These are only a few examples of many situations that can arise. Enquiries of various sorts may be initiated by governments, and the results usually enter the public domain.

  • *Patents.* If an organization wishes to protect its inventions it has to apply for patent protection in its home country and in others where it wants the protection to apply. Many companies today apply for international patents right away. A study of the patent documentation of a competitor may reveal useful information about products (although not all patents may be used by the owner), and give some clues to new product strategies. The Canon example given earlier would have involved a detailed study of all the Xerox patents.

  • *Freedom of information Acts.* In some countries, most notably the USA, there are Freedom of Information Acts, which mean that much information which would have remained confidential moves into the public domain and can be accessed.

Activities of Outsiders

Not every piece of information available about a competitor comes from voluntary or legally driven causes. There are sources which come from organizations and sources that obtain and disclose information that might otherwise have remained hidden. Investigative journalists are one example, although more does not need to be said about this, as the sources have already been discussed. Similarly, disclosures by lobbyists or disgruntled employees which find their way into the media will also be found along with other articles on the competitor.

Not everything is reported in this way, and various web sites on the Internet may be the only source of such information. Some is published in books and reports assembled by a pressure group. For example, organizations appear from time to time, such as Counter Information Services, which in the late 1970s produced critical reports on industries and companies, and Social Audit Ltd, which used unofficial sources to compile a social audit on a number of organizations. Remember that any pressure group, or organization with a particular social or political bias, may not always be fully objective.

The international trade unions have also, from time to time, used their members to compile detailed reports on the activities of selected companies, and sometimes these can be purchased.

Competitor Analysis on the Internet

The Internet was born during the cold war, as a military project, a conduit for communication in the event of attack. In the private domain, the Internet has become one of the most significant mechanisms for information search and retrieval in competitive analysis, and has forever changed marketing intelligence. Today, a single analyst equipped with a computer and an internet connection can accomplish more than an entire planning department could achieve just 15 years ago. The enlargement of the Internet has meant the immediate and continuous availability of information stored on databases thousands of miles away. Whether the analyst is pursuing a one-time project or intends to establish on-going monitoring of a competitor or an industry sector, the Internet provides important gains in efficiency.

Search engines such as Google allow the user to specify a word or string of words of interest, for example, "enzymes and animal and feed". This in turn generates a list of possibly relevant databases where the word(s) appear in documents. These search engines are based on extensive logarithms, which are soon to become every IT company's tool. The single biggest challenge for the analyst is the overload of information, which means that several screenings must be performed. Suddenly, screening (not the actual search per se, but knowing how to pick out the good apples from the bad) has become a major analytical ability: "I have 10 million hits, now how do I narrow this down?"

On-going surveillance of a particular competitor or industry sector often combines on a regular basis the above type of enquiry with the use of automated procedures, which consistently scan various sources of information about the target. Instead of doing the search yourself, there are more and more companies who do it for you.

There are companies who can tell how many have visited your site, how often, and from where. There are services which will scan all newspapers for you for specific key words such as the name of a competitor or a product. There are easy ways of entering all this data into databases, and extracting from it any information you would need (data mining). Then there are the supportive business intelligence systems, which frequently work together with similar software within Sales, Customer Relations Management and Knowledge Management. The trend is that more and more of these systems are integrating and sharing information with each other to produce joint reports. The goal of all this is real-time competitive intelligence, preferably from a mobile phone-sized personal computer, requested by an employee from some airport lounge. That reality is not far away.

Conclusion

In this book, we have presented a framework for how to work with Intelligence Analysis in organizations. Starting with the ideas of Michael Porter, we have developed over the years a model for how to conduct an assessment of a company's Competitive Advantage based on two sets of analyses: the company and the industry analysis. We have presented our working model in a Management Strategy perspective, as we see a direct line drawn from Competitive Advantage to Strategy and Intelligence Analysis. We understand intelligence work to be an integrated part of overall management and production, at least for now. It is quite possible that this will change in the future as companies adapt fully to the consequences of the Information Age, but we still seem to have one foot in the Industrial Revolution and the corporate structures it created in the first half of the twentieth century. Intelligence analysts and intelligence departments are still mostly found in state and military organizations. Due to the significant increase in articles and training on Market Intelligence, knowledge on intelligence work has been widely disseminated in the corporate world over the past decades, but at least for now its use seems to have taken on a more organic form. There are a number of reasons for this. First, there is the sensitive nature of the subject matter. However, there also seems to be a feeling, based on actual experience, that Market Intelligence capacity is better served and more efficient when it is an integrated function in the organization.

Our goal has been and is to provide for these knowledge workers tools for intelligence analysis. It remains for you, the reader, to decide to what extent we have succeeded.

REFERENCES

Akerlof, G. (1970). The Market for Lemons: Quality, Uncertainty and the Market Mechanism. *Quarterly Journal of Economics*, 84, pp. 488-500.

Brennan, M.J. (1994). Incentives, rationality, and Society. *Journal of Applied Corporate Finance,* 7, pp. 31-39.

Dasgupta, P. (1988). Trust as a commodity, in D. Gambetta (Ed.); *Trust: making and Breaking Cooperation Relations*. N.Y.: Basic Blackwell.

Diamaond, D.W. (1984). Financial Intermediation and Delegated Monetoring. *Review of Economic Studies*, 51, pp. 393-414.

Gulliver J. (1990). How Scotland lost out to back street Hammersmith. *The Times*, 31 August.

Hussey, D.E. (1988). *Management Training and Corporate Strategy*, Perganion, Oxford.

Jensen, M., Meckling, W. (1976). Theory of the Firm: Managerial Behavior, Agency Costs, and Ownership Structure. *Journal of Financial Economics*, 3, pp. 305-360.

Myers, S.C., Majluf, N.N. (1984). Corporate Financing and Investment Decisions when Firms have Information that Investors do not have. *Journal of Financial Economics*, 13, pp. 187-221.

Porter, M.E. (1980). *Competitive Strategy*, The Free Press, New York.

Porter, M.E. (1985). *Competitive Advantage*, The Free Press, New York.

Rasmusen, E. (1989). *Games and Information*. Cambridge, MA: Blackwell.

Solberg Søilen, K., Huber, S. (2006). *20 Fallstudier för SMF*. Studentlitteratur: Lund.

Solberg Søilen, K. (2004). Wirtschaftsspionage in Verhandlungen aus Informationsökonomischer und Wirtschaftsethischer Perspektive - Eine

Interdisziplinäre Analyse. *Dissertation.*
Wirtschaftswissenschaflichen Fakultät der Universität Leipzig,
Deutschland.

Solberg Søilen, K. (1995). A Type of Moral Hazard with Hidden Action: Di-
versifying Moral Risk Among Managers with Asymmetric Information - A
Contribution to the Cynical Perspective of Business Ethics. *Working Paper.*
Norwegian School of Management (BI), Oslo.